Praise for *The Baby Scoop Era*

Karen Wilson-Buterbaugh has broadly and richly mined the adoption, social work, and psychological literature of the last seventy-five years to document the ways that many authorities participated in the degradation of thousands of white girls and women in the United States. At the same time, The Baby Scoop Era poignantly and distressingly documents the impacts of coerced adoption on the lives of so many vulnerable people. - *Rickie Solinger, Historian. Author of "Wake Up Little Susie: Single Pregnancy and Race before Roe v. Wade" and "Beggars and Choosers: How the Politics of Choice Shapes Adoption, Abortion and Welfare in the United States."*

This account of compulsory, historical adoption in the USA has the capacity to bring about long overdue change by educating adoption social workers and other 'helping' professionals of the harm they continue to perpetuate by failing to understand the past. Twenty years of research has produced undeniable truth. - *Joss Shawyer, Author of "Death by Adoption," 1979*

The era of maternity homes, systematic punishment of unmarried mothers and forced child relinquishment should be common knowledge to anyone concerned about the rights of women. Yet the post-war decades that made up the Baby Scoop Era too often remain a missing chapter in the story of feminism. For years, Karen Wilson-Buterbaugh has labored to correct this gap, doggedly uncovering and preserving the history of the modern adoption system and its invisible victims. With the care of an historian and the passion of a survivor, Wilson-Buterbaugh brings her research together here, in a book that should be read by anyone who cares to understand the full story of women and family policy in the 20th Century. - *Kathryn Joyce, Author of "The Child Catchers" and "Quiverfull"*

This book ought to be included in Women's Studies Programs across the nation. Karen exposes the Baby Scoop Era and its crimes against women. She has identified many of the cultural elements that shamed and silenced young mothers. That silence, in turn, contributed to a fertile ground in which the adoption industry spun its myths and became a billion dollar industry. Adoption preys on our most vulnerable population of women and children, living in poverty, in America and around the world. This book is the non-fictionalized version of "The Handmaid's Tale." - *Leslie Pate Mackinnon, LCSW*

Karen Wilson-Buterbaugh's thorough and perceptive analysis clearly shows how the exploding adoption industry herded unmarried women in the decades after World War II into giving up their babies. She shines a shaft of light on the creepy and deceptive policies of supposedly good-intentioned social workers and the adoption agencies they worked for, revealing how the focus shifted from keeping mothers and babies together to separating them, all in the name of 'good intentions.' A much needed scrutiny of policies that continue today. - *Lorraine Dusky, author of "A hole in my heart, a memoir and report from the fault lines of adoption"*

In her exposé of the fateful coercion of pregnant women, Karen dares to tell the horrible truth, the punishment bestowed upon millions of women, a punishment worse than death, led like lambs to slaughter, to a trauma worse than the horrors of war. Their beloved children were ripped away from them, an act of violence causing them and their children a lifetime of pain. Do you dare to read the truth? - *Joe Soll, Psychotherapist, Author of "Adoption Healing: A Path to Recovery"*

Karen intermingles stories of single mothers who lost children to forced adoption practices with historical accounts of how society treated these mothers and their babies. Her research goes to the depths of what was known about the complex mental health issues of people separated by forced adoption and what was known about the lifelong suffering of young women "cast out" by their families, society and the institutions initially set up to keep newborns with their mothers. During the BSE, infant adoption was sinister, illegal and punitive, inflicting lifelong trauma. People today cannot comprehend a society that condoned an evil that affected millions across the world. It is the only period in history where millions of single mothers supposedly "gave their newborns away" en mass and willingly to strangers. Adoption promoters ignored the harm it inflicted on those whom it was their moral duty to protect. The Baby Scoop Era is a tool that should be studied by every adoption professional, social work student and prospective adopter involved in child welfare. An activist for decades, Karen writes with authenticity and offers cold hard facts. A well written book that deserves a place on any library shelf in any country of the world. - *Lily Arthur, Director, Origins New South Wales Australia*

Karen Wilson-Buterbaugh shares both her own traumatic experience and, from her exhaustive research, a wealth of others.' revealing voices from and about this painful part of our past. - *Elizabeth J. Samuels, Professor, University of Baltimore School of Law*

This is the most thorough book about the history of adoption which I've ever read. The author takes you on a journey back to the 40s and up through the Baby Scoop Era. With her use of statistics and quotes, you will be astonished to realize how many unwed mothers faced horrific scorn and shame. As an unwed mother during the early '50s, I was sent out of town and made to feel as though I had committed the unpardonable sin and given no other way for me to be redeemed, except to surrender my first born! In this powerful treatise, the author has succeeded in producing an historic, though shocking, book; one which every reader will be able to relate to whether it be as an accuser, a supporter, or the one condemned. - *Sandy Musser, Author, Activist, Founder, ALARM Network. (Adoption Legislation for Adoption Reform Movement)*

THE BABY SCOOP ERA

Unwed Mothers, Infant Adoption, and Forced Surrender

KAREN WILSON-BUTERBAUGH

Cover photos: Photo of "Admission Requirements"
courtesy of the Directory of Residences for Unwed
Mothers (1969). All other photos courtesy of the
Florence Crittenton Association of America

DISCLAIMER

This book is presented solely for educational and informational purposes. The author is not offering any legal or other professional advice herein. While best efforts have been applied in the preparation of this work, the author makes no representations or warranties of any kind and assumes no liabilities of any kind with respect to the accuracy or completeness of the contents or fitness of use for a particular purpose. The author shall not be held liable or responsible to any person or entity with respect to any loss or incidental or consequential damages caused, or alleged to have been caused, directly or indirectly, by the information contained herein.

DEDICATION

To my raised daughters
Brandi Wilson Brown and Trinity Wilson
and my husband, Grant
for their support, encouragement,
understanding and love.

To my dad, the late Lt. Col. Donald E. Beebe, USAF
My best friend and biggest fan.

To Kate Waller Barrett,
the Mother of all Exiled Mothers.
A woman far ahead of her time with tremendous
wisdom and a huge, generous heart.
She had the right vision and approach.
How tragic, wrong and unethical that her passion to help
single mothers keep and raise their own infants became
corrupted by the advent of so-called child welfare
"professionals."

To all Exiled, Natural Mothers and their taken children
who have suffered immeasurable loss
at the hands of those who appointed themselves
"the experts."

And Mostly and Eternally,

To my taken daughter Michelle Renee aka "Maria"
without whom this book would not, and could not, have
been written.

TABLE OF CONTENTS

ACKNOWLEDGMENTS

This work would not exist without the very accomplished skill, wisdom, support, encouragement and generous assistance provided by
Joss Shawyer, Joe Soll, Ann Fessler, Debbie Warila, Vicci Kitzberger, Mary O'Grady, Patricia Selinger, Leslie MacKinnon, Elizabeth Samuels, Lily Arthur, Lorraine Dusky, Rickie Solinger, Cedar Bradley, Sandy Musser, Kathryn Joyce, Becky Drinnen, Carla Marie Rupp, Connie Marie Pitts, Priscilla Stone Sharp, Nancy Lambert.

Thanks to Darian Brown
of Richmond Signs & Designs
for the book cover

With Deepest Appreciation
To My Incredibly Skilled Editor
Stephanie Korney

PREFACE

Consider The Precedent

Between 1945 and 1973, more than 1.5 million white, unmarried mothers lost their newborn infants through the ubiquitous, fraudulent, unethical and coercive practices of churches, maternity home administrators, adoption caseworkers, and the public social welfare system. In 1970, a United States court confirmed the existence and impact of these practices and returned custody of the infant child to his unmarried mother.

The Case of

METHODIST MISSION HOME OF TEXAS

v.

N_____A.____ B____,

Court of Civil Appeals of Texas, San Antonio

March 4, 1970

451 S.W. 539 (1970)

In 1968, a young, pregnant female (unnamed in this case) was deposited by her family at the Methodist Mission

Home of Texas, a licensed adoption agency operated by the United Methodist Church. On November 23, 1968, the young mother gave birth to a boy at a local hospital. Four days later, she returned to the Home, called her mother, and declared her intention to keep her son.

According to the details provided in the appeal, the original lawsuit, which was filed by the mother to retain custody of her son, ended with the jury finding that "...the execution of the instruments by the plaintiff was the result of undue influence exerted on her by Defendant's [Methodist Mission Home's] agents and employees."

The Methodist Mission Home of Texas appealed the jury's verdict, and the appeals court upheld the original trial court determination: the young mother was exposed to undue influence when making her decision. The court found sufficient evidence in the case to support the following conclusions:

- It was the policy of the Home to encourage unmarried mothers to release their children to the Home for adoption.
- The Home's counselor attempted to persuade mothers to release their children for adoption.
- During the time before the birth of the Plaintiff's son, the Home's staff, believing she intended to surrender, made no effort to convince her to reconsider her decision.
- After the mother changed her mind and announced she intended to keep her child, the Home's counselor arranged a series of interviews with her over several days, which

resulted in the mother giving consent to
release her child for adoption.

- Even though the adoption worker testified
  that she discussed the pros and cons of
  keeping the child with the mother, the
  worker's contributions consisted only of a
  recital of reasons why the mother should give
  up her baby.

- The adoption worker "emphatically stressed"
  that if the mother was "any sort of person,"
  she would release her child for adoption.

- The mother was subjected to "excessive
  persuasion" and "emotional distress during
  the critical period following the birth of her
  child..."

- An unwed mother who has just given birth is
  often emotionally distraught and particularly
  vulnerable to any effort, well-meaning or not,
  to convince her to give up her child.

The court reiterated that the mother was wrongly
advised that she had no right to keep her child, and the
adoption worker accused the mother of being selfish,
telling her that if she "was any kind of person" she would
consent to the adoption. The mother was subjected to an
endless recital of "only the cons" and "a repeated
monologue of the reasons why she should not keep her
child."

- The Home told the Plaintiff [the mother] that
  she should pay reasonable costs of the
  services of the Home; however, no applicant
  was denied admission to the Home because

of an inability to pay. (The Plaintiff [the mother] had stayed at the Home for more than fifteen weeks, made a payment of $150… she has not made further payments, nor has the Home made any effort to collect any additional amount.)

- The Home's Resident Handbook, which was issued to each resident, included a statement explaining why, in most cases, the adoption of a baby born out of wedlock offers both the child and the mother the best chance for normal development.
- The Home's counselors repeatedly said that an unwed mother should give up her baby, and the policy of the Home was to encourage mothers to release their babies for adoption, explaining to the mothers why they should surrender their children.
- The Defendant accused the Plaintiff of being selfish and said she had no right to keep the child.

According to court documents, the arguments made by the Defendant to convince her to release her child included the following:

- The fact that the mother loved her son was not reason enough for her to keep him.
- The Plaintiff could have other children.
- The adoption worker claimed that the adoptive parents would love the child more.
- Dire consequences would occur if the Plaintiff kept her child, such as the child would always be a burden

to her and would make it difficult for her to find a husband.

- If the mother married at a later time, her husband would probably resent the child.
- The mother would have to confront a situation in which her son returned home from school and asked, "Mommy, what's a 'bastard'?"

After review, the Court of Appeals affirmed the trial court's ruling that the mother was coerced and pressured by the adoption worker employed by the Methodist Mission Home of Texas to surrender her son for adoption. The court then ordered the Home to return the mother's infant son to her.

The information in this book corroborates the facts presented in this case, and more. This very important and precedent-setting legal case can be applied to the plight of over 1.5 million young, defenseless, unmarried mothers and the babies they lost, the babies wrongly offered for adoption simply because, in the overwhelming number of cases, their mothers were not married. History has shown that these horrendous, abusive, improper, and unethical separations of mother and child would have very negative effects on them for the rest of their lives.

Fraudulent adoption practices continue. Adoption is big business. An industry analysis of fertility clinics and adoption services in 2001 valued the adoption services industry at $1.4 billion, with a projected annual growth rate of 11.5% between 2001 and 2004. This is the only analysis of the adoption services business sector ever undertaken (Ashe, 2001).

Will state, federal, and international laws ever be written to support women and children? Will the Equal Rights Amendment ever be passed in the United States? Will the United States ever pass the 14th Amendment of the Human Rights Commission, which has already been passed in all other industrialized countries? Or will the business of buying and selling human beings continue to be an option for those who cannot conceive children?

A MOTHER'S STORY / *Connie*

Coerced adoption caused permanent damage to my life.

I became pregnant in 1969. Because I was unmarried, and prior to *Roe vs. Wade*, there were no options besides adoption unless one's parents or family members were willing to help. My parents were not willing to help, and I was told not to speak of my pregnancy to any of my relatives. No one knew but my immediate family and a few close friends. As soon as I started to show, I was forced to leave my school and went to live at a maternity home, the Salvation Army Booth Memorial Hospital and Home for unwed mothers. The social climate then was very different than today.

It was soon evident I was there to be punished. All us girls/women were segregated according to our ages. I had one roommate. We shared one toilet, sink and shower. Passes were required if we were to leave the building for any length of time, and we had to be back by 8:30 pm, and in our beds and quiet by 10:00 pm. Someone roamed the hallways every evening to be sure we were all in our assigned rooms. We were given chores to do. We were forced to attend Mass one night every week.

Since I was still a high school student, I attended Emily Dickinson Opportunity School, which was adjoined to the building. The labor rooms and the delivery room were in the same building as well.

Meetings with my social worker were embarrassing. She never discussed keeping my baby, or discussed any rights I might have had at the time. She was more interested in my sexual experience. Conversing with her was extremely awkward for me.

Early in the morning of March 14, 1970, I was washing sticky, syrupy pans from that morning's pancake breakfast. I was in a lot of discomfort, but didn't realize I was in labor. My mother picked me up, only to take me right back. I was frightened and asked if my mother could stay with me. We were told "no," so my mother left as I was taken back to one of the labor rooms. I was left alone most of the time and spent my entire labor on a gurney.

In the delivery room, my legs were put in stirrups, and my arms were tied down by my sides. During delivery, a second doctor was called in. Apparently, doctors resided near the hospital. The second doctor was called as there were complications, and my son was born with the help of forceps. When I started asking questions, the doctor who arrived later abruptly and rudely told me to "Shut up."

Had I not asked over and over again, no one was going to even so much as tell me if I'd given birth to a boy or a girl. I didn't get to hold him and didn't see him until the next morning. The glass wall of the nursery kept us divided. He had bruises on each side of his face from the forceps.

My day in court was scheduled for March 25, 1970. Absolutely the worst day of my life! I was asked to read and sign the relinquishment papers in Denver Juvenile Court. Judge Philip Gilliam, now deceased, asked me if I was being pressured by anyone and if I'd like my social worker and my Dad to leave the room. Judge Gilliam could clearly see my eyes were swollen from crying.

The night before my appearance in Denver Juvenile Court, I begged my parents to let me keep my baby boy. I pleaded with them that he needed me, his mother! I told them this would ruin my life too. I'd never know what happened to him, and he'd never know me or know how much I loved him. My mother didn't know what to do with me, so my Dad came into my bedroom. I expected some sympathy and kind words, but what I heard was quite the opposite.

My dad told me I was being selfish -- that if I loved my baby so much, I'd see to it that he got both a mother and a father. He told me if I didn't do as he said in court the next day, he would throw me and my baby out into the cold snow with no place to live, and what kind of mother would that make me? I went numb temporarily. I couldn't believe the words I had just heard.

So even though I wanted desperately to tell the judge I was being immensely pressured and threatened, I was terrified of my Dad, and I had no one else to turn to. My relatives lived in Oregon, and I had been told early on not to contact any of them as my parents did not want them knowing I had a baby out of wedlock.

The judge did not read the relinquishment papers to me out loud. I was instructed to go to a table to the left to read and sign the papers. I was so upset I did not read it. I was not given a copy after I signed the papers either. I finally received a copy of the relinquishment papers I signed and my son's original birth certificate in 2015, as Colorado had recently become an open adoption records state.

Approximately two weeks after the signing of the relinquish papers, I called Booth Memorial Hospital while my parents were out of the house. I asked them if my baby had been adopted yet. I was put on hold, and then a gal took it upon herself to tell me he was already adopted by a loving couple. I was never informed of any rights I may have had, so that statement made my heart sink, and I fell into a deep depression. I slept most all the time.

Years later, when I found out searching was possible, I obtained non-identifying information, and I learned that my son was adopted at around six months of age. So while I was inquiring about whether he was adopted or not, a week after coerced relinquishment, he was actually being cared for at a foster home. Learning this news made me physically ill. Many years would pass, while I always, and still do feel a deep sense of loss, and a void that can never be filled.

When my son would have been six years old, my brother's wife was expecting their first baby. I threw a baby shower for her in the "big room" at my apartment's clubhouse. I entered the room and noticed the cake said "Welcoming Our First Grandchild." I was devastated! I left the shower early, went to my apartment and cried for hours on end. Was my child simply forgotten? Was he nothing to my parents?

My parents both expressed remorse over the years, and they did eventually both admit that I was never the same, and if they had to do it over again, things would have been different. I appreciated their remorse and apology, but the damage was already done. My Dad told me nothing was more important than family and not to blame my Mom, as she had tried to talk him into letting me keep and raise my son. I replied to my Dad, my son WAS family!

He is right about one thing -- I never will be the same.

INTRODUCTION

The bond between a mother and her child is naturally sacred. It is physical, psychological and spiritual. It is very resilient and very flexible. It can stretch very far – naturally. Any artificial or violent injury to this 'stretch' constitutes a psychic trauma to both mother and child – for all eternity. This means that children need their mothers and mothers need their children – whether or not the mother is married or unmarried.

Phyllis Chesler

This is a critical examination of closed infant adoption practices and the experiences of unwed mothers, which also examines the historical literature of the years just after World War II through 1972, which are called the Baby Scoop Era (BSE).

This research focuses on the beliefs of adoption professionals, their methods of operation, their attitudes and how they shared their views and practice standards with others. It is not only about those who worked in the adoption industry and the individuals and organizations who benefitted from mother and child separation, it is also about those who grew concerned and issued warnings that were systematically ignored.

Did these professionals really operate with the best interests of the mother and her baby uppermost in their minds? Did the methods they use negatively impact these vulnerable mothers, especially those who were housed in maternity homes? What negative emotional after-effects might these mothers and their babies have suffered as a result of being separated from each other? Who was involved? What did they say, think and feel? What didn't they do that they should have done? What did they do that they should not have? How and why were they able to remove so many newborns from these new, unmarried mothers and then turn around and offer their babies for adoption? If there is blame to be placed, where might it lie?

The content is intentionally presented as clearly and simply as possible with the hope that the reader will focus on the actual words spoken and published during the BSE – and on those who reflected back upon it. Each chapter is arranged by category and year to reveal the evolution of the beliefs, principles, procedures, and practices of adoption social workers. Each chapter also includes the views and opinions of those who interacted professionally with adoption workers.

This work was not created to entertain. Instead, it is offered to educate and stimulate conversation. Many exiled natural mothers (the author included) hope that the information presented here will spur a federal government hearing to examine whether these entities operated properly, ethically and legally on behalf of unmarried mothers during the Baby Scoop Era in the United States.

This is an exposé.

PART I

THE PRECIPICE

THE BABY SCOOP ERA

CHAPTER 1

THE BABY SCOOP ERA

In the pecking order of America, unwed mothers are perhaps the most despised minority. They are the targets of abuse from legislators bent on punishing them. They are the scapegoats of moralists crying an alleged lapse in public morality. They are the butt of jokes by school children and adults... Ironically the barbs are thrown at only one half of the duo responsible for illegitimacy. There are few burning indictments of unmarried fathers...although they can produce far more out of wedlock children than women.

Alex Poinset

The period between the end of World War II and early 1973 is generally known as the Baby Scoop Era or BSE. The BSE formally ended with Roe v. Wade and pertains to closed infant adoption practices. At no other time in our history have such huge numbers of newborns been surrendered to adoption by unmarried mothers.

The BSE has been documented in such publications as *Wake Up Little Suzie* (Solinger, 1992), *The Girls Who Went Away* (Fessler, 2006), and the documentary *A Girl Like Her* (Fessler, 2012). It is also the subject of the Australian documentary *Gone to a Good Home* (Berkman & Shapman, 2006) and the Academy Award-nominated movie *Philomena* (Frears, S. & Coogan, S. & Pope, J., 2013), which tells the story of Philomena Lee, an unmarried, pregnant girl imprisoned in an Irish Catholic laundry that also served as a maternity home, who was forced to surrender her son to closed adoption.

The Adoption History Project has estimated that, during the BSE, approximately four million children were adopted. However, that figure could include babies adopted through Kinship Care (familial) and other types of adoptions other than newborn. It is possible that up to two million newborns were surrendered by unmarried mothers during the BSE. That number could be larger because it has been speculated that a good number of unmarried, pregnant females checked into hospitals under false names and wearing fake wedding rings. In addition, early in the Baby Scoop Era, record-keeping methods were lax and not generally required by agencies, hospitals and other entities. Often, the information provided was not easy to verify.

For example, there was no written record of the names of unwed mothers at the Florence Crittenton Homes in South Carolina prior to 1942. The lack of an accurate count of the number of unwed mothers before or during the BSE in the United States was attributed to a strong surge in the birthrate during the 1950s. More young women between the ages of 15 and 19 married at this time than during any other comparable period. According to estimates, 78.3 million Baby Boomers were born during these years. In the decades between 1946 and 1966, there was also a significant increase in the number of illegitimate births, with the U.S. National Office of Vital Statistics giving 133,200 as its best estimate for 1949. This estimate is considered low since illegitimate births were often reported as legitimate deliveries in this period (Cupp, 2013).

Between 1957 and 1970 there was a steady increase in the number of nonrelative adoptions, from 47,000 in 1957 to 89,000 in 1970. However, toward the end of this period the rate of increase was limited. The annual adoption rate remained steady at 20-21 per 10,000 children under age 21 for the period 1968-71. The actual number of nonrelative adoptions in 1970 was almost the same as in 1969. The trend was reversed in 1971 when, for the first time since 1957, there was a decrease in the number of adoptions. This downward trend was continued through 1975 and is likely to continue for the foreseeable future (Turner, J., 1977).

Unmarried females had little access to birth control methods and protection. They were generally unable to obtain information about reproduction, and sexual issues were not taught in schools then as they are today. In public libraries, books and other materials on these topics were stored behind locked doors. The BSE was definitely not a time of easy access to reproductive information. There was no "Information Super Highway."

After the soldiers returned home at the end of World War II, society witnessed a bumper crop of babies, a group known today as the "Baby Boomers." There were 2.858 million babies born in 1945. The number rose to 3.411 million in 1946, and the number continued to rise steadily, reaching a high of 4.300 million in 1965 when births began to progressively decrease. Some soldiers returning from war may have brought home sexually transmitted diseases that could have caused infertility, not only for them, but for their wives as well.

When young, unmarried females became pregnant, adoption workers convinced the public through the media, that there was a real and growing crisis in unwed motherhood. An epidemic. However, since the population of teenagers increased during the Baby Boom period, the growth rate was simply a matter of an increase in population (Vincent, 1962).

In a perfect storm of trends and events, the BSE experienced an increase in the number of teenage girls due to overall population growth, very limited access to birth control and little information about reproduction available to unmarried adolescents and young adults, an increase in infertility rates, and the "sexual revolution" of the 1960s.

During the 1940s, illegitimacy slowly came to be viewed in terms of a psychological deficit on the part of the unwed mother rather than as a moral problem. At that time, there was a more sexualized society that provided little information about birth control methods and that imposed restrictions on their availability. This society experienced an increase in unwed pregnancies. The dominant view among professionals in psychology and social work was that the majority of these mothers were best served by taking their babies away from them at or shortly after birth and offering them for adoption.

According to Regina Kunzel (1993), these years were marked by an evolution in the perception of unmarried mothers among social workers, changing from "seduced and abandoned" to "feebleminded" and then to "sex delinquents." Social work professionals began to see unmarried mothers as dangerous rather than as endangered.

By using the labels of both feeblemindedness and sex delinquency, social workers could operate within prescribed boundaries that favored adoption: if mothers were too intelligent to be considered "feebleminded," they remained sufficiently defective as "sex delinquents" to be separated from their children.

Over time, the perception of unmarried mothers as being sex delinquents caused a breakdown of the boundary between unmarried mothers and delinquents until these status designations became synonymous. Instead of helpless victims, these women were viewed as willful violators of moral norms. This effectively shifted the burdens of guilt associated with unwed pregnancies from men to women. While social workers claimed to approach the subject of unmarried mothers with objectivity, public discourse ultimately coalesced around normalcy and deviance, and social workers more actively suggested that unmarried mothers surrender their children.

After World War II, there was a new market for babies, and adoption workers strongly encouraged unmarried mothers to release their children for adoption. At the same time, adoption was generally viewed by social workers and society as a means of controlling the behavior and sexuality of women in order to perpetuate the patriarchal nature of the family (Wegar, 1997).

The mission and philosophy of maternity homes changed in the 1950s and 1960s. The homes served as

e pregnant girls could be sequestered until they
vith the staff making concerted efforts to
y unmarried mother who was unsure or
.............ed in the option of adoption that this was the
best and even only course of action (Fessler, 2006). There
was little effort to help these mothers keep and raise their
babies (Mandell, 2007).

The BSE was characterized by specific conditions, social
structures and criteria designed to facilitate the removal of
white newborns from white, unmarried mothers, which
were then offered to married, white couples for adoption.

These conditions included:

• The creation of a new professionalism in social work in
the United States allowed workers to define and operate in
the specialized field of infant adoption, regardless of their
previous experience or training, and to declare themselves
experts in unwed motherhood.
• The expansion of maternity homes in nearly every
major city throughout the United States, particularly the
Salvation Army and Florence Crittenton Homes.
• The evolution of staff at maternity homes from
religious women whose aim was to help mothers keep their
babies, to professional "adoption workers" interested in
pressuring the mothers to surrender their children to meet
the growing market demand for white infants among white,
married adopters.
• A change in foster care from efforts to support both
the mother and her child, who remained together, to a
system of care that provided only for the newborn,
effectively separating the mother from the child.

• An increase in infertility rates attributed to soldiers who might have returned from World War II with sexually transmitted diseases.

• Difficulties experienced by teenagers and other unmarried individuals in obtaining birth control methods like condoms or the pill.

• Lack of readily available or accessible information about reproduction among adolescents and young adults.

• Societal pressures to have a "perfect family" of two or more children tended to stigmatize childless married couples.

• The so-called "sexual revolution" that occurred in the 1960s.

> The Baby Scoop Era left a generation of young mothers stripped of their firstborn children and a generation of adopted individuals embroiled in conflicts of identity. The ramifications of the adoption epidemic leave aftershocks in our society today. The wounded mothers have lived for decades in shame and silence over their secret children (Cunningham. 2010).

CHAPTER 2

A HELPING HAND

*For in the same way you judge others, you will be judged,
and with the measure you use, it will be measured to you; John
8:1 - 11 He that is without sin among you, let him first cast a
stone...*

Matthew 7:2-5

Before the BSE, society and those employed by maternity homes believed that it was best for unmarried mothers and their children to remain together. The policy of the first and largest of the maternity homes, such as the Salvation Armies and the Florence Crittentons, firmly reflected this view.

Dr. Kate Waller Barrett and Charles Crittenton co-founded the Florence Crittenton maternity homes in 1895 with the goal of keeping mother and child together. By 1897, when 51 Crittenton homes had been established, Dr. Barrett was still expressing strong feelings about the importance of this goal (In Kunzel, 1993):

> Were I going to make a text for this subject
> ...I should take the sentence from the
> marriage service: Those whom God hath
> joined together, let no man put asunder.
> Sometimes we may have very grave doubts as
> to whether God has really had any part in the

making of a marriage, but we cannot doubt
that he joins together mother and child by the
strongest of all human ties.

Emma Lundberg and Katherine Lenroot (1920), the first
Director and Assistant Director, respectively, of the Social
Services Division of the United States Children's Bureau
(See Appendix C), writing about illegitimacy as a child
welfare problem, emphasized the value of the bond
between the natural mother and her child, as well as their
concerns about preventable separations:

> Of increasing interest is the question as to
> whether in being separated from the mother,
> the child is not deprived of something that
> society cannot replace even with the best care
> it can provide, and whether this most
> important consideration may not outweigh all
> others...Often separation occurs when it
> might have been prevented, and when it is
> contrary to the best interests of the child and
> the mother (Lundberg & Lenroot, 1920).

This philosophy was apparent in staffing the homes as
well:

> When a social worker applied to the NFCM
> [National Florence Crittenton Mission] for
> maternity home employment in 1930, Reba
> Barrett Smith's response testified to the
> strength of that commitment at the same time
> that it betrayed an anxious defensiveness. 'I
> would like to know,' she wrote, 'whether or
> not you believe that a mother and child

should be kept together whenever possible -
that it is God's divine plan that they should
not be separated, and the training and
encouragement will often make it possible for
a girl to keep her baby…and that in the long
run it is better for both mother and child if an
attempt is made for them to spend their lives
together?' (Kunzel, 1993).

In response to widespread deviations from principles
established for adoption casework and concerns about the
growing number of independent adoptions, the Child
Welfare League (as cited in Carp, 1998) issued its first guide
for adoption practices in 1938. This list of safeguards,
consistent with the philosophy of the Crittenton and
Salvation Army homes, emphasized the importance of
keeping the natural family intact, stating, "The first
safeguard for the child could… be considered one for the
natural parents: the child was not to be unnecessarily
deprived of kinship ties."

The Child Welfare League's standards (See Appendix
D) presented a model of the most desirable practices to
which adoption agencies should aspire. At that time, the
newly emerging adoption workers seemed to agree with
that standard. Within a decade, however, adoption policy
concerning unmarried mothers began to change
dramatically.

Andy Hardy's Dilemma, a 1940 film short from the
Community Chest, a precursor to the United Way, shows
how Andy and his father explore the idea of charitable
giving. In the film, the narrator specifically discussed a
Salvation Army Home for Women, stating that the hospital:

…is happy to indulge any mother who wishes to be known by her first name only and once baby and mother are both healthy, the organization will find the mother a job where she can keep her infant nearby with the belief that with her own child growing up beside her, a girl isn't going to make the same mistake… A fundamental principle here is that, after the baby is born and started in life, and after the mother is well and normal, every effort is made to find work so she can keep her baby. You see, this magnificent principle of tolerance and understanding is based on her own child growing up beside her. She is unlikely to make the same mistake again… and oh, I didn't say anything about the babies' fathers, did I? And no, I'm not going to.

Just a few years later, in 1942, a brochure from the Washington, D.C. Florence Crittenton maternity home described the Home's actions to help residents begin caring for their children during the six months or more that a mother was permitted to stay at a home:

[Question] What does the Home do for a girl…?
[Answer] Training in care of her baby. If she cannot be restored to her own home, our caseworker finds a job for her. If she cannot have her baby with her, provision is made for the baby to be cared for while she is working…' [The Big Sister Group] gives material aid in the form of clothing, baby

carriage, furniture or temporary assistance in boarding the baby... She helps in the solution of problems. She stands by as long as she is wanted... These girls... are encouraged to keep their babies... girls leaving the Home are not turned at random into the world again, to rise or fall... the [maternity home] Society watches over and befriends them as long as seems necessary, sometimes for a period of years... In the usual case, both mother and baby leave the home when the baby is five weeks old. Plans for both are worked out before they leave (Crittenton Brochure, 1942).

This brochure further stated that it would be best for the mother and child if they remained together, noting that loving and caring for a baby strengthened the mother's character and that social workers and psychologists had learned that no material advantages compensated a child for the loss of its mother. *"Better a home with mother love... than an adopted home in luxury"* [emphasis added].

While, according to the language in the brochure, it was stated that adoption workers held this view, once adoption workers firmly established themselves in maternity homes around the country, they began to change adoption policy and practice and to pressure mothers into surrendering their babies instead of giving them the help they needed to keep them.

Maud Morlock of the United States Children's Bureau, explored the use of foster homes to care for *both* the natural mother *and* her child. In this situation, a single mother lived in the private home of a married mother who would instruct her in proper childcare. The new mother was expected to help clean and cook in return for room and board so that she could keep her baby with her. This arrangement was very effective in providing a place where the mother and baby can live together. The foster mother's experience in the physical care of babies and her willingness to teach the [new] mother are of vital importance (Morlock, 1946). Morlock appeared to suggest to adoption workers and maternity home personnel the safest and most ethical approach to mother and baby:

> There must be sufficient money available so that the economic motive will not force the mother to a hurried decision regarding separation from her child. Provision should be made so that *boarding care can be guaranteed for the baby for a 6-month period at least before a decision must be taken regarding adoption...* Particularly it is easier...for her child's father to see her if both desire this [emphasis added].

In 1947, maternity homes began shifting their operations and control away from the religious women who wanted to help mothers keep their babies to a professional class of adoption social workers who were introduced into the maternity homes. Bernice Brower, the director of the Women's Service Division of the United Charities of Chicago, sounding as if she was reminding others to support past "helping" policies, stated:

> Maternity home procedures were planned so as to encourage formation of an emotional bond between mother and baby, and from this developed such requirements as compulsory

> breast feeding by the mother, an insistence
> that all mothers give personal care to their
> babies, and requirements that the mother and
> child live together in the maternity home for a
> stipulated period of time after delivery ...
> Many people today, both in social work and in
> the outside community, feel that the
> unmarried mother should be encouraged to
> keep her child... (Brower, 1947).

Dr. Robert Barrett, the son of Crittenton Home co-founder Dr. Kate Waller Barrett, became president of the Florence Crittenton Homes after her death in 1925. He objected to the placement of social workers in the maternity homes and was concerned about their qualifications for handling the problems of unmarried mothers:

> I do not think that...the great majority of
> social workers (especially young, unmarried
> women) are competent to handle the problem
> of the unmarried mother and her child. A
> master's degree in social work does not always
> qualify a young woman to deal with the
> intricate problems of social behavior... An
> unwed mother must not be rushed into a
> decision to give up her baby for adoption until
> every other avenue has been explored and
> every other door opened (In Solinger, 1997).

Tragically, history subsequently revealed that, in most cases, no other avenues were explored, and no other doors were opened. Adoption had not been a part of the Crittenton care philosophy, but some of the homes allowed young women to surrender their babies for adoption or into foster care on a temporary and informal basis. The national organization was not in favor of this practice however, and in 1943, after some ten years' of debate, a path opened to change Crittenton's basic belief that it was necessary to keep mother and child together (McConnell & Dore, 1983).

In one case, a social worker at an Anchorage home tried to admit a pregnant unmarried woman who was planning to place her child for adoption, "but the Board refused, citing the Crittenton philosophy of keeping mother and baby together… The South Carolina home required the promise of a year's residence. The rationale for this practice was to insure a healthy start for the baby and to prepare the mother to support herself and her child… While commitment to serving young women in need remains the primary purpose of Florence Crittenton Services, the emphasis shifted… This shift began in the 40s with the provision of case work services… Seventy-six percent (76%) of Crittenton residents were placing their children for adoption by 1954" (McConnell & Dore, 1983).

Writing in 1952 to Virgil Payne, the first national director of a newly formed Florence Crittenton Association of America, Robert Barrett made his feelings clear:

> I feel very badly that a girl in our homes
> shall not be given every opportunity to help
> keep her baby if she wants to. Often a girl
> who has made up her mind to give up her
> baby feels different when the baby comes and
> her mother's instinct is aroused. Not to give

her that chance seems a cruel and unnatural proceeding (In Solinger, 1997).

In language both critical and reproachful directed at those working in child welfare, a report from the U.S. Department of Health, Education and Welfare presented at a Children's Bureau conference emphasized that the rights of an unmarried mother are the same as those of a married mother:

> The mother of a child born out of wedlock has the same rights, moral and legal, as the parent of a legitimate child. *A mother should not be forced by financial pressure to give up her child... The caseworker must utilize the skills of other professions to meet the needs of mother and child, and to help the mother to make a decision she can live with the rest of her life...* Adoption is one... accepted practice of handling the placement of infants of illegitimate birth. *Another alternative is providing the necessary* <u>total</u> *services that would enable the unmarried mother to rear her own child...* [emphasis added] (Children's Bureau, 1955).

Salvation Army Colonel Jane Wrieden warned others in her field in the 1950s that maternity homes themselves might become a problem in the future, noting that maternity homes were part of a "whole service to a whole person in a whole community" and that their effectiveness were a function of their personnel. She was concerned about this, stating, "This is the rub... I wonder to what extent we can consider the 'agenda of opportunities'...*Is it possible that the maternity home itself may become a social problem?*" [emphasis added] (Wrieden, 1951).

Sociologist Clark Vincent, issued an amazingly accurate and dire warning about what he observed and expected for the future:

> If the demand for adoptable babies continues to exceed the supply... if the laws and courts continue to emphasize that the 'rights of the child' supersede the 'rights of the parents,' then it is quite possible that, in the near future, *unwed mothers will be 'punished' by having their children taken from them right after birth. A policy like this would not be executed nor labelled explicitly as 'punishment.' Rather, it would be implemented by such pressures and labels as 'scientific findings,' 'the best interest of the child' and 'rehabilitation of the unwed mother'*... [emphasis added] (Vincent, 1964).

The agencies began to pressure mothers to place their children for adoption. Records kept by a Crittenton caseworker revealed how the agency, originally going to "great lengths and expense to compel a woman to keep her child, *now applied great psychological pressure upon a mother to place her child for adoption*" [emphasis added] (Morton, 1997).

As time went on, the Crittenton Homes moved away from their original philosophy, ending an era, and signaling the "victory of the professional ethos of social workers over the founding ideals of religious women reformers. Social workers used the ideology of professionalism to carve out creative careers for themselves" (Kunzel, 1993). Other maternity homes, both private, religious and state, also slowly began their evolution away from the earlier policy of supporting the unmarried mother to keep their babies to pressuring them to surrender thereby ending the helping era.

CHAPTER 3

THE "EXPERTS"

When confronted by evil, the wisest and most secure adult will usually experience confusion. Imagine, then, what it must be like for a naïve child who encounters evil in the ones it most loves and upon whom it depends. Add to this the fact that evil people, refusing to acknowledge their own failures, actually desire to project their evil onto others, and it is no wonder that children will misinterpret that process by hating themselves. …evil is 'live' spelled backward. Evil is in opposition to life. It is that which opposes the life force… the desire of certain people to control others – to make them controllable, to foster their dependency, to discourage their capacity to think for themselves, to diminish their unpredictability and originality, to keep them in line…

F. Scott Peck

Over time, the policies of the Florence Crittenton Homes slowly evolved, with the Florence Crittenton Mission adapting to the changes and reevaluating the policies at work in its network of sixty two (62) homes during the 1930s. As the first legitimate adoption agencies emerged, adoption became a more feasible option, and the homes began to discourage unmarried mothers from keeping their children. Following World War II, there were ever more social workers entering the field with college degrees, and they replaced the occupational staff members at the homes (Baumler, 2003).

As discussed earlier, a major change began to take place in the 1940s. Religious women, who offered a helping hand, were pushed out of the maternity homes by adoption workers who claimed to be adoption specialists and experts in unwed motherhood.

Jane Wrieden of the Salvation Army expressed her concerns about the lack of education of adoption workers in the maternity homes, believing that before any caseworker went to work in a maternity home she should have "experience in a casework agency of high quality" in addition to obtaining a graduate degree from an accredited school of social work. She noted, however, that maternity homes tended to allow individuals without professional education or experience to work as caseworkers "and expect [them] to do a professional job" (Wrieden, 1951).

The fact was that in 1950, 40 percent of child welfare workers in non-institutional public child welfare programs did not have advanced social work education. The situation was particularly acute for caseworkers; 50 percent had no graduate education in social work, and 20 percent of public assistance workers, who had significantly less professional education than child welfare workers, held positions in child welfare programs (Shapiro, 1955).

According to a paper presented at the National Conference on Adoption in January, 1955:

> *About 75 per cent of their workers were without graduate social work education...*These agencies employed 1,608 caseworkers: 429 or nearly 27 percent of them were either high school or college graduates only...[I]n some instances

*the blind are being led by those with poor
vision...*they are likely to bring about poor
service to some clients at some time in some
way...Even these scattered statistics indicate
that *a large number of the social workers serving
children are without graduate education in social work*
[emphasis added] (Shapiro, 1955).

In fact, there was criticism of social workers in the mid-
1950s noting that the workers did not have adequate
knowledge of babies and caused them more pain than was
necessary as they did not empathize with the babies or
realize the terror they experienced moving into unfamiliar
environments and situations (Charnley, 1955).

In 1964, Barbara Costigan in her dissertation, "The
Unmarried Mother - Her Decision Regarding Adoption,"
noted that adoption workers favored surrender:

The emphasis on intra-psychic disturbance
of the unmarried mother appears to have led
the social work profession clearly in the
direction of favoring relinquishment of the
baby... The conclusion that recent social work
professional opinion generally favors the
relinquishment of the unmarried mother's
baby is supported by a review of the literature
from 1950 to the present... It was believed
that the social worker should decide on the
plan and carry it out... [T]he preponderance
of social work professional opinion has been
that, in most instances, it is a better solution
both for the mother and the child if the child
is placed for adoption (Costigan, 1964).

It became increasingly obvious by the 1960s that there was a real need for a close examination of adoption social work, particularly concerning the lack of innovation in the field and the reluctance to review its own practices (Perlman, 1971).

Many adoption workers did not have sufficient experience and knowledge in working with unmarried mothers nor did they make plans with unmarried fathers. It was the case that social work staff had only limited training, with little planned for fathers and no understanding of their needs. Adoption workers had only limited resources available for addressing the fathers at all, and neglecting the needs of a baby's father remained a major problem in the 1970s. The lack of considerations for a baby's father was related to cultural attitudes that accepted the role and behaviors of unmarried fathers while at the same time labeling pregnant females as social deviants (Klerman & Jekel, 1973).

As previously stated, there was a marked transition from the original goals of the National Florence Crittenton Mission (NFCM), which worked to keep mother and child together, to the strong mandate coming from social workers after World War II that unmarried mothers should surrender their children for adoption. Few social workers continued to view these women as their "unfortunate sisters" whom it was their duty to "save." Instead, social workers began to see themselves as professionals with an interest in reshaping perceptions of illegitimacy and unmarried mothers (Kunzel, 1993).

Maternity homes were under increasing pressure by the newly professionalized adoption social workers to replace their missionary zeal and religious charity with a "professional, scientific approach" that favored adoption. The change began in 1943, with the NFCM taking a major step for an organization whose member agency had, *only a few years earlier, denied a local social worker's plea to admit a girl who had been thinking about placing her child for adoption...* By 1954...76% of Crittenton residents were placing their babies for adoption..." [emphasis added] (McConnell & Dore, 1983).

A few social workers were frustrated at what they perceived as the "punitive" attitudes of some of those working with unmarried mothers in separating them from their children, which were readily admitted in some cases. In 1954, Sara Edlin, long-time director of the Lakeview Home for unmarried mothers, acknowledged her frustration, saying she was "deeply discouraged at the punitive attitude of many social workers, and their resistance to any legislation that would make life easier for mother and child..." Many social work professionals justified their actions by describing them as in the best interest of the mother and of her child. In answer to the concerns of those social workers who were unsure that pressuring a mother to surrender her child was the right thing to do, Dr. Leontine Young, an educator, author and social worker who adopted, provided assurances, writing:

> [A] worker may ask, 'what happens
> afterward? Doesn't the girl regret giving up
> the baby?' That is quite possible and... even
> probable...The unhappy girl continues to
> dream of what *might have* been, but at least she

is spared the grinding disappointment of experiencing what *would have* been...Because the girls are so unable to take any decisive action, *the responsibility falls far more heavily upon the worker... one often finds workers worrying that they may be putting pressure on the girl to decide... almost always this is pressure to surrender the baby - and that they are making up her mind for her.* They fear that they are in effect 'selling her a bill of goods' which she does not really want to buy and which once bought she will regret... [emphasis added] (L. Young, 1954).

During the 1950s, adoption social workers began to see unmarried mothers as "sick:"

We know a great deal about the unmarried or natural mother...that she is not bad, but rather *that she is sick*...Not only is one attempting to help the unmarried mother develop more mature methods of solving her problems than through her solution of getting pregnant, *but one also is usually able to help the unmarried mother give up her baby for adoption...* [emphasis added] (Littner, 1955).

By the end of the decade, adoption workers had gone further, perceiving unmarried mothers as troubling, unfit and needing punishment:

The applicant who wants none of the agency or the caseworker is obviously the hardest one to reach, engage or even tolerate... [I]t is this client...who is troubling the

community's peace of spirit (such as the
unwed mother)…What is social work for…if
not to make social beings of these
unfortunate *misfits* or to protect society against
their depredations? Where can they be helped
or dealt with, if they are not to be put in
places of confinement and *punishment?* …Of
the several professions that use psychological
means of influence, that of social work
consistently encounters the *problem of the
unwilling client.* Caseworkers…work out ways by
which to engage *the unwilling person* [emphasis
added] (Perlman, 1957).

In 1984, Edwin Shur, professor of sociology at New
York University, discussed how social workers defined
segments of the population as deviant to keep them "in
their place." According to Shur, it happens that:

[For] supposedly 'helping' professionals…
definitions of deviance operate to impose
control… by defining the latter's behavior as
deviant… to keep women under control or in
their 'place'… [W]e also began to observe
more directly the role of social control
agents… Through the interpretations and
classifications they use in dealing with
possibly problematic behaviors, social control
and 'helping' agents… play an important role
in 'producing' deviance… These processes
also involve converting specific individuals
into 'cases'… (Shur, 1984).

It was even recommended by the professionals that if an unmarried pregnant female was unwilling to surrender her baby for adoption, the social worker should be "decisive, firm, and unswerving" in finding a "healthy solution to the girl's problem" by targeting that woman's mother to make sure the baby would be surrendered. According to Dr. Marcel Heiman, clinical professor of psychiatry at the Mount Sinai School of Medicine, *"The 'I'm going to help you by standing by while you work it through' approach will not do. What is expected from the worker is precisely what the child expected but did not get from her parents - a decisive 'No!'"* [emphasis added] (Heiman, 1960).

This kind of pressure and coercion placed upon a vulnerable young mother by a caseworker, an adult authority figure, was frequent and usually quite effective. According to social worker Barbara Costigan (1964), there was an acknowledged tendency for social workers to influence unmarried mothers to release their babies for adoption, and the more contact the mothers had with adoption workers, the more likely they were to surrender their babies; gaps in communications between adoption workers and pregnant women before birth were linked to a mother's decision to keep her child. If the mother ultimately did not surrender her baby, that outcome was viewed by the adoption worker as "a failure:"

> [I]f a majority of the caseworkers shared the prevalent belief in the social work profession that 'in most instances the best solution, both for mother and child, is relinquishment,' this belief got across to the unmarried mother... The fact that social work professional attitudes tend to favor the relinquishment of the

baby, as the literature shows, should be faced more clearly. Perhaps if [this] were recognized, workers would be in less conflict and would therefore feel less guilty about their 'failures' (Costigan, 1964).

Recognizing the dangers facing unmarried mothers, Helen Terkelsen, a pastor and counselor in the United Church of Christ, expressed her concerns about the pressures they faced:

> [W]hen the unwed mother is brought to the counselor, she will repeat what she has already said to her parents. 'I want to make my own decisions'... Unfortunately, many of the unwed mother's enemies are more real than the Christian pastor cares to admit... She may consider her enemies [as]... *Those who are ready to snatch the baby from her* [and] those who would send her away from home...unwed mothers may have placed their children for adoption [because] they *were advised or pressured to release the baby*... [emphasis added] (Terkelsen, 1964).

By the 1960s, social workers, adoption counselors, and legal consultants began to examine the attitudes and practices of the social work profession in applying pressure on unmarried mothers to surrender their babies. It was determined, that in the United States, adoption agencies - and the general public - expected unmarried white mothers to release their children for adoption, with the workers having different reactions to statements of intention from the mother: "that she wishes to give up the child and the statement that she wishes to keep him. The first... they take at face value, the second in a very challenging way" (Isaac & Spencer, 1965).

> The double-edged sword aspects of authority meant that it was useful to the social worker and sometimes necessary to effect appropriate outcomes ("...*the use of the client's trust in the worker as a vehicle for influencing his behavior is sometimes a very useful form of treatment...*"), but when used inappropriately, it could cause great damage in people's lives. The inherent power of an adoption caseworker over the behavior of the "client" (mother) was described "as effective as a court's threat of imprisonment" [emphasis added] (Nicholds, 1966).

Concern about the misuse of authority continued into the 1970s, with some social workers questioning the practices of others. Rose Bernstein, a social work pioneer, warned:

> The implication is that having conceived a child out of wedlock, *she has forfeited the right to control significant aspects of her life. She must accept the decisions of others...* [emphasis added] (Bernstein, 1971).

It was also observed that an unmarried mother could feel that, while her needs were met by an adoption worker, it was not out of that worker's concern for her, but only because she was the source that could supply a child that someone else would take from her (Costin, 1972).

There have been few studies verifying the assumptions and dogma on which adoption social workers base their practices, but those that have been done indicate that these beliefs tend to "deny or neglect the true feelings and experiences of all those involved" with the adoption process. Some social workers have called for the profession to challenge *"the traditional assumptions and practices of social workers that have labeled certain feelings and desires 'abnormal' and have distorted the experiences and needs of adoptees, birth mothers* and those who adopt" [emphasis added] (Baran & Pannor, 1990).

The "double-edged" role of female social workers was again noted. Adoption workers generally may have had humanitarian motives as their inspiration, but the way they treated [natural] mothers was shaped by societal assumptions about what constitutes "good mothering." The policies governing their work are also shaped by attempts to gain professional status, authority, and influence in a society that has traditionally devalued the work of women (Wegar, 1997).

Critics of adoption practices, who changed with the professionalization of social work, have gone so far as to characterize the actions of some adoption workers as being akin to fraud. They further justified policies that they imposed. Two Australian criminologists have stated that fraudsters display no real remorse for the actions they take, but superficially justify themselves by blaming their victims as "being stupid or deserving of their fate." They also minimize the harms that arise from what they do, or they show an "arrogant indifference" to the consequences they bring. While an ethical approach may stem some of these elements, there will "always be a hard core of people who, with full knowledge of the difference between right and wrong, will opt for the latter" (Duffield & Grabosky, 2001).

CHAPTER 4

ILLEGAL MOTHERHOOD

Make that Mother look like a Saint. Then blind side her,
she won't know what hit her. When I had to be NICE to
[the] girls mother I just about died inside, but once the
termination was over, I just told her what a piece of crap she
was. I don't know your story. But, I will pray that you get to
keep [her] child.

Anonymous on Internet

In the 1950s, traditional children's institutions were "retooled" to provide treatment rather than punishment for children deemed delinquent, neglected, or disturbed, and welfare authorities recognized that old-style maternity homes should also be revamped to provide "a thorough treatment job" for every girl or woman who entered (Lourie, 1956). As late as 1964, social work professionals remarked that "illegal coition" was widespread in the United States and increasing because it was being encouraged by the culture and by social patterns (Kahn, 1964). Illegitimacy was still considered a crime and a delinquency at the end of the 1960s (Kammerer, 1969).

By the late 1960s white unmarried females had not attained 'sexual freedom'... even after the 1973 Roe v. Wade decision. But one result of the rapid 'de-criminalization' of youthful,

female sexuality and even of unwed
pregnancy between 1965 and 1973, was that
white broadly middle-class girls would not be
forced to go behind the fence... to serve time
for the crime of pregnancy (Solinger, 1992).

Joss Shawyer (1979) described adoption as violent and
aggressive:

> Adoption is a violent act, a political act of
> aggression towards a woman who has
> supposedly offended the sexual mores by
> committing the unforgivable act of not
> suppressing her sexuality, and therefore not
> keeping it for trading purposes through
> traditional marriage. The *crime* is a grave one,
> for she threatens the very fabric of our
> society. The penalty is severe. She is stripped
> of her child by a variety of subtle and not so
> subtle maneuvers and then brutally
> abandoned [emphasis added].

Phyllis Chesler (1986) explained that nonconformity was
viewed as a crime and wondered who it served to remove a
baby from its mother:

> Is it in the interest of the state, the family,
> or the child to remove it from its own
> mother's custody if her only *crime* is
> nonconformity? Whose interests are being
> served? Since a mother loses her rights not by
> mothering poorly but by violating patriarchal
> rules for women, then 'parent's rights' are but
> a subterfuge for men's rights, such as they are.

David Howe, Phillida Sawbridge and Diana Hinings (1992) also described the criminal aspect of unmarried motherhood:

> Having got pregnant under morally censured circumstances, the unmarried mother compounds her *'crime'* by not bringing up her own child. A climate of punishment and censure often seems to surround the mother... There is a price to be paid... the reactions of people to the unwed mother not only create feelings of stress, trauma and shame in the mother-to-be, but those same reactions lead her to conclude that adoption is the only way out of her increasingly complex situation... She also realizes that her *'crime,'* the conception of an out-of-wedlock child, has shrunk to a commonplace event [emphasis added].

PART II

THE SCOOPING

A Mother's Story / *Nancy Ann*

Pain and Sorrow for What Should Have Never, Never Been

Skip and I truly loved each other. Our love resulted in a pre-marital pregnancy. Unfortunately, my sister, who was interning for Catholic Charities through the College of St. Teresa, got involved and claimed she knew how to handle the dilemma at hand. That is when Catholic Charities got involved.

My pregnancy as an unwed mother (as I was called) was very typical of most stories during that time; brow-beaten with names, stereotyped as neurotic, sent away to a ghetto in St. Paul, and left alone to fend for myself. All of the things that are written about the Baby Scoop Era apply to me.

My clothes were taken away, my name was changed and I was not able to connect with the outside world. I compare my stay there to anyone who is abducted by a cult. I was brainwashed with propaganda of how sinful I was. I was treated like a second-class citizen who deserved to be treated as such for my sins and given tasks to do that no one nine months pregnant should be allowed to do, such as working in a laundry where the temperature exceeded 100 degrees. All of this was referred to as my punishment.

The nuns at the home made reference to my unworthiness and to how grateful I should be to them for saving me. The social worker who visited me several times could not handle my unwillingness to surrender the baby to CC. My precious baby girl was never referred to as my baby because in the mind of the social worker I could never be a fit mother; perhaps someday, if I could be, I would have a baby of my own. But not this baby. This baby would go to people who were capable of being a real mother and father. After all, it was reiterated to me over and over again that I had nothing to offer my child. However, a married couple had plenty to offer my baby.

The day of the delivery finally came. I was never given any information as to what would happen during my delivery except that I would be whisked away by a taxi and taken to St. Joseph's Hospital in St. Paul. Upon being admitted, I was taken to a labor room to labor by myself. The crude nurse checked on me several times, but left me alone, to suffer as that was part of my punishment.

When the time came for delivery, a cold-hearted doctor came in and demanded that I be shackled to the bars of the delivery table. I turned to the nurse with an anxious look, and she told me it was for my own good. The delivery came, and my beautiful baby was taken to a corner where I could not see her. I remember trying to get up to just see a glimpse of her, but she was kept sheltered from me doing so. And so the hospital stay went on with no association with *anyone*.

Several days before the delivery I was informed that when I got to go home, my dad would come and get me alone. I questioned why my mom would not come, but was given no real answer. Contrary to the direction given my mom, she did come along with my dad. They both saw my beautiful baby girl through a glass door at the Catholic Infant home. Years later I figured out it was so my mom, grandmother of my child, would not see her and become weakened to the decision that my baby would go to an unknown family.

Well, CC knew what they were doing. My mom did entertain the idea of keeping my precious child with one condition. Skip and I would have to be married. Skip and I did work on this idea to see if this could become a reality. We talked, attended meetings at CC, both together and separately. We needed time to make an informed decision. Of course, we did not get to see our child during this time. She was tucked away in a foster home at a location unbeknownst to us (civil rights issue).

Several days later, my mother got a phone call from Margaret Driscoll, the head of Catholic Charities in Winona. The call consisted of my mother listening and Margaret talking. She was degrading my mother as I was degraded while in the home in St. Paul. After the call I was informed that I had one day to make the decision and that was that.

Needless to say, my mother was also coerced to make the "right decision." After all, who did my mom think she was to be able to make a decision about our child?

I believe CC was aware that we were very close to making a decision to keep my baby, but they already had another family in mind for her (as I found out several years ago when reading the official notes about my case.) I have read about treating the grandmother as they did me, and I believe this is what happened. CC wanted my baby for themselves so they could deliver her to the family they promised. (For $ of course!)

I can remember how my heart sank when I realized I had no recourse of action to keep my baby. All support (the little I had) was removed by a simple phone call. My life was forever changed. Am I still sad? Of course. Nothing can ever replace someone you love. (Both my baby and her father.) It is something I live with daily. I have tried many things to help me overcome my feelings. However, reality is reality.

It is so easy for others who have not gone through a trauma of this nature to ignore it. People tell me, "You should be get over it, that's what they did back then, be grateful for what you have, I'm proud of your strength for doing that, I could not have ever done that," etc. Why are comments like that made by others? Because that is the easiest way for them to deal with the reality of what happened.

CHAPTER 5

THE GOD PLAYERS

Power tends to corrupt and absolute power corrupts absolutely. Great men are almost always bad men, even when they exercise influence and not authority; still more when you super-add the tendency of the certainty of corruption by authority.

Lord Acton

Did adoption workers enjoy their power and the opportunity to "play God" as they took babies from unmarried mothers and placed them into the arms of wealthier, mostly infertile, married couples? Some claimed that adoption workers had little in the way of specialized training. Did the lack of training impact their attitudes? A chronological review of statements by social work professionals of the BSE period shows that they well understood the kind of power they wielded in the adoption process.

In 1955, a social worker acknowledged that anyone responsible for making decisions on the placement of a child is "playing a God-like role." In 1962, a discussion of power and the adoption worker (Ferard & Hunnybun, 1962), noted the "zeal" demonstrated by some workers "in going to the rescue" and how that might reflect a hidden desire for power that was satisfied by managing other people's affairs. For some workers, the difficulties experienced by their charges provided justification for taking control of the situation, despite the fact that their actions could be detrimental to the client's capacity for self-help and independence.

A paper presented at a regional adoption conference in Georgia reiterated the idea that adoption workers felt as if they "played God," and also raised concerns about the lack of experience and training of other child welfare workers who had influence and authority over the lives of others (Roberts, 1964).

Throughout the 1960s, social work professionals acknowledged the actual and perceived power given to adoption workers. Caseworkers gloried in their power to give or withhold children (Rowe, 1966); said "yes" when asked if they were playing God (Benedict, 1964); and recognized that social work asserted both legitimate and coercive power.

In his paper "Changing Organizations," Warren Bennis stated:

> The social actionist starts from an operational base of expert power – the ability to develop or possess knowledge in some area that is considered important by the social system... depending on the problem focus and his role and status, [there are] two other kinds of power: legitimate power, "the capacity to invoke the authority of position which is accorded by institutional norms and practices" and coercive power, "the capacity to reward and punish" (In Craigen, 1972).

By the early 1970s, guidelines for adoption stated the adoption agency receives its power to transfer the custody of a child from the court, whether through voluntary surrender or legal termination of parental rights. The guidelines also stated that a natural parent's right of consent to any transfer of that responsibility should be included in the process (Ford, 1971). At the same time, some adoption professionals realized a manipulation of power manifested in the transfer of child custody, and it had a strong effect on clients and represented a force in society. In fact, the actual language used by social workers during this period was changing.

> The thrust is...from social workers as enablers to social workers as change agents, from client as having self-determination to clients as change *target*, from compromise to *manipulation of power... Power as a social force* has pushed its way into rank and uneasy recognition by community workers. Power structures, power conflicts, power play are considerations that must be in the very center of any community-wide *intervention strategy*, whether political, economic, or social [emphasis added] (Perlman, 1971).

Six years later, Julie Cheetham described the intensity that can develop in the relationship between the adoption counselor and the unmarried mother, an intensity that is compounded by dependency of the unmarried mother, who is facing a crisis in her life, and the power, authority, and influence possessed by the adoption worker. She emphasized the responsibility of counselors to be honest about their own prejudices and biases:

> People in a crisis are more dependent than usual and therefore *more susceptible to influence.* This presents counselors with opportunities they need to guard against suggesting courses of action to someone who is not in a state to explore their implications, and who feels it is easiest to do what others seem to think is best...*it is quite unethical to exploit individuals' temporary dependence...*because people tend to undermine decisions they feel have been thrust upon them, and also feel demeaned if responsibility is taken away from them, adoption counselors must help their clients make decisions they can live with [emphasis added] (Cheetham, 1977).

In the 1980s, discussions of power considered how members of marginal groups must address larger and stronger groups of people who enjoy advantages they lack and whose power is viewed by the marginalized as the source of their problems (Inglis, 1984). The potential for abuse in the worker-client relationship was even recognized by the professionals themselves. "Adoption work by its nature is seductive because of the amount of power it transfers to its practitioner" (Triseliotis, 1989).

"Whoever saw a human being that would not abuse unlimited power?" asked Phyllis Chesler (1986).

In the 1990s, women who had lived through the BSE began to share their experiences with adoption workers, agencies, and other authorities, but their stories did little to change conventional views of the dynamics. Their stories had little impact on what continued as the dominant narratives of single pregnancies. Natural mothers were considered "unreliable narrators" and "liars" by adoption authorities. Their narratives of their own experiences were not acknowledged as "legitimate" by adoption professionals (Kunzel, 1995).

At the same time, social casework, which brought its "morals-tested" aid to poor, single mothers, became an extension of the law, declaring single mothers unfit and petitioning the courts to remove their children from the home (Armstrong, 1995).

By the beginning of the 21st century, some adoption professionals encouraged counselors to view adoption as a part of the agency's "redemptive mission," which represented an "act of grace" to "redeem" women and children from lives of suffering. "If they see God's hand in adoption, they will regard women who choose adoption as loving mothers and themselves as faithful and competent for having presented the option" (C. Young, 2000).

Grace Duffield and Peter Grobosky (2001) described an important aspect of fraud in "The Psychology of Fraud:"

> ...motivation that may apply to some or all types of fraud is ego/power. This can relate to power over people as well as power over situations...*acting skills are advantageous if not essential to the deception inherent in face to face fraud...a lack of social conscience and conventional morality ... frequently deceive, exploit and manipulate*

others in order to achieve personal gain
for…power [emphasis added].

The modern age of social media has provided examples of how the notion of power among adoption counselors and social workers continues today. In 2014, "a social worker gloated about having three children taken into care on her publicly accessible Facebook page. Siobhan Condon, 41, bragged about the power she felt at breaking up the family and reveled in the judge giving the parents a 'massive rollicking'" (Levy, 2014).

CHAPTER 6

THE INDU$TRY

Adoption Loss is the only trauma in the world where the
victims are expected by the whole of society to be grateful.

Reverend Keith C. Griffith, MBE

Adoption is viewed by many as altruistic and saintly. However, it is really big business. Marketdata Enterprises estimated that the adoption industry took in "over $1.4 billion annually" (MarketData Enterprises, 2000). It is a market in all senses of the word, complete with brokers and buyers. The brokers are the facilitators and include adoption agencies and adoption lawyers. Buyers are potential adopters. The brokers locate and obtain the product, in this case newborn babies and infants; they also facilitate the adoption. The source of the product is the (mostly) young, vulnerable, unprotected, and unmarried mother.

By 1955, the U.S. Department of Health Education, and Welfare (HEW) Children's Bureau described the extensive use of advertising by commercial maternity homes, and in 1957, Mildred Arnold of the Social Services Department at the HEW acknowledged that there was no problem finding adoptive homes for white babies, but:

[T]he present 'market' is creating serious
problems for us in terms of independent
placements of these children without essential
safeguards in the study and selection of
homes. Some of this comes about...from the
feeling on the part of many people that just
any well-meaning person can find a good
home for a baby, from the denial of services
to unmarried mothers, and from the profit
that is sometimes made in such transactions
(Arnold, 1955).

Some social workers in the late 1950s acknowledged the
damage done to unmarried mothers by their profession,
which worked hard - in what they came to believe was the
kindest approach - to help these women "deny emotionally
the biological experience of pregnancy and to prevent the
emotional maturity to develop which should be the natural
consequence of the physiological changes in her female
body" (Bye, 1959). It was impossible for anyone involved
to ignore the physical changes attending a pregnancy, but
the social work professionals decided that focusing on the
needs of sterile couples who entered the adoption market
and its ready supply of newborns was the "least punishing
way" to help the unmarried mother - and themselves:

Our conscience as social workers is
appeased. The mother is helped to avoid the
social stigma. As citizens, we receive them
back into their homes, in their schools, in
their offices, in their professions, as if nothing
had happened. The fact that we, by this
process, have left them psychologically
immature and sociologically isolated entirely

too often has as yet not penetrated our
awareness (Bye, 1959).

It appeared that society in general preferred the status
quo, which continually supplied white infants produced by
white unmarried mothers for adoption, over any kind of
real solutions to the problems associated with illegitimacy.
Preventive efforts remained on the safe side by highlighting
conventional reasons for illegitimacy, such as poverty,
ignorance, youth, or psychological "disturbance." Society
continued its basically ineffectual approaches to
understanding or decreasing illegitimacy rates instead of
facing the real problem and making real changes to
attitudes and practices. Critics of this approach even said
that if this was the case "we might at least discontinue the
self-deception of believing we really want to do away with
illegitimacy...For the current illogical practice of enticing
the cause (pre-and extra-marital sexual intimacy) while
stigmatizing the result (out of wedlock pregnancy)..."
(Vincent, 1962).

A report from the United Nations Secretary General's
Commission on the Status of Women called for more
protections for unmarried mothers in 1971, describing
current protections as "far from adequate." According to
the report, every effort should be made to meet the unique
needs of unmarried mothers, and that professionals like
doctors, social workers, and lawyers should work together
to ensure the adequate health, social and legal protections
for these women.

It should not be considered as one likely to
encourage births out of wedlock and therefore
as a cause of a situation looked upon as a

social evil. If the unmarried mother is successfully helped, she and her child may well become useful and active participants in the life of the community rather than both being social outcasts… (United Nations, 1971).

White unmarried mothers became the prime source of commodities for the adoption industry and systems were developed to denigrate or eliminate programs that allowed some unmarried mothers to avoid the baby market. Programs such as Aid to Dependent Children (ADC) were targeted and downgraded as appropriate options for white unmarried mothers in order to feed the market of the hundreds of thousands of married couples who knew that healthy white babies were supplied by these women (Vincent, 1962).

Because a proprietary adoption agency was, fundamentally, a business, the Child Welfare League of America stated that it required safeguards to ensure that its services were not applied in ways meant only to "protect or enhance profits" (Child Welfare League of America, 1971).

The United States, which has been described as "an exuberantly mercantile nation," began to "merchandize" children in the early 1970s with newspaper ads, adoption columns and photos of the Adoptable Baby-of-the-Week to promote the growing industry of providing babies to infertile couples. In that market, there was no significant increase in the number of adoptions of non-white children, but there was a shortage of white babies, which were in high market demand. Potential adopters in some parts of the U.S. had to wait two years for a white baby, while in other places, the adoption agencies simply closed application lists for white infants, giving rise to a thriving black market. "The price per little white head may go as high as $1,000 in Michigan. In California, there are stories of couples who offer doctors and lawyers as much as $10,000 cash" (Morgenstern, 1971).

By the 1980s, the adoption market had matured so that it could be described as a "seller's market" for white couples who used a licensed agency: the low supply of white children coincided with a high demand from potential parents (Kirk, 1984).

Of course, adoption agencies tried to gloss over the unsavory aspects of baby selling in the adoption process. While some adoption workers grew alarmed at what was happening, many of the adoption agencies, so self-described at least, tended to blur the line between "financial support" offered to the unmarried mother and "baby selling," which was prohibited by law in most states.

> Many of these newer self-described 'adoption' agencies, which have sprung up in many states, gloss over the line between financial support to isolated and frightened unwed mothers and 'baby selling' forbidden by law in most states. Many lawyers have gone into the business of private adoptions, some more unscrupulous than the agencies... Meanwhile, impatient infertile couples now openly seek out desperate pregnant young women directly through advertising, often moving to states where they can escape

agency scrutiny (The New Bodies, Ourselves, 1992).

In 1992, Rickie Solinger described the business aspect of infant adoptions:

> The psychiatric explanation of white single pregnancy spared the male as it punished the female…it rehabilitated the… illegitimate baby; the baby was rendered adoptable and the adoption market was served…Over one in ten of all marriages are involuntarily childless …most of these couples must wait one or two or three years in order to adopt a baby…Under these conditions, white, pregnant, unmarried women and their babies became market commodities.

In 1995, Regina Kunzel also discussed the growing adoption market. She claimed that:

> 'The Terrifying Ordeal' defied the postwar consensus that denied single white women a rightful claim to maternity…The very notion that it was their choice to make ran counter to the growing conviction that the recovery of the reputation and mental health of white single mothers (and, importantly, a growing adoption market) depended on their surrendering their children.

In a weak attempt to regulate the adoption industry, the Family Research Council suggested that so-called pregnancy centers and counselors sell the idea of adoption to vulnerable, unmarried mothers and minimizing the factors that would keep women from taking the adoption route and maximize those who would motivate them to do so. However, they were cautioned to avoid conflicts of interest and being seen as obtaining profits from any arrangement.

> The demand for healthy, white babies was enormous in the United States, and its sheer size invited abuse. Evidence indicates that there was a broad and lucrative underground market for white babies, especially during the 1950s. Workers in child care agencies admitted that there was considerable abuse centered on the unmarried mother's release of her child. In the U.S., it was clear that some of the worst abuse of power involved the child welfare agencies themselves (Chambers, 2006).

The business of adoption evolved and brought along a significant amount of shady dealings and fraud. Most individuals who commit fraud try to find ways to rationalize or justify their behavior. They will use "vocabularies of adjustment" that create the reasons and extenuating circumstances for their actions and remove their guilt at the same time. They begin to view the victim of their fraud as the guilty party in some way, easily believing that the victim "had it coming." By generating a lack of respect and outright dislike of the victim, fraudsters have an easy time treating them badly. Once they begin to view their victims in this way, there are few restraints to inhibit continuing the crime (Duffeld & Grabosky, 2001).

The issues surrounding adoption and adoption practices involved the unpleasant factors of poverty, lack of power, social class and race. Despite the close links between these forces and their impact on unmarried mothers, adoption was under-represented in the mental health literature. There were both cultural and moral values involved, such as bad behavior, shame and secrecy; there were also economic factors such as the social status of the original parents, the business of providing children for adoption, and the cost of obtaining a child. During the period when only "bad girls" got pregnant out of wedlock, there were many white babies available for adoption, but according to Henderson (2002):

> [A]s adoption became an increasingly big business, the process also became correspondingly more expensive… As the supply of healthy white American infants dwindled, the desires of childless parents for a baby were harder to meet. Agencies had to go first to poor (often minority) American neighborhoods, and then later overseas, to find children to place, and a certain amount of real additional expense was created. In some cases these legitimate expenses are considerable. When agency profits are added into the mix, however, distressing questions about 'buying children' arise and discomfort around these questions may cause other issues of adoption to be ignored by all involved.

CHAPTER 7

IN WHOSE "BEST INTERESTS?"

There is no room in the civilized world for the barbaric and inhuman practices against children to continue, regardless of how well disguised under the auspices of 'best interests of the child.'

Maureen Dabbagh

In the mid-1960s, there was a recognizable change in the focus of adoption professionals. Instead of focusing on the needs of the child - the child's "best interests" - adoption practice centered on the needs and wishes of the adoptive parents. Where the motivations of adoption workers had been to find a good home for a child, they began to make providing children for potential adopters their priority. "One big difference in adoption practice which stands out immediately is that the focus was heavily on the needs and wishes of the adoptive parents" (Canada, 1964).

As the adoption field developed, it became increasingly obvious that adoption practices prioritized the best interests of the people who adopt and the adoption workers themselves. Developments in the field rarely occurred in response to the best interests of the child, but tended to arise from many external factors, including the number of childless couples who wanted to adopt and the

THE BABY SCOOP ERA

pursuit of professional advancement among social workers (Wegar, 1997).

The change of focus created a situation in which illegitimate births presented less of a problem because they served a "valid social function such as a supply of children for economically secure, but infertile families who constituted a sizable adoption market" for the babies of unmarried mothers, both of whom were raised in value by their status: *"an unmarried mother is at a premium and her offspring [is] a desirable possession"* [emphasis added] (Roberts, 1966).

There was always an uncomfortable reality behind the motivations of adoption workers, a reality of which adopting couples and the workers themselves claimed no knowledge. Behind every child available for adoption was an unmarried mother who provided that child to the system, and while workers and adopters tried their best to ignore the situation, they knew it existed.

A study by Iris Goodacre showed that adopters did not like going to a maternity home to pick up their baby because *"their acute awareness of the natural mother's pain spoils the pleasure of the day to which they have looked forward to for so long"* [emphasis added] (Rowe, 1966). Since society in general finds a mother who gives up her child to be "unnatural," there is little effort to understand her or her situation, including by those who adopted: *"No one finds understanding more difficult than the adoptive parents, who have waited so long for a child... One admitted 'I know there is a girl out there suffering, and I don't like to think about her'"* [emphasis added] (Benet, 1976).

Some adoption workers during the 1960s Baby Scoop Era admitted that the adoption practice of the times was oriented toward finding babies for childless married couples. They felt they had failed if "too many" of the unmarried mothers they counseled chose to keep their babies. Reflecting on his career, Reuben Pannor, an adoption worker and former Director of Community Services at Vista Del Mar Child Care Service in California, stated, "We supported the needs of the adoptive parents whom we saw as the primary clients" (Pannor, 1987).

As infant adoption practices concentrated on meeting the needs of the adopters, adoption came to be perceived by the general society in a very positive light as a charitable and altruistic activity that characterized the adopters as saviors. As such, it became common to believe that adopted children should be grateful because they were taken in by these saviors. Adopted children were told they were bad or disloyal if they are asked about their heritage or wanted to search for their original parents. They were told they had no right to know about the past and that they had a better life with their adopters than the "immoral" unmarried mother could have provided. However, this perception fails to recognize that the adoptive parents also received the benefits in having *their* needs met [emphasis added] (Marshall & McDonald, 2001).

While the adoptive parents were viewed as altruistic saviors, the unmarried mother found herself in a double-bind once her child was born. Many people were ready to advise her that adoption was the best option for her and her baby, often telling her that it was the only fair thing for the baby. In one instance, a new mother described a matron telling her:

'Stop thinking about yourself. Think of the baby. It should be brought up in a home with a mother and a father, and think of the joy he would give to this couple who want to adopt your baby. They can't have children, you can have plenty in the future'...However she looked at her situation, there was no way she and her baby could survive. In refusing to support her, the world left her no alternative (Howe, et al., 1992).

It was clear with this approach that the surrendering mother was lacking in what it took to raise a child.

For a mother, this is a devastating judgment and is calculated to undermine not only her confidence but her self-esteem... once the decision had been made to surrender the child, many mothers felt that the adoption worker lost all interest in them and concentrated entirely on the baby... Lurking beneath the surface of many of the discussions between the mother and the 'professionals' was a pernicious double-bind: If you really love your baby you will give him or her up for adoption; if you keep the child then that is proof that you do not sincerely have his or her best interests at heart and therefore you are not a fit person to care for the baby... (Howe, et al., 1992).

An additional element in the shifting focus of adoption practice was the growing emphasis and importance given by adoption workers to material considerations alone. Some professionals realized that adopters are not necessarily better than mothers who were not permitted to raise their children because of their marital status, age, or financial situation, "for many young women the only argument in favor of adoption is that they will have a better material life. In its starkest aspect, adoption means placing more value on cold hard cash than on a young woman's capacity to love" (Luker, 1996).

CHAPTER 8

THE RITUAL HAND-OFF

*Against the background of history, too prominent to
escape the observation from which it shrinks, stands a figure,
mute, mournful and indescribably sad. It is a girl holding in her
arms the blessing and burden of motherhood, but in whose face
one finds no trace of maternal joy or pride. Who is this
woman, so pitiable, yet so scorned? It is the mother of the
illegitimate child. By forbidden paths she has obtained the grace
of maternity, but its glory is for her transfigured into a badge
of unutterable shame.*

Albert Leffingwell

During the BSE, many adoption workers used a ritual in
which a new mother was encouraged to offer her
illegitimate newborn to the adoption worker who was a
stand-in for the girl's own mother. This practice reflected
the belief among adoption professionals that unmarried
girls intentionally became pregnant in order to gift the baby
to her own mother. Social worker Leontine Young offered
suggestions to others in her field in how to ensure that the
new mother would give her baby to them, including several
psychological inducement techniques. Young recognized
that a girl needed reassurance and permission; workers
needed to understand that unmarried mothers more readily
gave their babies to adoption workers when they trusted
them:

We need to see that when the girl trusts us and is able to use our help she gives the baby to us. Our great need is to see the unmarried mother as she actually is and relate this realistically to her life. We need to see that we do not take the baby away from the mother as we did when punishment was the motive, but that on the contrary the girl gives the baby to us and can do so because of her relationship to us... [emphasis added] (L. Young, 1947).

Throughout the BSE, adoption workers were continually encouraged to steer the unmarried mother toward making the "good" decision to surrender the child in a way that would make the woman want to give her baby to the worker, who would be taking on the role of the woman's "new" mother:

Material gathered during this experience has led us to believe that the caseworker should take an active, 'steering' role in helping the unmarried mother to make a good decision for herself and the child...when the pregnant girl admits the pregnancy by coming to the agency, she is frequently in a shocked and traumatized condition and requires a period of dependency on the caseworker before she can begin to work on the problem realistically. This new kind of mother can help to make and sustain decisions, can use her role to help the client to give up her baby to her...[I]llustrations used in this paper have indicated that we are more 'on the side' of having the unmarried mother relinquish her baby (Scherz, 1947).

In 1954, Young described the ritual "handing over" of a baby by a new mother as a "gift," stating that social workers needed to overcome their fear of the process or they could make it more difficult or even impossible for the girl to give the baby to her:

> ...even when that gift may be the one doorway to release for the girl. The psychological difference between stealing something from someone and permitting someone to give you something is enormous; and when that something is a baby, the emotional ramifications are tremendous... (L.Young, 1954).

Michael Shapiro (1955) noted the unusual quality of the ritual, in that it is the worker and her agency who finally become the recipient of the *"gift of the baby"* [emphasis added].

An example of how adoption workers thought about the actual physical hand over of the child by the unmarried mother illustrates their acceptance of the popular psychological theory of the 1950s:

> Social workers and psychologists analyzed Ellen's neurotic urge to pregnancy a little differently, although fundamentally it was also a subconscious solution to her emotional dilemma. Ellen sought to have a baby not as a revengeful act but as a means of healing the

breach between herself and her mother. *Ellen wanted to give the baby to her mother...* [emphasis added] (Erichsen, 1955).

The power and influence of adoption workers on new mothers was also rooted in the idea that unmarried women became pregnant in order to satisfy their own needs for approval from a maternal figure, represented by the worker and therefore worthy of trust.

> If the unmarried mother is able to form a close relationship with the *caseworker, she will probably want to give the baby to her...*the closer and more satisfying the relationship is with the caseworker, the more likely the unmarried mother may be to relinquish...[Quoting Pollack] ...the unmarried mother who surrenders her child to the social worker and agency does so not because of a wish to give a baby to a maternal figure but because the social worker and the agency have gratified early love deprivations [emphasis added] (Costigan, 1964).

It was still believed, in the 1960s, that the ritual of physically handing over the newborn to the adoption worker was necessary to help unmarried mothers handle the situation. "Many girls who release their babies for adoption *need to give the baby to their caseworker* either actually or symbolically as an important part in their working through their emotional problems" [emphasis added] (Rowe, 1966).

A detailed description of the handing over ritual from 1969 details the actual practice and illustrates the psychological elements involved in the interaction between the unmarried mother, the adopting couple, and the case worker:

> Usually the girl and her case worker will be in one room, the prospective adopters in another. *The girl is invited to give her baby to her own caseworker*, who will hand him to her colleague; she herself will not leave the girl at any time. The baby is shown to the adopters...if the mother wishes to see them the child is removed from the room before she is brought in. The meeting is just long enough for the adopters to thank and reassure her and the actual parting is over...*in particular the mother should never be asked at this late stage whether she wishes to change her mind and keep the baby. If the preliminary casework has been well done there is no need...* at this stage in particular the *worker must concentrate on supporting and strengthening her client to carry out* what is almost certainly the most crucial decision she has ever had to make [emphasis added] (Pochin, 1969).

CHAPTER 9

ADOPTER ASSESSMENTS

Although social workers frequently promised surrendering mothers that their children would be adopted by married couples who were mature and would make wonderful parents, the literature shows it was long known that, in many cases, agencies did not fully investigate the qualifications of hopeful adopters. Adoption workers were looking to feel good about taking a child from one woman and giving it to another. To justify their actions, the unmarried mother had to be viewed as "bad" while the adopters were perceived as "super parents."

As recently as 2002, the "feel good" and super parent models of adoption were explained as follows:

> In the 'feel-good' model, birth parents 'won' by being freed of parenting responsibilities for which they were (often repeatedly) told they were unprepared. An adoption...could minimize, or prevent altogether, the 'bad' reputation. Birth parents, after a 'feelgood' adoption, were typically told that they could resume their pre-pregnancy lives, free… of any consequences…
> Adoptees, facing a future in which they were typically an 'unwanted' and 'illegitimate' child,

'won' by being placed in a (presumably) better home…Adoptees, seen in the 'feel-good' model as the 'lucky bastards,' also 'won' by being sheltered from…the presumed sins of their birth parents…The adoptee, as the 'bad seed' of this 'bad behavior,' is seen as benefiting from a new start in a 'proper' family. Adoptive parents…'won' by being able to raise the child…Those parents who adopted for reasons other than infertility could bask in the positive light of 'saving' an unfortunate child…adoptive parents… are looked up to as if they were 'super parents' (Henderson, 2002).

Psychiatrist Dr. Irene Josselyn (1955) wrote that some agencies:

> …considered adoptive parents suitable if they were desirable citizens of the community *without consideration of what they were as people*. Still other agencies considered their responsibility for the child fulfilled if the child was placed in a home offering *financially or socially glamorous security* for the child, a placement that would reward the agency…[emphasis added] (Josselyn, 1955).

It is not difficult to believe that "rewarding" the agency meant providing it with some financial consideration in the form of higher fees and/or donations.

Social workers applied a double standard when dealing with married and unmarried mothers. The same traits that adoption workers claimed made unmarried mothers unfit to raise their own children were generally overlooked when they considered married women who were potential adopters. Any hint of neurosis or psychological need in the unmarried mother meant she should surrender her child, while married women seeking children to meet their various needs were considered worthy of motherhood.

> The child available for adoption was used as a means to give a bored woman something to do [such] *as a new toy with which adults could play, as a cure for the neurosis of a childless woman*, as a way to meet the lacks in a woman's marriage because her husband was too busy with business or too interested in alcohol to be interested in her, or as a tool for preserving a disintegrating marriage... [emphasis added] (Josselyn, 1955).

In some cases, potential placements failed the acceptability criteria, and adoption workers began to realize that couples looking to adopt should not automatically be supplied with children just because they wanted them.

> It is easy to blame adoption per se when further enquiry would show that the *placement was unsuitable* in the first place, *inadequately arranged or improperly safeguard*ed... adoption workers have come to the realization that couples who apply to adopt are seldom just worthy citizens...but usually people with a problem – their childlessness... The National Association for Mental Health investigation of 27 non-relative adoptions seen in two

other clinics disclosed 16 situations where there were obvious and serious *problems in the adoptive parents whose attitude to the children were often either hostile or lacking in warmth* [emphasis added] (Rowe, 1966).

Because many of those who adopted were not sufficiently investigated, many adoptions ultimately failed, but the lack of recordkeeping in social welfare departments allowed workers to avoid responsibility:

> Social Welfare Department does not keep records of adoption breakdowns and therefore does not know the total number of failed adoptions. Not recording mistakes is a novel way of avoiding the responsibility for having made them and an ingenious way to justify the continued perpetration of the same mistakes over and over again (Shawyer, 1979).

With inadequate screening of potential adopters by trained workers in officially authorized adoption agencies, families were torn apart unnecessarily.

> They described *common practices* in child-placing that adoption workers should avoid, such as needlessly breaking up families, *pressuring unwed mothers to relinquish their children* before they had recovered their physical and emotional equilibrium, and *failing to investigate the physical, mental, social and family history of the child and the adoptive parents before placement* [emphasis added] (Carp, 1998).

Some adoption workers in Australia also acknowledged the inadequacies of the screening process, including the investigations into the suitability of potential adopting couples:

> Much practice followed what could only be described as crude assessment methods in approving applicants for adoption. Largely, applicants were approved if they were married, had suitable accommodation, were employed and had no criminal record. Privately arranged adoptions, possible in most states, had often occurred in an equally haphazard fashion…It could not be assumed that all adopters had healthy child-centered motivation. The haste with which society, through its doctors and others, proposed adoption as a quick solution to infertility, or to compensate for the loss of a child at childbirth, often propelled grieving parents into application to adopt before their anguish was resolved (Marshall and McDonald, 2001).

THE BABY SCOOP ERA

CHAPTER 10

BOYS WILL BE BOYS

PATER IGNOTUS…special family situations such as illegitimacy may be observed or inferred from baptismal records. Although cannon law strictly forbade making special notations in case of illegitimacy parish priests in this country seem uniformly to have made such notations…Notations such as 'pater ignotus' (father unknown) or simply 'illegit' will occasionally appear.

There is no question that a pregnant girl is perceived differently and treated differently than the male who fathered her baby. The difference was particularly noticeable when teens are the unmarried parents. When an unmarried teenage girl learned she was pregnant, she tended to hide the pregnancy because she knew she would be immediately removed from school. Often, she delayed telling anyone about her pregnancy for this reason and would continue to attend school until she could no longer hide her expanding belly.

> Once a girl has discovered she is pregnant, in her terror or ignorance, she often delays even longer, out of fear of telling her family or school personnel. (She faces instant expulsion if her secret is known) (Allen, 1963).

...many schools did not 'allow a pregnant girl, married or unmarried, to continue in classes once her condition becomes obvious' (Lipke, 1973).

Unmarried mothers who were still in school during the BSE would be immediately expelled once the pregnancy was discovered:

In many schools, identification is further hampered by a regulation that requires a pregnant girl to be dropped from school as soon as her pregnancy is known...Pregnant girls may graduate from high school in ceremonies held for them in the maternity home... (Kelley, 1962).

While in the minority of educators surveyed, some of the responses given when questioned about providing public school education to unmarried mothers included, "Why award them for the problems they have brought upon themselves and society? I would not want them to attend school with my daughter" (Nelson, 1960).

In what might be viewed as an act of punishment, a pregnant teen girl would be denied an education as schools would remove the unmarried mother-to-be once the pregnancy became known:

Some schools discharge a girl when her pregnancy becomes known and provide no means of continuing education through home

instruction or any other plan. Limited
educational opportunities may be due to
…economic privation, community pressures
or attitudes, and stigma or *punitive school policies*
that virtually prohibit return to school. Any or
all these causes lead to termination of
education of the adolescent unwed mother
however good her potentials might have been
[emphasis added] (Journal of Home
Economics, 1963).

The plight of unmarried mothers confined to maternity
homes could be worse, as these girls were:

[S]eparated from family and friends,
excluded from school, employment, and
meaningful activities, and forbidden to
communicate with the institution if she again
becomes pregnant, would certainly
understand the attitude of those helping her,
and the expectation for her to repent and
emerge cleansed (Osofsky, 1968).

In these cases, to "repent and emerge cleansed" meant
the girl surrendered her baby and returned to society as if
nothing had happened, as if virginal and cured of her sin.
In other words, marriage material.

In 1996, Kristin Luker discussed a Reader's Digest article
from 1970, which stated, "Traditionally U.S. public schools
have felt that a pregnant girl should be expelled (1) to keep
her from 'contaminating' the rest of the girls and (2) as an
object lesson in the wages of sin. "Physicians Zackler and
Brandstadt gave a clear historical overview of the

unmarried mother and how she had been treated by her school once her illicit pregnancy was discovered, claiming that:

> Pregnant school-age girls throughout our history have had little or no help from society. Their treatment has been not only *neglectful but often punitive*…the family and the school system, have often been harsh and unresponsive… young women who became pregnant *were forced to leave school*…while the young men who caused the pregnancy were allowed to remain…society spoke of this as 'boys will be boys' and appeared to applaud a male youth sowing a few wild oats…the girl involved was viewed as disgraced, shamed, and unfit…[emphasis added] (Zackler & Brandstadt, 1975).

While it was common practice to expel or otherwise separate a pregnant teen girl from her school, unmarried school-boy fathers faced few repercussions.

> [T]here is no question about society's instinctive response to her plight. It is simply to ostracize her…she will probably be expelled from school…such swift action is not meted out to the unmarried school boy father…Says former U.S. Commissioner of Education, Lawrence Derthick, 'Many school systems …are prevented by law from providing teachers…or making homebound programs available from public funds for unwed mothers…there is no way a girl can

earn credits for any scholastic work she does
during pregnancy…there is no way by which
she can conceal the fact that the earning was
done in a maternity home…' (Rinehart, 1963).

There was a general disinterest in the unwed father, and
in many cases "…there was no serious consideration of the
father's status and the possibility of securing from him
voluntary or forced contributions. Public opinion permits
many fathers to shirk their duties… (Lundberg, 1920), and
while the experts believed that fatherless children suffered
"a great handicap," society tends to withhold protection
and gratification from the person who becomes a mother
outside marriage. "The absence of her child's father further
handicaps the mother in carrying out the maternal role…"
(Greenleigh, 1961). The unmarried fathers were permitted
to simply walk away. They became, and often still are,
completely invisible.

Discussing the role of the unmarried father in 1962,
Clark Vincent observed:

> The male is half the cause of illegitimacy
> …only about one study of fathers exists for
> every thirty studies of unmarried mothers
> …illegitimacy cannot be understood, much
> less solved, by studying only half its cause. To
> study, observe, and censure unwed fathers to
> the same degree we do their female
> counterparts …poses a dilemma; it requires
> changes in the conventional double standard
> by which we judge the sexual behavior of
> males and females. Semantically, we have no
> male equivalent of 'the fallen woman'… We

condemn and stigmatize unmarried mothers
far more harshly than unmarried fathers…
There is also the cherished practice of treating
a person as innocent until proven guilty, a
practice which penalizes the unwed mother…
because her guilt is made self-evident by a
protruding profile… The unwed father bears
no evidence… the unwed mother must
disclose her identity and sexual misbehavior…
the unwed mother poses tangible problems,
the unmarried father does not. It is she for
whom prenatal care, maternity homes, and
possible child support must be financed…The
male represents no obvious expense to
taxpayers and bears no evidence of
unconventional sex behavior (Vincent, 1962).

Social workers were charged with addressing the issue of
what was termed "the putative father":

Work with unmarried mothers followed…
certain principles designed to avoid creating
more social problems. How-to-do…involved
trying to locate the putative father to secure
some financial support (Reynolds, 1963).

As a 'putative father,' the male has no
rights… If his paternity is established, he can
be forced by the courts to contribute to the
support of his child and of the mother, but
he can make no decisions about his child's
future... little effort is made in this country to
hold the father to his financial
responsibilities... (Isaac & Spencer, 1965).

By the end of the 1960s, some experts believed that the State should step in when the issue of "illegitimacy" arose:

> At present the woman bears a disproportionate amount of the burden, for which the man is equally responsible... It seems equally logical and right that in the instances in which the father of an illegitimate child disappears, the State should assume the responsibility by assisting the mother in the support of the child (Kammerer, 1969).

Should, yes. The state should assume responsibility by assisting the mother, but in most cases, the state *did not* assume the responsibility of assisting the mother in support of her child. Instead, she was too often pressured to surrender her child.

In contrast to professionals' eagerness to address the unmarried mother, few adoption workers were interested in the father:

> The social worker and the rescue worker may have had different priorities, but both were more interested in changing unwed mothers than in changing the men who impregnated them or the economic and social conditions that permitted and then punished unwed motherhood... Women do not get pregnant by themselves, but their lack of economic and political resources has meant that *male sexual partners could abandon them with impunity*. When women consequently became

dependent on public or private aid, policymakers, like sexual partners, could afford to ignore them [emphasis added] (Morton, 1993).

Regina Kunzel (1993) noted the difference in attitude toward the "delinquent" boy and girl:

> Who has ever heard of a 'fallen boy'? One social worker asked…'when we speak of a delinquent girl we mean one thing, and when we speak of a delinquent boy we mean another,' and that 'when we speak of the delinquent girl we usually have in mind the sex offender.' Unlike social workers, evangelical reformers had always been careful to distinguish unmarried mothers from delinquents.

In 2001, William Bennett recognized the less than responsible behavior of unmarried fathers, stating:

> To the degree that out of wedlock births elicit any criticism these days, most of it is directed toward the women who bear these children… In almost every instance, a single woman will not abandon her illegitimate child… it is unmarried fathers who are missing in record numbers, who impregnate women and selfishly flee. And it is these absent men, above all, who deserve our censure and disesteem.

CHAPTER 11

THE GOLD STANDARD: IVORY SNOW

*[G]itelman helps the childless secure children – asking as
much as $250,000 for a healthy white, blonde haired, blue eyed
baby girl. When it comes to providing white children to the
wealthy at a premium, no one… has an incentive to talk.*
                                                    Jim Defede

American society after World War II and the start of
the BSE, put a premium on the myth of the perfect family.
Couples without children were viewed as incomplete,
without meaning or value. Childless couples were subject to
many and diverse pressures to have children as larger
families became increasingly respectable and not having
children became less socially acceptable (Reid, 1955).

> [T]he social and historical content of pro-
> natalism has defined women without children
> as unfulfilled and undervalued, and families
> without children as deficient. The standard
> view of the family as a married couple with
> children born to them has defined all other
> family forms and ways of building a family as
> 'less than,' deviant, or even 'improper' or
> 'wrong' …one in every six couples of
> childbearing age is infertile, a 100% increase
> in 20 years… The tension between the
> growing number of infertile couples and the

reduced availability of infants for adoption becomes clear as couples and unmarried adults search far and wide in their efforts to build a family (Valentine, 1988).

Because of the social stigma imposed on childless couples, they looked for ways to become more acceptable, to "complete" their families. They found themselves in the odd situation of wanting another woman "to meekly give her child to them," which left her childless, and then "conveniently" disappearing from their lives so they can live the fantasy that they were the natural parents of that child (Shawyer, 1979).

According to sociologist Edwin Schur, not having children could be viewed as a mental illness and as a psychiatric problem. Schur stated:

> [J]ust about any female behavior which diverges from general prescriptions is likely to be interpreted in mental illness terms. If a woman is too fat or too thin, if she is too aggressive or too passive, if she is an unmarried mother *or voluntarily childless*... some psychiatric theory will be put forward to 'explain' the behavior or condition [emphasis added] (Shur, 1984).

Psychologist Douglas Henderson described the plight of a couple who remained childless after being married for a certain period of time; they were considered to have "some sort of problem." Therefore, social workers tended to minimize the "importance" of an adoption and told adopters not to tell their adopted children about their origin.

> Particularly if the adoption itself was concealed, a couple who adopted might not have to reveal potentially embarrassing aspects of their most private relationship to others. Mental health professionals likely cooperated in maintaining this privacy by underplaying the importance of adoption both in the parenting process and in the development of the adoptee (Henderson, 2002).

Childless couples felt a real need to have children in their families in order to gain social acceptance and the appearance of "normality." This dynamic meshed easily with the ideas of maternity home adoption workers and physicians.

> Once the child was born, it would be adopted by a middle class couple so that it could be brought up in a 'normal' (two parent) family; and the young woman would likewise resume a 'normal' (childless) life. Of course, this 'treatment' was typically limited to white, middle class women, right up through the 1960s... (Luker, 1996).

The demand for healthy white babies among infertile married couples began to rise at the start of the 1940s. With this increased demand, the focus of adoption shifted from providing homes for truly homeless, orphaned babies to providing infants to childless couples. A number of reasons were used to justify separating mothers and their infants. These reasons were framed in terms of punishing unmarried mothers, preventing them from relying on public assistance (AFDC), and a plan to remove white infants from white unmarried mothers deemed by adoption social workers to be unfit for whatever reason, usually because the mothers were perceived as "neurotic."

By the end of the 1940s, there was a marked increase in the number of infertile white couples who wanted to adopt a white newborn. The huge demand for these babies and the desire for quick adoptions resulted in viewing unmarried mothers as breeding machines, as clearly stated by highly regarded and well-known adoption social worker, Leontine Young:

> ...the tendency growing out of the demand for babies is to regard unmarried mothers as breeding machines... (by people intent upon securing babies for quick adoptions) (L. Young, 1953).

The high demand coupled with a low supply of desirable white infants also created pressure on unmarried mothers to surrender their babies.

> Popularity has brought with it problems of supply and demand. Since the great demand is for young white babies, the Children's Bureau's explorations were concerned primarily with these babies. The number of such infants available for adoption has increased in recent years, but the rate of

increase has not kept up with the demand...
Many abuses have been reported around a
mother's relinquishment of her child
(Thornhill, 1955).

Describing the low numbers of white babies, especially
white, blue-eyed baby girls, on the market as a shortage of
adoptable babies was misleading at best.

> There is not so much a shortage of
> adoptable children as a surplus of would-be
> parents. Each year close to 700,000 couples
> try to adopt children but there are only 90,000
> children available. Besides, 95 percent of these
> couples want a white infant... The pool of
> adoptable babies consists largely of babies
> born out of wedlock. But the number of
> white children born out of wedlock is only
> about 54,100 each year... it must be
> remembered that few, if any, of the children
> in our institutions who might be made
> available for adoption are the *'blue-eyed baby
> girls' in so great demand* [emphasis added] (Reid,
> 1956).

Along with the growing acceptance of white unmarried
mothers as suppliers, their babies came to be viewed as
market commodities. After a while, these mothers were
regarded as a very valuable resource, supplying the white
babies to fulfill the growing demand. According to a
leading sociologist at the time:

> ...censure of white unwed mothers is
> tempered when they represent the largest

single source of adoptable infants and [they]
serve a useful social function by enabling
childless couples to achieve the cherished goal
of having a family. As physicians, lawyers, and
social caseworkers can testify, many of the
conservatively estimated one million
involuntarily childless, white couples in this
country would not be too happy if a major
source of adoptable white infants was to
disappear. This dilemma of having to choose
between either the continuation of
illegitimacy or a diminished supply of
adoptable infants... is not openly
acknowledged... (Vincent, 1962).

The stigma of adoption was lessening at the same time,
which also contributed to a greater demand for the right
kind of baby. Workers at the Child Welfare League of
America noted, "As knowledge about the influences of
environment in the development of children became more
generally known, the idea of adoption became more
acceptable, eventually growing into an overwhelming
demand for healthy white infants" (Mayo & Reid, 1962).

A 1964 study, made at a time and place that demand for
white adoptable infants existed, showed that its date had
little application to a population of African American
unmarried mothers, who still had very few outlets if they
wanted to surrender their children for adoption (Vincent,
1964).

It makes one wonder whose best interests were really
served by infant adoption - those of the mothers, the
agencies, or the adopters?

Welfare workers in the U.S. tended to discriminate between white unmarried mothers and the mothers of color. There was no question that the market for healthy, white babies was very strong, but there was no comparable market for black babies. Unmarried mothers of color were encouraged to keep their babies, while the white mothers were advised to surrender their children for adoption.

Traditionally, welfare workers encouraged non-white clients to keep their babies ..."this type of advice is different from what would be given to a white, pregnant teenager..." (Osofsky, 1968). In 1969, it was estimated that 70 percent of white children born to unmarried mothers were surrendered for adoption, compared to between five to ten percent of non-white children (Shiller, 1969).

The race of an unmarried mother became a large factor in decisions involving what to do with her baby. According to Lipke (1973), "...a girl's race sometimes influences the decision of what to do with the child. There are many couples waiting to adopt Caucasian babies so Caucasian girls may be pressured to give up their children... The unwed mother should realize that it is possible that some people who offer her advice may not have her best interests at heart."

Social workers increasingly recognized that unmarried motherhood performed a useful function in providing to white middle-class couples the children they were looking for. By the early 1970s, it was possible to state that, contrary to previous perceptions:

...unmarried motherhood is the mark, not of deviancy and degeneracy, but of victimization. It is the visible sign and outcome of a total pattern of inequality in... access to significant resources and reflects the intent of the dominant majority to keep the poor in their place [by] insuring that the life of the poor is hard... Illegitimacy is functionally useful to society. To eliminate it would be to eliminate the raw material of the adoption process, whose products are sought after by childless middle class couples...Society encourages illegitimacy not, as is generally thought, by encouraging premarital sex, but by discouraging responsible parenthood... (Ryan, 1971).

Obtaining a healthy, blue-eyed, white baby for adoption was considered a prize, and prospective adopters lived in fear of the mother reclaiming her baby. The agencies:

...tried to find the perfect adoptable baby... it had blue eyes... Its skin was white as Ivory Snow. Its health and intelligence... were covered by a money-back agency guarantee... [One adoptive couple stated that:] 'I don't even dare say where we got her, from what agency, state or country, for fear of attracting the natural mother's attention. Fear is endemic to adoption where we live... Adoption is a lottery, and we've drawn the grandest of grand prizes. To win and then lose would be intolerable' (Morgenstern, 1971).

With a reduction in healthy, white infants available, the costs for adopters increased, giving rise to advertisements in newspapers and magazines designed to attract unmarried mothers who might potentially surrender their infants.

> Applicants for white infants...can look forward to a two year wait...agencies are simply closing their application lists for white infants...The price per little white head may go as high as $1,000 in Michigan. In California, there are stories of couples who offer doctors and lawyers as much as $10,000 cash...The U.S. is an exuberantly mercantile nation, and now it is merchandising children. Newspapers run adoption columns and Adoptable Baby-of-the-Week photos (Morgenstern, 1971).

The pressure for a white, unmarried mother to surrender her child was intense, despite the stated beliefs of some social workers and psychology professionals that it was unadvised to make serious decisions during times of emotional stress.

> If the unmarried mother is white and not poor, she will be expected to surrender her baby for adoption... [C]ontrary to the usual admonitions that one should try to avoid making major decisions at a time of strong emotional distress, she is required to commit herself to a decision... when she is likely to be in a state of crisis... This denial of her right to make her own decisions may, in her mind,

have a... punitive connotation (Bernstein,
1971).

And so it was that as the decades passed after World War
II, the growing market for healthy, white babies altered the
perceptions of adoption workers, potential adopters, and
the general public. This prompted adoption workers to
pressure white, unmarried mothers to supply their children
to satisfy the market. The same pressures were not applied
to unmarried mothers of color, however (Wegar, 1997).

CHAPTER 12

PUNITIVE ATTITUDES & COERCION

...girls provide a crucial test of the caseworker's adjustment to the situation. Why does she hang back? Is it because she retains a trace of the wish to punish, and feels that the girl is being let off too lightly? Or is she afraid that the young mother will change her mind and recall her baby? ...traces of the old punitive attitude still exist both in the law and in social provisions, just as traces of the old fear and anger remain in our emotional reactions.

Jean Pochin

One of the reasons adoption social workers during the BSE favored the permanent separation of unmarried mothers from their children was to punish them for the sin of out-of-wedlock pregnancy.

Peter Kammerer, an Episcopalian minister with a PhD from Harvard University, published in 1918 the first comprehensive study of births occurring outside of marriage in the United States, collecting data on 500 cases, described the attitude of social workers and the general public toward out-of-wedlock births as falling into two categories, one of which looks upon illegitimacy as a manifestation of those forces menacing the home and monogamy.

Their attitude towards the unmarried mother is almost always personal. *She represents to them an individual who has sinned and who should be made to feel the full burden of her behavior...* A group of this kind... would oppose the extension of mother's pensions to unmarried mothers, regardless of the fact that an illegitimate child may be as much in need of such help as is his more fortunate brother, and that the mother may be capable of good care [emphasis added] (Kammerer, 1918).

Their pressuring and coercive attitudes had an influence on the type of services they provided and the way they provided them. From the 1940s into the 1970s, there was a prevailing opinion that unmarried mothers should "suffer" in one way or another for going outside the set social boundaries of motherhood. In addition to its punitive aspects, adoption workers also tended to view surrender of the child as part of the rehabilitation process for the mother, creating a confusing psychological situation for everyone involved.

In the past, it was felt that it must be best for an illegitimate child to be adopted because, according to Joseph Reid (In Reeves, 1993), "the concept that the unmarried mother and her child constitute a family is... unsupportable. There is no family." Jane Rowe, also quoted by Reeves, described those mothers who chose to keep their illegitimate children were viewed as "neurotically needy." Leontine Young (In Reeves, 1993) warned against emotional reactions when taking illegitimate children away because unmarried mothers were not as attached to their children as married mothers.

Legislation was enacted to allow children to be separated completely from their mothers.

> [Adoption]... continues to be viewed as an incomparably final method of reordering the deviant family through placing the mother in the hot seat of moral responsibility whilst refusing her access to the means (usually economic) to determine and control her environment (Reeves, 1993).

According to Reeves (1992), "demand and supply of adopters and adoptive children is central to the development and importance of adoption as an instrument of social control."

Reviewing circumstances during the Baby Scoop Era, historian Marion Morton (1993) described how social workers at the time decided which unmarried mothers should place their infants for adoption because "adoption was preferable to keeping mother and child together" and also rejected "the idea that all women who had borne children were suitable mothers" and that they must make a case-by-case determination as to which mother should or should not surrender her child. Maternity homes followed the social workers' recommendations, and rather than retain the mission they defined in the early 20th century - namely to keep mother and child together - the homes became almost exclusively places for unmarried pregnant females to become invisible in society while being persuaded to surrender babies through the maternity home mantra and visits from agency workers.

Ruth Brenner of the Child Adoption Committee recognized that the personal and negative attitudes held by social workers influenced the way they responded to unmarried mothers and how such an inappropriate case work attitude focused on punishment contributed to the hopelessness and confused reactions of unmarried mothers to their caseworkers, noting that:

> Every one of us reacts quite normally when our first and unprofessional response is the primitive taboo attitude of withdrawal: the untouchability, ostracism, and finally punishment of the evil one. Not one of us enjoys facing the full implications of such... unconscious and unprofessional reactions to unmarried parenthood...the attitudes... are society's response and therefore may be characteristic... of the workers who live in that society and constitute the personnel of the institutions (Brenner, 1942).

A 1947 article about unmarried mothers in the *Ladies Home Journal* described the experience of one of these young mothers living in a maternity home. This mother felt that she had been jailed:

> All of us had jobs. It was my job to scrub the ward floor and the bathrooms. There were about twenty-five girls there... It made me feel like a criminal. And a prisoner... One of the girls ran away. She left her baby behind; she couldn't have taken it with her even if she'd wanted to - the nursery was guarded against us except at feeding and bathing time. She

walked about two miles... in the snow, without a coat, because our coats were all in the storage room where we couldn't get to them. Finally she collapsed and some people picked her up and she was brought back. The next day the attendant said to us... 'You are very low girls or you never would have done this thing'... you can't call your soul your own once you've had a baby without a marriage certificate (L.Younger, 1947).

The prison-like and coercive atmosphere of the maternity homes continued into the 1960s:

...rules forbidding the use of makeup, reserving the right to inspect residents' belongings, or claiming the need to censor correspondence, may appear as an intolerable interference with personal liberty and privacy...some have locked doors, open all letters, and remove pocket money and note paper, [the Homes] are virtual prisons... none provided instruction [about birth] as a matter of routine, and for residents... it seemed the subject was sometimes not covered at all... Group after group wanted someone to tell them what to expect in labor. Many of the expectant mothers were frightened and confused about their approaching confinement...Their urgent wish for knowledge was apparent...preparation for motherhood was not well covered. Some of the mothers did change their minds, and others 'nearly go demented' making wild plans

for trying to keep the child although they
know it is really impossible... (Nicholson,
1964).

Experts like social worker Leontine Young emphasized
the duty of caseworkers during the BSE to make active
efforts in guiding the unmarried mother, whom Young
considered "seriously neurotic" toward surrendering her
baby to adoption:

> Most unmarried mothers are serious
> neurotics...How can we rationally expect the
> neurotic unmarried mother to make a realistic
> decision if we leave the total burden to her?
> ...the caseworker cannot escape the
> responsibility for participating actively in this
> decision (L. Young, 1947).

In 1954, Leontine Young continued to encourage
adoption workers to do everything they could to make sure
the baby was surrendered, as none of the mothers, in her
opinion, were able to take on the responsibility of being a
parent; workers should focus all of their efforts on ensuring
the legal surrender of the baby stressing that:

> *It is very important that the worker do everything
> in her power to see that the baby is legally
> surrendered...* Young also recommended that
> the worker cultivate the relationship with the
> unmarried mother to gain her trust because, if
> the mother liked the worker, *she may be willing
> to follow the worker's advice* [emphasis added] (L.
> Young, 1954).

Young warned other social workers to avoid using a baby in a "tug of war" with the new mother, however, acknowledging that the mother is vulnerable and exposed to society's condemnation and the "unscrupulous exploitation or well-meaning mistakes of those who want their babies... It is not always easy or possible to persuade the girl to surrender the baby."

Expressing her own view of the kind of "punishment" an unmarried mother faces, Young noted that a "sadistic, angry attitude" that could rob an unmarried mother of her child in order to punish her, "existed in the past and still exists" at the time of her writing. That scenario could result in creating confusion for a well-meaning worker. They should remember, Young said, that "if punishment is the objective, one may punish equally by trying to compel every girl to keep her baby and do penance for a lifetime for her supposed sin." In other words, for Young, punishment is just as easily imposed if the unmarried mother is counseled to keep her child, so encouraging her to choose adoption is actually saving the mother from punishment. A clever double-bind argument that eliminates guilt for the caseworker and leaves the unmarried mother in distress whatever she decides.

In 1952, psychiatrist John Bowlby grew concerned and subsequently warned case workers to avoid "the sentimental glamour of saving neglected children from wicked parents" and "not take impetuous actions to relieve parents of their responsibilities, and, by their actions, convey to the parents the belief that the child is far better off in the care of others." He went on to say that instead of focusing on what is best for the child and the mother, social workers and case workers were too often influenced by attitudes that promoted punishment towards the "erring mother" (Bowlby, 1965).

Sara B. Edlin, who began to work at Lakeview, a home for unmarried mothers on Staten Island, New York, in 1912 and later became its director, was "discouraged about the punitive attitudes of many social workers" attending conferences hosted by the Children's Bureau of the U.S. Labor Department and the social worker "resistance to any legislation that would make life easier for the unmarried mother and her child" (Edlin, 1954).

The attitudes of adoption workers and society toward unmarried mothers were also a concern of Pulitzer Prize winning novelist Pearl S. Buck. Buck herself adopted seven children and is now credited with coining the term "birth mother," first using it in 1955. She wondered what chance a child born and kept by an unmarried mother had to find a good family and community life when society overall, and social workers in particular, condemn, ridicule and judge her instead of trying to understand her (Buck, 1956).

The act of "renouncing her child for its own good" was viewed as a learning experience for the unmarried mother, according to social workers in the 1950s, as she has "learned to pay the price for her misdemeanor and this alone was punishment enough," according to Dr. Marion Hilliard, the chief of the obstetrics and gynecology department at Women's College Hospital in Toronto from 1947 to 1956. Dr. Hilliard, along with social workers of the time, believed that the fact that the child's father had no role in this was part of the woman's "rehabilitation" (Howarth, 1956).

The Honorable Justine Wise Polier of New York's Domestic Relations observed:

> The mother of the child born out of wedlock is frequently young, frightened and very much alone *when she is forced to make the momentous decisions about her future* and that of her child. The provision of proper medical care, casework service, a plan for her child, full and honest disclosure as to her legal rights and the consequences of surrendering her child for adoption are essential... It is when this is not done, when she is not helped to work through to the right decision, that *decisions made under duress may and often do lead to unresolved conflicts that may shadow her life...* [emphasis added] (Polier, 1956).

And Biestek (1957) noted:

> Caseworkers have differed in their evaluation of the capacity of unmarried mothers... to make sound decisions. Some feel that unmarried mothers are so damaged emotionally that they are incapable of arriving at a good decision themselves. These caseworkers have expressed the conviction that they must 'guide,' 'steer,' and 'take sides in' the final decision.

Unmarried mothers who were young and white with appropriate social ties were not subjected to the condemnations imposed on less socially well-positioned women in the same situation. It was understood that if the mother was willing to return to society and "act as before" the pregnancy, having surrendered her child, she would be accepted back into the societal fold. According to Lillian Bye, executive director of the Crittenton Hastings House in Boston:

> Where the girl is young, white, adequate, socially well accepted, *we do not show our wrath openly* even if she presents us with the obvious fact that she has broken our mores... The males will not permit her to bear children outside their social and legal control... We accept in silence that they often pay with their virginity. *We even accept the baby — if it is released for adoption and the mother does not openly claim it. We will accept her as before the pregnancy took place if she is willing to act 'as before,' and the maternity home and private agency has been pushed along in this trend of thinking,* reflected in the basic philosophy of their services [emphasis added] (Bye, 1959).

In 1959, Bye made a public appeal for professionals to review their policies of putting almost all the children born to unmarried mothers out for adoption, asking, "Are we doing the right thing... [pressuring] a young woman to give up her baby?" (Solinger, 1993).

Australian physician D.F. Lawson strongly believed that, for practicality's sake, obstetricians should encourage unmarried girls to choose adoption, even if that meant disregarding the law:

The prospect of the unmarried girl or of her family adequately caring for a child and giving it a normal environment and upbringing is so small that I believe for practical purposes it can be ignored. *I believe that in all such cases the obstetrician should urge that the child be adopted...* 'When in doubt, don't' is part of the wisdom of living: but over adoptions I would suggest that 'when in doubt, do' should be the rule... *The last thing that the obstetrician might concern himself with is the law in regards to adoption* [emphasis added] (Lawson, 1960).

In the U.S. as well, national social welfare conferences discussed how unmarried mothers might apply to placement agencies for aid when planning for their children. The process, which involved seeing an intake worker, waiting to hear from another worker, and frequently not even seeing the appropriate worker before the birth, made these women wonder if the agency was really interested in her well-being or perhaps, *"Are they only interested in getting my baby?"* [emphasis added] (Crockett, 1960).

The subject of unmarried mothers was even addressed by the mainstream advice columnist Ann Landers (1961) who believe that "single girls who hang on to their babies" displayed a "sick kind of love" and "an unwholesome blend of self-pity mixed with self-destruction and a touch of martyrdom."

The experience of an unmarried mother in a maternity home in 1963 described how she was illicitly allowed to hold her newborn: "When Margaret gave birth [August 26, 1963], she briefly considered keeping the beautiful baby boy. 'The nurse let me hold him, which was against the rules,' said Margaret. At the time, Florence Crittenton and other homes discouraged women considering adoption from bonding with their newborns" (Cupp, 2013).

The idea that unmarried mothers should suffer and be punished did not disappear even in the arguably more liberal 1960s. Some felt that helping these mothers only encouraged them to have additional out-of-wedlock pregnancies. They also believed that "Generally speaking, adoption is the best for both the mother and the child" (Pinson, 1964).

A paper published by the National Association of Social Workers in 1964 acknowledged that white, unmarried mothers were considered as the source of a very valuable commodity: healthy white babies. Illustrating a shift in the views of professional social workers, these babies born out-of-wedlock were "no longer considered a social problem, but a social boon" and an asset. In the words of social worker Helen Perlman (1964), "Because there are many more married couples wanting to adopt newborn white babies than there are babies, it may almost be said that they, rather than out of wedlock babies are a social problem. (Sometimes social workers in adoption agencies have facetiously suggested setting up social provisions for more 'baby breeding')."

Perlman (1964) went on to say that if the white, unmarried mother surrendered her baby and foregoes welfare assistance, she is no longer a problem. She contrasted this with a woman who keeps her child and is not sufficiently punished for her act. Perlman noted if the woman has "been able to give away the living symbol of her 'sin' or 'mistake'... she is 'solved' as a social problem... If she keeps her child but needs no economic support, she is lost to public view... The assumption is that she is paying for her transgressions - and this is a morally satisfying assumption. If ...she keeps her child and requires economic aids for the support of herself and child, she is not 'paying'."

Helen E. Terkelsen, a social worker involved with pastoral counseling and an adoptee herself, recognized that social pressures on the unmarried mother resulted in most pastoral counselors saying "frankly that they advised adoption for the babies of those unwed mothers who did not plan to marry at once. They advised this because they had little evidence to believe that an unwed mother could successfully raise her child in the community without incurring social sanctions" (Terkelsen, 1964).

As in previous years, there were some adoption authorities who did not believe they had the right to present adoption as the best, or even only, option for an unmarried mother. In regard to the field of family law, questions arose about whether demands that "captive clients" should surrender their babies because they believed it was for the good of the baby. *"If the mother feels that relinquishing the baby is to her detriment, that is, if she proves resistive to our approach* and we respect the integrity of another human being, we cannot insist on surrender, however well-intentioned we may be" [emphasis added] (Heiman, in Levy, 1964).

The means by which an adoption worker could encourage the "neurotic unmarried mother" to surrender her baby for adoption was outlined for professionals, recognizing that "...The worker... has to clarify for herself the differences between the feelings of the normal woman for her baby and the fantasy use of the child by the neurotic unmarried mother" (L. Young, in Levy, 1964).

The idea that unmarried mothers had to be "convinced" to surrender their children was part of the education of professional social workers. Instruction in "intensive" casework with the mothers provided by the Child Welfare League of America in 1963 emphasized that the release of the child was "one of the most crucial phases" in working with these women, and that workers should be aware that they may be "so concerned with her child's welfare that *she may encourage relinquishment precipitously*, thereby inviting another pregnancy."

For decades, workers continued to put pressure on unmarried mothers to surrender their children to adoption. The popular explanation continued to be that the mothers who release children to give them a chance to have the "normal" family life that they cannot provide and to give them the opportunity to get back to the "normal" life they had before the pregnancy altered it. In other words, *"the unmarried mother relinquishes her child because society expects her to do so..."* This does not mean that the mother does not want to provide her child with a normal family life and does not hope that her child will have a happier life than would be possible if she kept the baby, but that in a large proportion of cases the mother accepts adoption as the best solution for providing for her baby's future because she has been told it is the best solution" [emphasis added] (Isaac & Spencer, 1965).

They went on to say:

> ...should the proposition of adoptive applicants to available children drop even further, it is likely that there will be a change in the *present discouraging attitude to the mother who wishes to keep her child...* The director of a Boston maternity home has quoted a girl who felt *she was being pressured into surrendering her child*, 'It's not what Mrs. K says exactly, it's just that her face lights up when I talk about adoption the way it doesn't when I talk about keeping Beth'... [emphasis added] (Isaacs & Spencer, 1965).

So, if the demand by potential adopters drops, then unmarried mothers will be encouraged to keep their babies instead of surrendering them to a "normal" (married) family.

Most adoption caseworkers had little experience in handling such an emotionally charged situation. Many were not married, and had no children of their own, and yet they were considered "experts" in unwed motherhood. They were cautioned to be self-aware in their dealings with the unwed mothers:

> Caseworkers dealing with unmarried mothers have a particular need for self-awareness since they are dealing all the time with raw human emotions towards sex, love,

marriage, babies and parents, and with women who have broken the accepted code of social and moral behavior. These are subjects which touch deep feelings in us all and about which it is difficult not to have some prejudices... Many women social workers are unmarried and have not been able to fulfill the natural feminine urge for children... It is no good being 'professionally' tolerant and understanding if, underneath, we secretly and perhaps unconsciously feel that these women are wicked and need punishing to expiate their guilt (Rowe, 1966).

Adoption workers were warned to not reveal that their interests were really invested in the infant and how their attitudes could actively play a part in the mother's "decision."

[U]nmarried mothers and their parents would be quite unwilling to accept direct help with their problems, but welcome help in planning for the child. This is the caseworker's opportunity... *she must not give the impression that she is only interested in the child...* There is... a temptation to feel that we must not intrude but should leave the mother to make up her mind alone. But this is actually to fail the client at the time of her greatest need. Perhaps the first thing which all caseworkers... must grasp is that *it is impossible to avoid the responsibility of playing a part in the decision.* We are part of it either actively or by default [emphasis added] (Rowe, 1966).

By claiming that the child of a "disturbed" unmarried mother will only bring her disappointment, the caseworker could more easily convince the mother that she needed the strength and affection of the worker in order to surrender her baby:

> [A]lmost overwhelming pity can lead to the false hope that, through their children, these unfortunate women will find satisfaction and happiness. But to such a mother a child will ultimately bring disappointment... What she needs is someone to give to her a strong arm on which to lean, a steady affection on which she can draw, not the demands of a helpless baby... with no husband to support her... because the children raised by inadequate and disturbed mothers are nearly always maladjusted and difficult (Rowe, 1966).

Workers were told to use the conflicted state of a new mother to "bear fruit," meaning to convince her to release her child:

> Only too often such girls...having previously declared that the child must be adopted immediately...now insist on keeping him even when it will be a destructive situation... It is while she is in the midst of the urgent conflicts and indecisions that the skilled caseworker can be of the greatest help in enabling her to explore her ambivalent feelings. *It is at this point that the patiently cultivated relationship bears fruit* (Rowe, 1966).

In the 1960s, society "seemed more interested in punishing" unwed mothers "than in understanding the social, economic, and psychological forces which have placed them in a deviant position" (Roberts, 1966).

These punitive attitudes of adoption workers were evident in many maternity homes where residents were treated as sinners and criminals and where the punishment was the removal of their newborns for adoption.

> She is sheltered for the remainder of the pregnancy, often with little activity or education... she surrenders the infant for adoption and... has no contact with the infant during her stay in the hospital. She is told it is a mistake which has now been erased... she is sent home, supposedly having purified herself and having become absolved of her 'sins.' Many maternity homes advise the girls not to communicate with them... it certainly becomes difficult to divorce the attitudes of the personnel from those of a group of judges sentencing, condemning, and finally absolving a hardened criminal (Osofsky, 1968).

Osofsky suggested further that the desire of adoption workers to punish unmarried mothers led to inadequate counseling, especially a lack of counseling designed to help unmarried mothers keep their babies.

> [C]ounseling is oriented to white females pregnant out of wedlock...middle class white females...What one sees... is a gross inequality

of social service counseling for pregnant teenagers…One may question the reasons for this lack of adequate counseling…there are certainly smoldering feelings which condemn… their 'immorality.' It is this author's conviction that there further exists a…*desire on the part of 'helping' officials to punish such individuals who are pregnant out of wedlock. Often, these feelings are thinly disguised...* [emphasis added] (Osofsky, 1968).

Sometimes, an unmarried mother would return to the caseworker to reclaim her baby, much to the disapproval of the professionals:

According to the records of one adoption society, about three babies out of every hundred placed with adopters are recalled by their mothers… Even the most careful and thorough casework cannot always prevent this… The caseworker must… *confront the mother with all the practical difficulties that will face her if she recalls her baby, as well as exploring her deeper motives for doing so…* Here is another instance in which the legal concept of *'possession' of a child by his parents does not always work out for the child's good* [emphasis added] (Pochin, 1969).

Many single mothers were losing their babies to adoption because of the attitudes of others, including adoption workers, maternity home personnel, parents and society.

Throughout 1971, comments were offered on this matter by Bernstein and Lipke:

> [O]ne must question whether a prognosis made at a point of crisis should determine the granting or withholding of services… a decision that can have far-reaching consequences for an unmarried mother and her child… As a woman in crisis, she is prone to feelings of guilt and self-deprecation. If the attitudes of others, particularly those who act as agents of society, are demeaning to her self-esteem, her own image of herself is likely to be correspondingly depreciated. One of the outstanding hallmarks of a devalued person in our society is the restriction of choices and decision-making (Bernstein, 1971).

Bernstein, raising concern, continued stating that:

> The first thing the unmarried mother is likely to lose is her right to make important decisions. The agency or community tells her what she must do if she is to receive the services she needs… In most instances the plan for the baby is pre-determined. Often these matters are decided without her being able to state her own preferences… decisions have to be made under conditions of restricted maneuverability and abnormal pressures – pressures of time and emotion that do not allow for testing, exploring and other procedures that are ordinarily essential to sound decision-making (Bernstein, 1971).

Lipke weighed in, too, saying that:

> An unwed mother must face some
> disapproval during pregnancy as well as later
> if she keeps the child. Society generally
> disapproves of unwed parenthood or
> illegitimacy... (Lipke, 1971).

Several years later, in 1973, Lorraine Klerman and James Jekel in "School Age Mothers, Problems, Programs and Policy," claimed:

> Clear evidence of the effect of early
> pregnancy on the psychological health of the
> mother and child is even more difficult to
> obtain because of the overwhelming weight of
> social factors. Certainly young pregnant girls
> and mothers exhibit a high rate of adverse
> psychological conditions, but little is known
> about the cause (Klerman & Jekel, 1973).

Punitive treatment of unmarried mothers by society, health care staff, schools and other institutions continued, with school-age pregnant girls receiving little help: families and schools being harsh and unresponsive and banishing the girls from pursuing education, and with health care staff making frightening and confusing experiences of pregnancy and birth even worse. In fact, health care workers tended to provide prenatal, delivery, and postpartum care "in an unfeeling manner," believing that if "they [pregnant unmarried females] suffer enough, they'll know not to do it again" (Brandstadt & Zackler, 1975).

In addition, according to Benet (1976), "...legislators and taxpayers are still unwilling to condone immorality by giving unmarried mothers adequate support... the encouragement of adoption can be used as one means of punishing the mother while avoiding the accusation of punishing the child."

Many mothers from the Baby Scoop Era subsequently worked and paid into Social Security for decades after surrendering their babies. An argument could be made that they had the right to use welfare assistance when they needed to. That was, and still is, the right of every American citizen. However, for unmarried mothers of the BSE it appeared not be a right that, for them, was protected or respected.

Case law reflected the punishing attitudes common in the late 1970s, with cases addressing the constitutional rights and coercion of unmarried mothers relevant to the matter of consent to the adoption.

> Harry v. Fisher involved not an agency but a private adoption. Here a natural mother executed a written consent to the private adoption of her child, and was held unable to regain her child from its adoptive parents, even though she alleged duress in the circumstances of her consent. The Virginia Supreme Court rejected her argument of duress, and held that once a valid consent was shown, the adoptive parents could keep the child if they showed that its best interests would be served... A mother such as this might well be held unable to regain her child,

but if she had a cognizable constitutional right under <u>Stanley</u> to rear her child, *she could still sue the agency for damages for violation of this constitutional right, if her consent had been extracted through duress...* but if such a right can be claimed, it becomes doubly important to avoid any appearance of nondisclosure or high pressure tactics on natural parents -- tactics that might later be interpreted as duress...Clear explanations should be given to any parent ...with respect to the *possible consequences in later termination procedures, and the continuing rights of the parent to visit and otherwise maintain contact with the child...*Where the parent consents to termination, *clear explanations of alternatives should be given to the parent prior to consent,* so that later charges of coercion may be avoided [emphasis added] (Rose, 1978).

By the 1980s, it was clear that in the United States mothers were being robbed of their rights to parent their own children for the simple reason of not being married. Phyllis Chesler (1986) pointed out that if children have a right to be wanted, then natural parents who are willing to parent them must also have the right to raise them:

This means that no one (male or female) should be unwillingly or unknowingly sterilized, *forced into an abortion against her will, or forced to give up her infant at birth* either because she is too young, unmarried, impoverished, unemployed, or underpaid or because she is denied access to basic family support services [emphasis added].

The effects of surrender on the unmarried mother were severe. She is shamed rather than congratulated after the birth of her child, and once the baby is placed for adoption, she is expected to return to her previous life as if nothing important had transpired. "To all intents and purposes, her pregnancy was made 'invisible'" (Howe, Sawbridge, & Hinings, 1992).

Hospitals adopted punishing attitudes when required to care for unmarried mothers. In a specific example provided by Howe, et al. (1992):

> ...in this hospital there was a policy... that mothers who were going to have their babies adopted should not see them. The babies were removed and it was not expected that the mothers would care for them. When Helen asked to see her daughter she was told that it was not allowed... More typical were the mothers who felt that a punitive atmosphere surrounded the birth of their baby. Medical staff treated the mother in a rough, condemnatory fashion that was both physically and emotionally very hurtful.

After a child was born, the family of the unmarried mother often wanted to forget it ever happened. The mother went without emotional support, and pressures were exerted upon them to make "decisions" that they might have been ill-prepared to make at the time. When discussing their experiences today, many natural mothers report feeling "coerced" into making a choice for adoption (McColm, 1993).

Social workers continued to have unacknowledged and contradictory interests and attitudes toward unmarried mothers, despite the fact that discussions of social work and adoption generally present the workers as neutral and knowledgeable providers of a service designed to benefit children without parents, couples without children, and the "child-burdened natal mothers. However, the fact that social workers have seen the interests of natural mothers as subordinate and contradictory to the interests of their children (and therefore expendable) has been rarely admitted within the profession" (O'Shaughnessy, 1994).

The so-called counseling of the natural mother often involves pressuring them to sacrifice themselves for their children; in other words, adoption acts to punish the mothers of out-of-wedlock children by taking their children away and to apply "discipline" through the pregnancy to "enable them to become orderly women, if not wives (where they would be under the discipline/jurisdiction of their husbands) and less of a threat to the sexual, social, cultural and economic fabric of society" (O'Shaughnessy, 1994).

Issues of economic class and psychosocial concerns also contributed to the attitudes of adoption workers. According to historian and sociology professor Katarina Wegar, "Researchers have argued that because teenage pregnancies have serious economic and psychosocial consequences for the mothers, it is the social worker's professional duty *to press for relinquishment*" [emphasis added] (Wegar, 1997).

There is no doubt that single mothers were encouraged, pressured, and coerced into surrendering their children to adoption between the end of World War II and the early 1970s. Social workers and adoption authorities believed "that unwed mothers were as a rule *pushed to relinquish their children, pressured by societal stigmatization* of single parenthood and a shift in trends in the field of social work favoring stranger adoption over helping birth mothers raise their children" [emphasis added] (Tyree, 2013).

By 2014, it could be said that the professionals recognized the separation of mothers from their children via "forced adoptions" was neither moral nor legal:

> During the mid to late twentieth century (1940s to 1980s), it was common practice for babies of unwed mothers to be adopted by married couples. Many of the infants were taken from their mothers at childbirth *as a result of extreme pressure and coercion that they experienced from family, social workers and hospital staff*...The adoptions that occurred in this way have been termed forced adoptions ...*It has now been recognized that the separation of a child from its mother in this manner was neither moral nor legal* [emphasis added] (Higgins, 2014).

CHAPTER 13

LIKE LAMBS TO THE SLAUGHTER

When a mother is forced to choose between the child and the culture, there is something abhorrently cruel and unconsidered about that culture. A culture that requires harm to one's soul in order to follow the culture's proscriptions is a very sick culture indeed.

Clarissa Pinkola Estès

During the Baby Scoop Era, many unmarried mothers, by virtue of their marital status and age, were at the mercy of their parents and society. Jobless and mostly of school age, they had no income. Many were not told about assistance available to them through federal or state agencies such as welfare and child support. They had little, if any, emotional or economic support. The perception that unmarried motherhood constituted a moral sin overshadowed any economic, social and emotional considerations.

While there were discussions of the role of poor economic conditions in out-of-wedlock pregnancies, the general view was that economic pressures and requirements were only secondary factors. The early maternity homes, which originally tried to address some of these issues, such as providing the residents with vocational training to provide them with a means of earning a living in order to

153

keep their newborns, were subjected to a change in focus as the field of social work professionalized.

Maternity homes provided the solution for unmarried mothers faced with the need to find a place to have their babies. By 1947, there were about 200 maternity homes in the U.S., most of which were linked to private agencies. Some of the "homes" based their programs on the latest advances in social work theory, while some continued to operate on the basis of religious tenets dating back at least to the days of *The Scarlet Letter*. The two major maternity home chains at the time were the Florence Crittenton homes and the Salvation Army homes, which traced their lineage to the organization's 19th century mission work with so-called "lost" women. Writing in 1947, *Ladies Home Journal* reporter Joan Younger stated:

> It is only recently that *the birth of a baby to an unmarried woman has been considered as an economic, social and emotional problem as well as a moral one,* and the problem of the baby's future life as a separate individual considered independently of his mother's 'mistake.' In spite of this altered focus, most maternity homes were plagued by a lack of skilled staff and old building facilities located in geographically isolated areas, making the residents "walled off and cloistered" [emphasis added] (Younger, 1947).

> [T]he girl whose baby is adopted has the formidable task of reintegrating herself in the society which cast her out...From the time she becomes pregnant until she is able to

return to society the American unmarried
mother travels a route of namelessness… says
Charlotte Andress, the able director of
Inwood House …'the girls are known only by
their first names and last initials to preserve
anonymity…our society isolates the offender
and loses interest in her once she is out of her
'state of sin.' We spend paltry thousands on
researching illegitimacy's causes and, as Clark
Vincent says, 'Nobody even thinks to ask
what the unmarried mother's problems are ten
years later'… (Rinehart, 1963).

Responding to the fact that unmarried mothers faced
significant, negative social pressures, some professionals
attempted to emphasize the contributory legal and
economic problems and to criticize legislation that tried to
"*to limit financial assistance available to women who are pregnant out
of wedlock*" (Osofsky, 1968) in actions that were entirely the
opposite of what was needed to change the situation of
these women.

Many an unmarried mother who would have chosen to
keep her child was "*compelled by sheer economic necessity to part
with him*" (Pochin, 1969) and trying to reconcile the conflict
between thinking the child would be better off if adopted
and her own instinct to mother the child herself.
Professionals acknowledged that it might be "possible" that
the most unselfish mother would choose the strongest
opportunity for the child's security and happiness by
deciding on adoption despite any grief or sense of loss she
might feel. Caseworkers needed to be able to "assess the
kind and degree of love her client is capable of" (Pochin,
1969) when dealing with these situations. Workers played

upon the unmarried mother's sense of shame by focusing on the fact that the out-of-wedlock birth could be hidden from society if she did not keep her baby. In cases of "more perceptive" clients, however, workers were counseled to help the mother "go on to reflect that *even if she parts with him it will not make any difference to the fact that she had an illegitimate child...*" (Pochin, 1969).

William Ryan, a sociologist who did pioneering work on society's tendency to blame the poor for their own predicaments, noted that unmarried mothers were not degenerates or deviants, but victims of poverty and the visible proof of a "pattern of inequality" in how resources are distributed and accessed, a pattern that reflected an intent by society's dominant majority to "keep the poor in their place." In contrast, the product of illegitimacy - the baby - was held in high value by society at large, and "to eliminate it would eliminate the raw material of the adoption process." In a particularly stinging criticism of the system, Ryan stated, "The great surplus of unadopted illegitimate children is…an untidy bi-product of the process, substandard material that is to be thrown back onto the resources of the hopelessly inadequate child welfare and public assistance system" (Ryan, 1971).

The Children's Bureau cited the United States Constitution as the source of the rights of all citizens, regardless of their place in society, to obtain child welfare services from the public and voluntary social agencies authorized by law or charter to provide these services. By the early 1970s, some states had enacted laws establishing a policy of public responsibility for children, and all had some elements that required certain services be provided in order to ensure the general well-being of children.

According to the Children's Bureau, "These services should be defined and established as rights by law, *legally enforceable and available without respect to economic or social status*, ethnic or national origin, race, color, creed or limitations of residence."

Policy makers and social work professionals were concerned that, if an unmarried mother and her child returned home, particularly in the case of school-age mothers, both would "become *economically dependent upon her parents or upon some form of welfare…*" Because American society had strong opinions about setting social norms like a stable family life with two married parents in the home and attaining a basic level of education and achieving economic independence for every family, unwed pregnancies of school-age girls were problems "to be denied or hidden" [emphasis added] (Klerman & Jekel, 1973).

Derek Gill, professor and chairman of the Department of Sociology and Anthropology at the University of Maryland and an expert in health care and the welfare state, emphasized that unmarried mothers and their children suffer adverse effects from some established social attitudes and policies. Such policies often mean that the mothers and children don't have enough money or adequate living conditions, and that they often face humiliation at the hands of the courts, supplementary benefits offices, and even social isolation. These factors only make the deprived and under-privileged status that women experience overall even worse, and they may stop "unsupported mothers from raising or caring for their children effectively" (Gill, 1977).

Describing the social stigma that remained attached to illegitimacy in 1977, Professor Juliet Cheetham at Oxford University's Department of Social and Administrative Studies also noted the continuance of the perception that *"women who fit themselves in this position must expect to suffer the consequences of their action (and that) single mothers share the economic and emotional hardships experienced by all groups of unsupported mothers."* However, deserted wives and widows usually received sympathy and support from their family and friends, but the unmarried mother was often required to handle her situation without receiving support or sympathy. Cheetham went on to say:

> It would be possible in our society, if we had the will, to ensure a decent standard of living for families with one parent... these are not our priorities, and while they are not we have to live with the logical inconsistencies, the moral ambiguities, and the human unhappiness and conflict which surround unwanted pregnancy and the methods we have evolved for dealing with it (Cheetham, 1977).

Standards for Adoption Service, a 1978 publication of the Child Welfare League of America, provided clear guidelines on the proper method of practice when dealing with children and their natural family members. The gold standard was that "no child should be deprived of care by his natural parents." However, in the case of newborns taken from unmarried mothers, rarely, if ever, was a mother tried and proven to be neglectful or abusive. Rather, it had been a normal course of action, and a systematic practice, for unmarried mothers to be expected, guided, pressured and coerced to surrender their babies for adoption as soon after birth as possible. In addition, rarely were there any discussions about alternative means of care that could help the mother keep her baby, nor were there any efforts to find such means.

Clearly, the published standards mandated that the natural family (father, mother, and their children) be preserved whenever possible in order to maintain the best means of giving children a stable family life. According to the standards, no child was to be deprived of care by natural parents, unless it is in the child's best interest to take other measures: "No *children should be deprived of care by their parents solely because of their economic need, or their need for other forms of community assistance* to reinforce their efforts to maintain a home for them" [emphasis added] (CWLA, 1978).

Because unmarried mothers had no husbands to protect them, they faced considerable financial challenges if they tried to keep their children. A mother had the traditional responsibility of caring for children, but an important element of the traditional model presupposed a husband who would supply financial support that allowed her to do so. Most unmarried mothers were economically disadvantaged in several ways: they were young in a society whose structures favored mature individuals, and as women, they had to fight an income structure that favored men. Without the protection of a male, the moral status of an unmarried mother was made untenable, and she and her child had virtually no societal identity.

"Being a mother while not a wife, she was excluded from the private economy between mothers and fathers

and from the wider economy by the belief that mothers
do not work for money but for their children and their
children's fathers, who must of course be husbands.
She was in trouble… She had no place" [emphasis
added] (Inglis, 1984).

Researchers in the adoption field understood how
economic stress regularly forced unmarried mothers to
release their newborns to adoption as the best recourse.
They found that a lack of financial resources was a major
cause of surrender, since external factors that removed
economic and social support for these women tended to
move them inexorably toward the decision to surrender
their babies. When "illegitimacy" was stigmatized by
society, it resulted in public economic assistance becoming
unavailable as unmarried mothers were categorized in social
policies as being among the "unworthy poor" (Pelton,
1988).

Adoption always had a connection to economics, given
that healthy white babies have always been the "products"
most in demand by the adoption industry, while children
who did not fit this category were relegated to foster care
(Schaffer & Lindstrom, 1989). One unmarried mother
stated that she had been "numb" since discovering her
pregnancy; she felt powerless in the face of economic and
social pressures, and felt that she had no choice but to
release her child (LaVonne, 1996).

It was easy to convince frightened, young females who
were pregnant and unmarried that they did not have the
essential qualifications to be mothers, and if a woman
rebelled once she had agreed to adoption, she faced feeling
responsible for family anxiety and "incurring the

displeasure" of the social worker on whom she had to depend during the process. Workers often felt that they had failed in their duties if a mother chose single parenthood rather than adoption, as they knew the mother *"lacked the material and social support to keep her child...* she was taking away a baby from parents who had waited and longed for a child. She was *being selfish when she could offer her child so little.* Workers assumed that the relinquishing mother would soon forget all about her child" [emphasis added] (Sawbridge & Hinings, 1992).

> Single mothers who were not offered any help in keeping their babies were ultimately "worn down and worn out" by monumental societal and economic pressures; many lost the energy to fight. These women became passive and acquiescent, tired, defeated, and demoralized. Everyone around them showed a strong determination to have the child adopted, and for the mother, it seemed there was "a conspiracy of silence" surrounding her. She wanted to express her feelings, "but no one wanted to hear" (Sawbridge & Hinings, 1992).

The unmarried mother's inadequate financial support meant she was scapegoated and punished for her poverty. Female reformers devised a new way of addressing so-called women in trouble. These "unfortunates" who included prostitutes, abandoned mistresses, or unmarried mothers, became defined as "victims of social and economic circumstances rather than moral pariahs." The reformers said that teenage parents in particular were vulnerable due to their poverty, but there was a moral risk for society in symbolically punishing teen mothers "for trying to solve the problems everyone faces and solve them with more limited resources than most Americans" (Luker, 1996).

Freelance writer and adopter Lois Gilman noted that when natural parents have limited financial resources they are more likely to surrender their baby for adoption (Gilmore, 1998), and Katarina Wegar, a sociology professor at Old Dominion University in Virginia, said the prevailing view throughout the history of adoption, was that social workers should "press for relinquishment" because unmarried mothers experienced terrible economic consequences (Wegar, 1997). Did she raise this issue to point out that social workers are entrusted with the duty to help all American citizens regardless of age, income, gender or marital status? Should unmarried mothers have their babies removed from them simply because they are economically stressed or not married?

Conservative spokesperson William Bennett was actively working against the provision of benefits to teenage mothers as late as 2001, stating that:

> My own hope is that at least one state will pass legislation cutting off future benefits to a particular subset of the population (say, unmarried teen mothers) while also actively expanding group homes for pregnant single women; promoting adoption... Terrible human wreckage has been left in illegitimacy's wake. We need to ask ourselves whether we are prepared to do anything about it, and we

need to ask ourselves, and answer ourselves,
soon (Bennett, 2001).

It is interesting to note that in comparison to children or
adults, teens are more likely to take risks, partly because
they experience a "mismatch" between two major brain
functions. The development of the limbic system, which is
fueled by hormones and drives emotions, becomes more
intense with the onset of puberty (usually between 10 and
12 years of age). However, the prefrontal cortex that
controls impulsive actions does not fully develop until at
least ten years later. This imbalance experienced during the
teen years contributes to teens' inability to control their
impulses and make reasonable judgments of the risks and
rewards of a given situation (Giedd, 2015).

Teenage unmarried mothers were vulnerable and
defenseless during the Baby Scoop Era. Even the
physiological development of their young brains worked
against them. Neuroscientist and life science patent
attorney Gargi Talukder has described the differences in
how teenagers and adults make emotional decisions, stating
that "teenagers are simply not yet equipped to think
through things in the same way… 'Good judgment is
learned, but you can't learn it if you don't have the
necessary hardware'."

CHAPTER 14

AID TO FAMILIES
WITH DEPENDENT CHILDREN

*...proposals that have come forward from time to time to
control or punish the unwed mother...usually it is the ADC
mothers for whom critics proscribe sterilization, imprisonment
or - most common of all – denial of subsistence...Ironically as
the clamor for sterilization on one hand – equally insistent are
the forces blocking the dissemination of information and
education for birth control.*

Alex Poinsett

The overall view of the general public toward unmarried
mothers has been described as follows:

As social welfare programs were
elaborated, casework became legitimized
surveillance... Once formalized as Aid to
Families with Dependent Children by the
Social Security Act of 1935, welfare for single
mothers became increasingly entangled with
an issue that had a separate, but more
forthrightly authoritarian history: the issue of
the state in its role as super-paternalist... This
was the history of the doctrine of *parens
patriae,* which gives the state the right to
intervene and remove children... Along with

the issue of welfare, the issue of state removal
of children from women who are 'maritally
challenged'...Child welfare is not and never
has been about children. It is and always has
been about welfare (Armstrong, 1995).

Through the 1960s and 1970s, society became
increasingly resentful of unmarried mothers who received
Aid to Families with Dependent Children (AFDC), a
federal social welfare program that provided support to
dependent children and their parents. Some mistakenly
believed that the availability of AFDC encouraged
unmarried motherhood. This led to changes in the program
that increased the pressure on low-income, unmarried
mothers to surrender their children to adoption.

Jane Hoey, who spent 17 years as the director of the
Social Security Board's Bureau of Public Assistance, tried
to explain that AFDC did not cause teenage pregnancy,
recognizing that the general public tended to lump all
families receiving assistance with the few whose situations
were "complicated" by a member who did not behave in a
"socially approved manner," such as a daughter who bore
an out-of-wedlock child. Hoey warned about imposing
punitive sanctions on single parent families. According to
Hoey, contrary to what the public might believe - that some
women deliberately become single mothers to get AFDC -
this was not the case and proposals seeking to deny
assistance to unmarried mothers, put them in jail and place
their children in institutions would do nothing to stop out-
of-wedlock pregnancies (Hoey, 1952).

The attitude of the public toward unmarried mothers and AFDC tended to consider these women as belonging to one of two categories:

> One of the arguments that has been raised… is whether… Aid to Dependent Children – encourages illegitimacy… usually lumped together clinically as a kind of sociological freak, the 'unwed' mother actually falls into two sharply delineated categories: the promiscuous woman with 8 or 10 illegitimate children all collecting ADC funds, and the new good-bad girl more typical who has her baby in secrecy, at no expense to the public, gives it out for adoption, either privately or through an agency, and returns to her self-supporting or family supported role in society (Browning, 1959).

The attitude of the public in 1959 is illustrated through a complaint made in New York alleging that many of the women on the "payroll" of Aid to Dependent Children had more than one child out of wedlock and that policies should be changed to allow a claim for the benefits for one child only; if a woman got pregnant again, she would lose her rights to ADC. Some policymakers suggested that women who had more than two children out of wedlock be sterilized (Pinson, 1964). Massachusetts asked "Does the state underwrite or subsidize immorality?" (Bye, 1959). A study of the ADC program in Cook County, Illinois, in 1961, was conducted at the direction of the board of county commissioners who worried about the rising costs and criticisms leveled at the program. The results of the study "baffled" the commissioners as it showed the number of ADC recipients increasing during a period of economic prosperity; they were especially concerned about the growing number of illegitimate children on the rolls (Sandusky, 1961).

In the early 1960s several states initiated efforts designed to keep mothers off welfare. In 1960, Louisiana passed a law barring any woman who had an illegitimate child from receiving ADC, and all homes in which illegitimate children lived were declared to be "unsuitable." A major concern in Maryland also involved the number of illegitimate children receiving public assistance. A newspaper in Connecticut published a series of eight articles under the title "Illegitimacy: Who Pays?" in response to public consternation about the number of illegitimate children on ADC rolls (McCalley & Greenleigh, 1961).

Approaches to unmarried mothers in the 1960s ranged from forgiveness to punishment, with some policymakers happy to include the woman's child in the punishment by withholding public assistance from both, while others favored allowing a woman "one mistake" before taking away ADC. Professionals commented on the "problem" of confusing the provision of help to a person in need with condoning the actions of that person (Adams & Gallagher, 1962). As time went on, the public's attention was increasingly drawn to the provision of public assistance to unmarried mothers and their children by continuing attacks on the ADC program disseminated in the press (Costigan, 1964).

While the press and the public were convinced that the availability of welfare encouraged unwed parenthood, the actual benefit amount of an AFDC payment was not sufficient for any "sane woman" to willingly take on the anguish of unwed pregnancy just to receive the "pittance" provided in an AFDC check (Pinson, 1964). Despite evidence dispelling this myth, policymakers continued to worry about the burden that "a rising tide of illegitimate children born to promiscuous women and irresponsible men: children who become dependent upon the public for support" imposed on taxpayers who ultimately paid the AFDC bill (Wiltse & Roberts, 1966). An estimate of the costs of providing aid to an unmarried mother and child in 1968 placed the average expense to a welfare department for 100 teenage girls at $10 billion over the course of the girls' lifetimes (Osofsky, 1968).

By the late 1960s, social workers acknowledged that while the public expressed hostility toward unmarried mothers receiving AFDC, there was a general tolerance for those who surrendered their children for adoption. In contrast, unmarried mothers in Denmark were treated with dignity, respect, and the provision of social aid and protections. There were "Mother's Aid" programs that provided prenatal, childbirth, and aftercare services, followed by counseling, housing, educational and vocational training geared toward individual needs." The goal of the assistance was to give the unmarried mother what she needed to become a self-sufficient, productive member of society, and the children of these mothers suffered no legal or social stigma. In fact, "over 90 percent of the unmarried fathers in Denmark give (their children) their names and some financial support." While social workers in the United States were aware of the methods in place in the Scandinavian country, they tended to disregard the information and did not implement any of the approaches that had proved so successful in Denmark (Shiller, 1969).

The issue of public support for unmarried mothers and their children remained significant for social work professionals and policymakers into the 1970s. Concerns were raised about how an unmarried, school-age mother and her child would become economically dependent on someone else after the birth, either on her parents if she returned home or on taxpayers in the form of public assistance (Klerman & Jekel, 1973). They used statistics noting the increase in illegitimate pregnancies to support this position and recognized the differences in "punishment" for unwed mothers according to their age and economic status. For example, in 1961:

> ...an effort to control illegitimacy by cracking down on welfare is unlikely to have any more effect in the future than similar efforts have had in the past...The degree to which each punishment will be experienced by... the unwed mother will vary according to her age and economic status at the time of pregnancy. If the woman does not experience pregnancy and illegitimate childbirth she will not be sanctioned... elimination of effects of some punishments can be obtained if the woman releases the child for adoption (Zackler & Brandstadt, 1975).

A *Newsweek* article in 1994 article stated that:

> Commentators on the political right and left have argued - sometimes provocatively -

> that more single teenage women should be
> encouraged to place their children for
> adoption… Prospective parents have to wait
> at least two years on average to adopt. Some
> pay fees of $50,000 to more than $100,000 to
> get babies through private adoption.

Society came to view out-of-wedlock children and their mothers as "problems" that needed support from the public in terms of money and care; therefore, they were targeted for governmental investigation and reform. This was a new attitude that began with the creation of the federal Children's Bureau in the United States. In 1926, one of the Bureau's researchers found that one-third of the illegitimate children born in a large city relied on public or private child-care or child-saving agencies. In other words, they depended on welfare (Luker, 1995). African American unmarried mothers received different treatment than white mothers after World War II and before Roe v. Wade. Black women were seen as "socially unproductive breeders, constrainable only by punitive, legal sanctions," but white mothers were viewed as "socially productive breeders" who could give infertile married couples a chance to construct "proper families" (Solinger, in Babb, 1999).

The negative perceptions of unmarried mothers on welfare was strongly promulgated by the politically conservative critic of American society William Bennett in 2001, when he wrote:

> …for decades we have had in place a
> welfare system that has deliberately subsidized
> out of wedlock births. The program called Aid
> to Families with Dependent Children (AFDC)

which began in the 1930s to help 'widows and orphans,' was transmuted over the decades into a vast government system that in effect has paid poor, unmarried women to have children. Whatever its good intentions, it ranks among the most destructive social initiatives ever.

Bennett even went so far as to say that the "large numbers of unmarried women who are having babies" represented "the major problem confronting American society" and stated that:

A reasonable person could well conclude, with University of Pennsylvania Professor Elijah Anderson, that *'in cold economic terms, a baby can be an asset.'* Perhaps, then, welfare does have a significant negative effect on the unmarried birth ratio... Even former Secretary of Health and Human Services Donna Shalala... has said: 'I don't like to put this in moral terms, but I do believe that having children out of wedlock is just wrong'... *Since we began subsidizing out of wedlock births in the 1960s, the federal government has compiled an astonishingly brutal record...* And the ratio continues its relentless march upward - meaning that things have to change if we are to avoid even greater social ruin [emphasis added].

CHAPTER 15

REVOLVING DOORS
& CONVEYOR BELTS

Maternity homes, which were once shelters dedicated to the
redemption and reclamation of 'fallen women', were now
redefined by social workers as places of scientific treatment.
Rather than unfortunate 'sisters' to be 'saved,' unmarried
mothers became 'problem girls' to be 'treated.'

Regina Kunzel

Many unmarried mothers-to-be were confined in maternity homes, where they were isolated from the outside world and pressured to surrender their children. There were hundreds of these homes scattered about the country; the most common were the Florence Crittentons and Salvation Army homes. A woman who experienced life as a young, pregnant, unmarried female in one of homes in 1947 described how it felt:

> ...(the) agency suggested I go to a
> maternity home and get some rest, and
> meanwhile they'd find me a foster home... the
> agency said rest, and I thought that's what I
> was going to do. I was so very tired. But all of
> us had jobs. It was my job to scrub the ward
> floor and the bathrooms. There were about
> twenty-five girls there when I first went there;
> all of us sleeping in one big room... It made

me feel like a criminal. And a prisoner... We
were all beaten. And even if we did get out,
where would we go? Getting out meant
someone wanted you, and who wanted us?
(Younger 1947).

For the most part, unmarried mothers relegated to
maternity homes were forbidden to have contact with the
fathers of their babies. Social work professionals believed
that paternity hearings should not be insisted upon because
it was better for the girl and "for the future welfare of the
baby" that all connection with the father be eliminated; it
was "clearly indicated for all situations in which adoption
was considered that a 'clean break' with the father was
preferred" (Bower, 1947). This meant that the mother-to-
be was actively prevented from knowing if the father of her
child wanted to marry her or, at least, wanted to help raise
their child.

Margaret Hickey (1958) of the Public Affairs
Department claimed that:

> Every year some 6,000 of the young
> women who become pregnant out of wedlock
> (193,500 in 1956) turn to Florence Crittenton.
> Girls may remain from two to four months
> before delivery until ten days to three weeks
> after. Many are able to pay the full fee...
> which may range for $2.84 to $10.61 a day...

It was clearly understood that expectant unmarried
women who were confined to maternity homes would
surrender their babies to adoption. In fact, living in a
maternity home for a significant period of time during that

final three months of pregnancy was strongly associated with surrender, as the maternity home environment was "conducive" to child surrender (Costigan, 1964).

Another unmarried pregnant 18-year-old described how one maternity home's personnel punished the "inmates" in 1966 by taking away their choice of television programs watched in the evening. The home was a "prison without bars," and its entire philosophy was that the girls were sinners who were being punished (Wiemo, 1966).

The homes imposed severe limits on the leisure time activities the women were allowed to pursue. There were no games, record players, or television, and the radio could by played only for one hour in the afternoon. The women were forced to do the washing and ironing for staff members. The freedom to leave the home was regulated, and few homes allowed residents to go out in the evening. Some matrons required residents to ask permission before going out, and that permission was not always provided. Residents were not allowed to make their own choices as their residence in the home removed their "client status" and they had to accept whatever "fixed and predetermined type of service" was chosen for them. "Perhaps the most apt term to suggest their status while in the Home is 'girl,' the word used by the staff of the Homes and the social workers. 'Girl' conveys the denial of adult status and responsibility, and the expectations of conformity and obedience..." (Nicholson, 1968).

Prison expert Dr. Howard Osofsky commented on the restrictive nature of maternity homes and the pressure placed on unmarried mothers to surrender, claiming that the girls confined to the homes experienced separation from their friends and family, could not attend school, get a job, or participate in any meaningful activities. They were also prohibited from communicating with the institute if they became pregnant again. In this situation, these girls would "certainly understand" the attitude of the home's staff and their expectation that she "repent and emerge cleansed" from her time there (Osofsky, 1968).

Some religion-based maternity homes expected unmarried mothers to surrender their babies. For example, Catholic Charities stated in 1969 that the admission of an unmarried, pregnant female to one of their maternity homes required surrender of the baby and apparently provided no opportunity for a mother to change her mind as her pregnancy progressed or after her child was born. The organization stipulated as a requirement of admission to a home *"the requirement that the child must be surrendered for adoption."* Other requirements included being a Catholic, being unmarried, and that the woman's pregnancy was her first. Catholic Charities stated up front that if an unmarried pregnant "girl" had definitely decided to keep her baby, she should not be referred to one of the organization's homes for care, as the home *"does not take... repeaters or girls who do not plan to surrender the baby for adoption"* [emphasis added] (Catholic Charities, 1969).

Maternity home residents were discouraged, and sometimes even prevented, from seeing their children. One mother had been advised to see her baby but not feed it, and when asked during a group therapy session why the social worker offered this guidance, the girl said, "I think maybe she's afraid that if I do too much, I will change my mind about adoption." Another girl in the session said that the social worker didn't think any of the girls in the home were capable of raising a child and didn't want any of them changing their minds about adoption (Rains, 1971).

It was easy for institutions to depersonalize the individuals under their control. Studies in the sociology of deviance have shown that the most dramatic examples of objectification involve ritual "mortification" or "identity-stripping" experienced by new inmates of "total institutions." Once the personal effects, clothing, and even normal physical appearance are taken away, the person effectively becomes a "prisoner," "mental patient," "recruit" (Schur, 1983).

CHAPTER 16

MOTHER OF MOTHER

She [unwed mother] cannot take advantage of the period of pregnancy... because of her preoccupation with the additional problems of social censure and the undivided responsibility for the child. Instead of having the help of her mother and the community, she is entirely alone; in addition, she must face condemnation by her family and the community.

Babette Block

Unmarried mothers were often kept from their children after the delivery. Sometimes, an unmarried mother's own mother or older sister would raise the child as her own, and the natural mother would have to live in the family as an aunt to her own baby. In these situations, the mother's family would adopt her child, and the child was never to know the real story. In a 1947 case, a girl's family planned to adopt her child and raise it, while sending the girl away to live with an aunt (Younger, 1947).

However, it was known that "...if the grandmother takes the baby, the girl may find herself more unsatisfied than ever, and be back in a year with another baby" (Hickey, 1958).

In a case from the 1960s, a girl's parents barred her from seeing her baby. She had given birth at age 17, and her parents insisted that she not see the child, so it was taken

179

away directly from the hospital. The girl felt that she had been "robbed" of her baby, and when she became pregnant a second time, "it was clear that this second pregnancy was in great measure the result of her agony of deprivation. 'I never even knew what my baby looked like,' she exclaimed. 'It was just snatched away from me...'" (Edline, 1960).

Dr. John Bowlby cited research indicating that a high percentage of unmarried mothers were "psychologically disturbed women, who may be unfitted to give a child the emotional stability it needs, and that to leave them to struggle alone with the child's upbringing or to return it to the grandparents' home - commonly the source of the mother's own emotional difficulties, may perpetuate a vicious circle" (Wimperis, 1960).

In the view of some adoption workers, the unmarried mother's mother should be "pressured" to tell her daughter to surrender the baby to adoption, in essence advising case workers to target the baby's grandmother if the mother showed any resistance to surrendering her child for adoption:

> It is essential that the parent most involved, psychologically, in the daughter's pregnancy also be dealt with in a manner identical with the one suggested in dealing with the girl. Time is of the essence; the maturation of the fetus proceeds at an inexorable pace. An ambivalent mother, interfering with her daughter's ability to arrive at the decision to surrender her child, must be dealt with as though she (the girl's mother) were a child

herself… there is a direct relationship
between the severity of a girl's emotional
disturbance and her inability to surrender her
child. The sicker the out-of-wedlock mother,
the greater her need to hold on to the child…
the family members must be treated with the
same firmness that the worker must use in
helping the girl arrive at a healthy solution
(Heiman, 1960).

Family members had a variety of reactions to the news
that there was a pregnant, unmarried female in the family.
An illegitimate pregnancy had a serious impact on all family
members, and often, rather than come to the aid of a teen
mother, they did not respond in "ways that would enhance
her ability to recover from the experience" or to handle it
emotionally, or to take steps to resolve their problems
(Greenleigh, 1961).

The attitude of family members also had an impact on
the services provided to unmarried mothers, and workers
found that they had to "service" the parents of the
unmarried mother in addition to the mother herself
because the parents' attitudes had a direct influence on the
effectiveness of the services provided to their daughter
(Adams and Gallagher, 1962).

It was believed that if the parents of the unmarried
mother withheld their consent to an adoption, this would
cause damage to both the mother and the child. States had
different laws calling for the necessity of consent from
parents or guardians of the unmarried minor before the girl
could surrender for adoption. Minority was not a bar to
consent in Arizona, the District of Columbia, Kansas, and

Maryland. Some adoption workers favored this situation, noting that *"Sometimes parents can do great damage to their child and their illegitimate grandchild by withholding their consent"* [emphasis added] (Katz, 1962).

Many adoption workers believed that if an unmarried mother took her baby to the home she shared with her parents the baby's grandmother would end up taking on the role of "mother" and raise it herself. It was thought that, at her parents' home, the unmarried mother would have to "share" the child with them, particularly if she went to work all day, which would encourage the child to become more attached to the grandmother. In such cases, the unmarried mother could "feel almost an outsider in the relationship. If it is hard for two women to share a kitchen, how much harder for them to share a child!" (Rowe, 1966).

Several factors influenced the unmarried mother to surrender her baby:

> ...a negative attitude on the part of the maternal grandparents... other factors which she found to encourage the decision in favor of adoption were... that the mother was under eighteen years of age... the intensity of her [the mother's] loss is seldom realized. The worker should be at pains to prepare the grandparents for their daughter's return home, and to ensure that she is given time to mourn. Too often she is expected to take up the threads of normal life again as though nothing had happened (Pochin, 1969).

In a 1918 study, the recommendation was that the best situation for an unmarried mother is one in which she can care for her child herself while living with a relative. In such cases, children who grow up among their own relations have the best chance of growing up in a stable environment (Kammerer, 1918).

One of the basic issues that unmarried mothers must overcome is human nature. Researchers have found that when confronted by "evil," even the most secure person becomes confused. It is easy to see how a child, who "encounters evil" in those upon whom he or she most loves and depends, experiences deeply confusing emotions (Peck, 1983).

If reactions from other people toward the unmarried mother and her child were hostile and characterized by rejection, the mother understood that she was essentially alone in her predicament. It was often the case that parents and partners expressed greater concern about how the pregnancy would impact them than putting themselves in the place of the natural mother to try to understand what she was going through. Parents were chiefly worried about the shame that would fall to them as a result of her pregnancy, and they had a strong influence on whether the unmarried mother would surrender her child. "A feeling of isolation began to haunt those mothers who were told that they had made their bed so they would have to lie on it. This was particularly hard and frightening for those who were young..." (Howe, et al., 1992).

These mothers were essentially forced to conclude that adoption was the only choice, since they could not contemplate how they would care for a child without any economic or personal support. Often, the parents were put in charge of the adoption arrangements; they would also threaten their daughters with various negative actions if she did not surrender her baby. For the unmarried mother, the most important decision of her life was taken away from her control (Howe, et al., 1992).

It was considered better to place the children in new families and establish a "clean break" from the family of origin…adoption workers held to the view that it would be confusing for the child to be formally adopted by a grandparent…. The workers also believed that providing a "small foster fee" would improve the situation considerably, as it would "completely transform the picture: the mother regains her self-respect, the grandparents relax and are more tolerant towards her, and the child grows up free of strain, secure and happy among its own relatives" (Marshal and McDonald, 2001).

The parents of young, unmarried women had considerable influence over the decision to surrender the children to adoption, chiefly because of their fear of the "shame" they expected the family to experience, and because they were reluctant to take on the raising of an additional child. During the period of time in which many thousands of children were surrendered, it was very unusual for parents to change their minds. Only in the cases where parents decided to take their daughter and her child back into the family home did social workers feel that the natural mother should see her baby after birth. In all the other cases in which the baby was surrendered for adoption, the professionals strongly believed that it was "most unwise for the mother to see or have any relationship with the child after birth" (Marshall and McDonald, 2001).

CHAPTER 17

UNEQUAL PROTECTION

Adoption practice works on the premise that in order to save the child, you must first destroy its mother.

Dian Wellfare

To further decrease an unmarried mother's chance of raising her own child, social workers often convinced her to surrender early in her pregnancy, long before her baby was born. They often encouraged a mother to surrender before she was in a good mental and physical state of health, having recuperated from giving birth, and before she was able to make a fully informed decision.

Social workers were advised to develop tentative plans for separating mother and child in order to perform as much of the preliminary work "of carrying out the plan" before the baby was born. The "preliminary work" included "casework treatment aimed at making socially and psychologically possible" for the mother to surrender her child (Clothier, 1941).

Many times workers did not take into account the physiological changes experienced by women during pregnancy; that they could have an impact on how mothers felt about releasing their babies after they were born. Workers felt that a plan to surrender by the unmarried mother early in her pregnancy, on the basis of what seemed to be "the only intelligent thing to do," could be at odds with the feelings that came about with psychological changes occurring as her pregnancy progressed (Boole, 1956).

When services were available to help unmarried mothers keep their babies, adoption workers often kept that information hidden or strongly discouraged mothers from accepting such help.

Some social workers expressed concerns that providing payments for the expenses of an expectant, unmarried mother would affect her ultimate decision about what to do with the baby. For unmarried mothers who made plans early in their pregnancies, and who accepted payments for medical care or living expenses understanding that taking the money constituted a "moral, if not legal, obligation" to fulfill the promise to surrender their children, found themselves in a "tragic plight" if they were unable to part with their babies after birth (Boole, 1956).

The legal establishment tended to support pre-birth relinquishment plans, and a "majority of district judges responded in favor of making plans for adoption before the child is born" (Dean, 1958). As a result, most of the children of unmarried mothers were surrendered to adoptive homes directly from the hospitals they were born in, at least at the end of the 1950s.

Lillian Bye, the executive director of the Crittenton Hastings House in Boston, noted that, between 1934 and 1959, the philosophical motivations of adoption workers had changed from attempts to help unmarried, pregnant girls "accept their motherhood" to its "extreme opposite" of trying to prevent a female who was pregnant out of wedlock to "evolve beyond the state of impregnation." According to Bye (1959), "We help her deliver her child with as little conscious orientation towards maternity as possible. In some instances, we even tell the impregnated girl that she does not need to see her baby, to touch it, or to have any conscious knowledge of it, even including its sex at birth."

Bye was concerned enough about the way the social work system was taking away from unmarried mothers the rights that any other mother had intrinsically that she wrote:

> A woman is an individual as well as a woman, and… she has *individual* 'equal rights,' according to the American Constitution…but if she exercises her 'rights' in the area of sex and as a consequence conceives a child although not traditionally married she finds that the American Constitution does not include her as a *woman*…she finds herself more or less an outcast…a *discrimination* which seriously affects her child also, psychologically and *economically*…Social workers…react with conscious or unconscious fear as women in spite of their technical training, and politicians, doctors, ministers, lawyers and police react as men…Only when we understand and accept this fact…will we, as social workers representing social agencies, be able to set up adequate services for unwed

parents and their children [emphasis added] (Bye, 1959).

The *rights of the mother* of an illegitimate child *are weaker than those of legitimate parents* (Rowe, 1966).

Acknowledging the bonding that occurred between mother and baby during pregnancy, some experts believed that separating the child from the unmarried mother was "unnatural," but despite this belief, continued to recommend that infants be removed from their mothers as soon as they were born. A case in point are the remarks of the psychiatrist Dr. H.G. Gianakon, who wondered:

> At what exact and certain moment should the separation be accomplished? ...Planning for the details of delivery and care for the separation of mother and baby should begin as early as possible... Too rapid separation at certain periods leads to biological damage... Their separation... is unnatural and can never be a harmonious and happy event. The least that can be done is *to ensure that the decision for separation be made early, as far in advance of the delivery date as possible...* [emphasis added] (Gianakon, 1960).

In some cases, the baby would be removed from the mother right after birth:

> [M]any mothers would not be allowed to see their baby. It is *not unusual for doctors, midwives and social workers to discourage mothers*

from forming a relationship with their baby...
hospital staff and relatives, adoption workers
and friends sponsor a *'conspiracy of silence'...*
[emphasis added] (Howe, et al., 1992).

Some adoption workers felt that the decision to
surrender should be made long before the birth of the
baby and that such a decision was too important to be
made by the unmarried mother. They believed that it was
possible to determine which women would make good
mothers and which should be advised "from the start" to
make no effort to keep their children.

Social worker Virginia Wimperis referred to the
expertise of psychology professor Virginia L. Binder when
she wrote, "The whole tendency of Professor Binder's
book is to suggest that *such a prognosis can sometimes be made
even before the child is born...*[emphasis added] (Wimperis,
1960).

Even though the Children's Bureau "described common
practices in child-placing that adoption workers should
avoid, such as needlessly breaking up families, pressuring
unwed mothers to relinquish their children before they had
recovered their physical and emotional equilibrium..."
(Carp, 1998).

Reflecting the belief that it was best to take a child away
right after birth, caseworkers would encourage mothers to
sign papers surrendering their parental rights before or just
after giving birth and before fully recovering from labor
and delivery. Wimperis objected to this practice, noting that
it did harm and that only "unscrupulous or thoughtless

people" would separate a mother from her baby before she was in an appropriate condition to make a good decision. She also noted that placing a child in foster care with a view toward adoption was "contrary to the spirit of the Adoption Act, which lays down that consent to adoption may not be given until a baby is six weeks old." She pointed to the fact that many unmarried mothers feel unhappy and disturbed during their pregnancies and that their maternal feelings may not be evident until after they give birth. "Moral welfare workers point out that a mother who has parted with her baby hurriedly or even from necessity may even grieve so much afterwards that she has a second illegitimate baby" (Wimperis, 1960).

Wimperis emphasized the importance of *allowing* mothers to see and care for their children before making a decision about surrender, believing that once a mother can see and feed her baby, she may realize that she could care for her child and that "it is clearly important in general for a mother to feel that she has reached a decision of such importance without external pressure, freely, realistically and responsibly. For this, time may be necessary... The records show that many of the mothers who had cared for their babies during the greatest period of dependency found it impossible to release them..." (Wimperis, 1960).

Unfortunately, pleas by Wimperis for attention to this issue apparently fell on deaf ears.

By the mid-1960s, it became clear to some social work professionals that unmarried mothers were victims of discrimination and punitive policies due to inadequate resources that were hard to access and to frequently humiliating aid procedures. Income maintenance assistance was particularly inadequate and "surrounded by *punitive administrative policies*." Additionally, the treatment of unmarried mothers varied according to their economic, social and ethnic backgrounds, with some policies reflecting what Columbia University social work professor Alfred Kahn described as *"continuing outright discrimination."* According to Kahn, "Programs are affected by the view that they must not excessively decrease existing guilt, and are often deliberately or unconsciously shaped so as to create or increase it" (Kahn, 1964).

Illustrating the legal approach of many states at the time is this description of Tennessee's law applying to welfare as provided by a deputy commissioner of the state's public welfare department at an adoption conference:

> The basic law under which we operate in Tennessee… is the Welfare Organization Act of 1937, which places responsibility upon the Department of Public Welfare for supervising the care of dependent and neglected children in foster homes or in institutions, especially those placed for adoption or those of illegitimate birth…Within this legal framework we have built a program of services to unmarried parents and their children based on the belief that the parents *should be guided toward the decision* which will help them to adjust as persons and, at the same time, a decision which is reasonably protective of the baby's welfare [emphasis added] (Yeatman, 1964).

Upholding this position was case law cited by law professor Robert J. Levy, which emphasized the rights of parents:

> ...the right of a parent to the custody of a child is paramount or superior to that of any other person: that a mother is presumed to be a fit and suitable person to be entrusted with the care of her child; and that *the burden of disproving this presumption rests upon the person challenging it...* (M.S.A. 260.11) that 'In no case shall a dependent child be taken from its parents without their consent unless, *after diligent effort has been made to avoid such separation*, the same shall be found needful *in order to prevent serious detriment to the welfare of such child...*' [fn 4]. (Levy, 1964).

It was also the case that unmarried mothers residing in maternity homes did not understand or hear about available alternatives to surrendering their newborns to adoption. There was widespread ignorance among these mothers about services like child support, temporary fostering or nursery care, even though most social work professionals had to have known that many maternity home residents would not have been there if they knew about any alternatives for keeping and caring for their babies. It was well known that the lack of financial capacity to raise the children was a major cause of relinquishment... such external factors probably served to cut off economic and social support thus forcing the adoption decision (Pelton, 1988).

Maternity home inmates had no concept of how the surrender would affect their lives in the future, let alone the impact it would have on the children themselves. According to Jill Nicholson, "All the residents we saw were within weeks of deciding whether to keep or to part with their baby. Yet *they had only the haziest notions of what either solution would mean in practical or emotional terms. In all but a few cases they were ignorant of the most basic facts about adoption or the facilities they might find helpful if they kept the baby...*" [emphasis added] (Nicholson, 1968).

Nicholson also stated that the unmarried mothers in the homes wanted to know about the practical and emotional consequences of surrendering their children, but:

> There was little evidence to suggest that much was done to help in this direction...In one Home, the residents described how the difficulty of handing over the baby for adoption was made worse by the knowledge that the matron was standing watching. If they showed any sign of being upset, she would say, 'Well, it's your own fault. If you're upset about the baby you shouldn't have given it away' (Nicholson, 1968).

It was very unlikely that an unmarried mother would be told about welfare or be supported in her decision to accept it. Services available to unwed mothers often consisted of minimal financial aid via the Aid to Families with Dependent Children (AFDC) program, welfare or child support, and most unmarried mothers did not receive any of these services or resources. In the early 1970s it was "very unlikely" that a pregnant, unmarried girl would find an official pregnancy counseling program that would provide her with all available programs and support her in reaching the decision that was right for her (Rains,1971).

A 1971 report from the United Nations Commission on the Status of Women recognized that:

> Article 25(2) of the Universal Declaration of Human Rights provides, <u>inter alia</u>, that 'motherhood and childhood are entitled to special care and assistance'... Article 10 of the Declaration of the *Elimination of Discrimination* against Women... principle 4 of the Declaration of the Rights of the Child, in its Article 11(b), refers to the protection of the rights of mother and child, concern for the upbringing and health of children... of measures to safeguard the health and welfare of women... the Declaration of the Rights of the Child... principle 6 according to which wherever possible, the child should grow up in the care under the responsibility of his parents, and, if in tender years, *shall not, save in exceptional circumstances be separated from his mother*... unmarried mothers... *are often subject to legal and social discrimination in violation of the principles of equality and non-discrimination*... efforts should be made, through all possible means, to promote respect for all inherent dignity and worth of the human person, so as to enable all members of society, *including unmarried mothers*, to enjoy the equal and inalienable rights to which they are entitled... *take all possible measures to eliminate any prevailing*

*legal and social discrimination against the unmarried
mother and to accord her all necessary assistance…*
and that they seek to obtain a greater
comprehension by society of her problems
*with a view to doing away with prejudice against her
and to secure the acceptance of her and her child on an
equal footing with other families… the unmarried
mother… shall enjoy in all cases, as a parent, the
fullest set of rights and duties provided for by law…*
The unmarried mother should be vested in
law with full parental authority over her child,
in all cases, as an automatic consequence of
the fact of birth… Maintenance *rights and
obligations as between the unmarried mother and her
child should be the same as between a sole parent and
a child born in wedlock…*All possible assistance
should be given by the State to the mother to
help her (a) establish paternal filiation, (b)
obtain an agreement by the father or a
decision by the competent authority *for the
support of the child by his father…*The unmarried
mother… *should enjoy all the measures of social
assistance and social security devised for mothers in
general and for single parents in particular*
[emphasis added] (United Nations, 1971).

By the end of the 1970s, criticism of the status quo in
regard to adoption started to arise, particularly focusing on
the failure of authorities to consider the rights of
unmarried natural parents and their ties to their children
(Turner, 1977).

More attention was placed on the rights of minors –
many unmarried mothers had that legal status as well. In a
1976 legal case cited by Carol M. Rose of the Child Welfare
League of America:

> In the 1976 case of *Planned Parenthood of
> Central Missouri v. Danforth,* the Supreme Court
> stated...Constitutional rights do not mature
> and come into being magically only when one
> attains the state defined age of majority.
> Minors, as well as adults, are protected by the
> Constitution and enjoy constitutional rights...
> The implication of this case... seems to be
> that courts are no longer to view children and
> adults as two dichotomous categories, with
> the latter having constitutional rights and the
> former not... Recent cases have held that the
> *in loco parentis* status cannot be used to
> overcome a child's constitutional rights. *In local
> parentis*: 'persons and institutions caring for
> children are said to occupy the legal position
> of the children's parents, or at least to have a
> substantial portion of parents' rights and
> immunities vis-a-vis children' (Rose, 1978).

It was thought that *in loco parentis* would no longer bring
a blanket immunity from cases involving legal damages:

> ...based on the constitutional rights of
> children... children need their own
> independent legal representation in a variety
> of situations... the level of intrusiveness of
> the treatment, and especially the potentialities
> for conflict of interest between the child and

the adults claiming to speak for him…
persons and institutions with a state-
authorized *in local parentis* status may not use
that status as an excuse for violating children's
constitutional rights (Rose, 1978)

.

CHAPTER 18

COLLUSIONISTS

Collusion: a secret agreement, especially for fraudulent or treacherous purposes; conspiracy... 2. Law. A secret understanding between two or more persons to gain something illegally, to defraud another of his or her rights, or to appear as adversaries though in agreement.

Dictionary.com

Social work professionals after World War II had strong views about what they perceived as the common condition of unmarried mothers. In 1949, Virginia Frum, senior case worker at the University Hospitals in Cleveland, Ohio, claimed that, "Promiscuity, illegitimate pregnancy and venereal disease, are associated, in our minds, and rightly so" (Frum, 1949).

Psychoanalyst Dr. Paul H. Gray stated his concern at the end of the 1950s "that mothers are not given time to experience their maternal instincts before their babies are whisked away." This situation was in direct contrast to the strong position of maternity home pioneers Kate Waller Barrett and Charles Crittenton, who believed that unmarried mothers should be given whatever help they needed to allow them to keep their babies. In essence, their original view was being systematically ignored. Dr. Gray, who acted as a consultant to the Florence Crittenton League Maternity Home in Washington, D.C., asked, "What are we actually doing to the unmarried young mother by purposely not permitting the emotional maturity of the pregnant girl to develop according to the biological and physiological laws of her female body?" (Bye, 1959).

Charles Crittenton and Dr. Kate Waller Barrett viewed an unwed mother and her child as a unit "never to be torn asunder." In the early days, the mission of a maternity home was to help young women exercise their rights to be mothers. In 1959, Lillian Bye said, "It is now time to ask… Why did this orientation come to be looked at in the 1959 casework approach as a 'punishment'?" (Bye, 1959).

Bye felt that professional counselors should question why they "discriminated so acutely in regard to the individual's experience of motherhood." She asked whether the professionals were really being as kind as they thought they were and whether they really approached the mothers without punishment in mind. She wondered if they had become punishers in a more serious way that did damage "to the total personality development of our young womanhood by simply ignoring the fact that they are mothers?"

> [W]e ask ourselves whether our own professionalism and (usually) unmarried status are determining factors in our philosophy… if we are using the psychological distress and need of the sterile couples to avoid facing the crucial question: 'If the mother unwed would insist in keeping her child could we accept her in our social ranks, should we support her through our tax money, and should we expose the natural father to where he… would have

to face his responsibilities towards his child, acknowledging the fact that all children *have* a father and that we do not have to give some children a father through the artificial process of adoption?' (Bye, 1959)

In 1962, physician Morris Wessel suggested that "rules often… prevent an unmarried mother from seeing her baby" and are too restrictive and "cruel" when they deny a mother seeing her baby and that it is too easy for workers to transfer her baby to potential adopters.

> [D]ecisions are too often based on… punitive feelings on the part of individual professional staff members…*An argument that is raised against a mother seeing her infant is that the sight of her baby may awaken conflicts about giving up the child for adoptive placement. This may delay or interrupt placement proceedings…Legal papers may even be presented to a mother before she has recovered from the physical and emotional impacts of delivery…* Many physicians…*may feel that permitting the mother to see the infant interferes with placemen*t and prevents, rather than facilitates, adequate resolution of psychological difficulties… [emphasis added] (Wessel, 1962).

Law professor Robert Levy feared that unmarried mothers were being held captive by those who want her to surrender her baby to adoption.

> Imagine…a hospital that serves accident cases is in the charge of social work personnel, and the medical specialists serve as

consultants...Each patient is offered help with whatever injury he has incurred. But, as he lies flat on his back and helpless...a captive, he is approached with the idea of delving into motives which led to the accident, and it is suggested that he enter treatment in order to avoid future accidents. Because in our agency situation the symptom results in a baby *which biologically and legally belongs to its mother...can we demand* that this *'captive' client relinquish her baby* because we believe it is for the good of the baby? If the mother...*proves resistive to our approach* and we respect the integrity of another human being, *we cannot insist on surrender*, however well-intentioned we may be [emphasis added] (Levy, 1964).

Irene Phyrydas, a psychiatrist at Emory University, quoted Dr. F. Ernest Johnson, saying that "the conscious exercise of choice is the essence of the freedom. If, in a crisis, a person knows or can think of only one thing to do, he is not free... Freedom thus means, in part, the ability to stop and think before committing oneself to a particular line of activity. It means the ability to place before oneself other satisfactions or courses of action besides the one suggested by the immediate environmental situation..." If this is true, she postulated, then social workers who can help people and communities in trouble to see potential alternatives to a problem that had not existed before, it must also mean that "freedom and liberty at their best are based not only upon choice but upon the *freest possible choice, the greatest possible absence of duress*" [emphasis added] (Phyrydas, 1964).

In addition, medical doctors had a potent influence on unmarried mothers, with most doctors who attended unmarried mothers favoring independent adoptions (Pringle, 1967).

Condon in 1986 said:

> The forces working against the ability of unmarried mothers keeping their babies in the 1980s included a continued high demand for adoptable infants in the face of a dwindling supply; financial pressures, and the social stigma imposed by family and professionals all made women feel that surrender was their only option. "Their perception of 'informed consent' is... a charade designed to obfuscate society's guilt at society's *forcing' them to relinquish*... [T]heir child continues to exist... while remaining inaccessible to them... The situation is analogous to that of relatives of servicemen missing 'believed dead'... [L]ack of knowledge of the child permits... disturbing fantasies, such as the child being dead, or ill, unhappy or hating his or her relinquishing mother" (Condon, 1986).

Adoption social workers assured the unmarried mother that she would forget her baby. They said that she would forget her maternity home (or other) confinement experience, that she would forget giving birth and the surrender of her baby. These workers hoped to avoid anything that might interfere with the release of her baby for adoption. Social workers advised her that this was the price she paid for unmarried pregnancy. The worker held the expectation that she would surrender the baby. The mother was pressured by authority figures such as maternity home and agency adoption workers, doctors, family members and others.

> Until recently, birth parents *were told that they would forget*, would just get on with their lives, and could have other children…*the grief reaction might jeopardize the signing of the adoption papers*, and might risk disproving the assumption that adoption was the 'best' alternative for everyone…*In the past, adoption was viewed as the price to be paid for the shame of having an out-of-wedlock child*…birth parents have felt that *they were deprived of choice* because of pressures from family, friends, doctors, social workers, and society…Even if you are being *influenced and pressured by social workers, doctors*, family, boyfriends, friends…it will be your signature on the adoption papers…a teenager or young adult would be *intimidated and pressured by those in authority*, and would give in to the wishes of someone more powerful…[emphasis added] (Roles, 1989).

Researchers have identified some reasons why people who mean well do not necessarily do well. According to a 2012 study, "scientists have shown that people may actually cheat more when their cheating benefits others but not themselves. If we are acting solely for others, it is hard to see ourselves in a negative light and much easier to rationalize unethical acts. People who work for nonprofit foundations, schools or other public benefit organizations may be relatively more inclined to bend the rules because the charge of enhancing social welfare seems to justify the dishonest behavior" (Ariely, in Benaforado, 2015).

CHAPTER 19

STRANGERS & STATISTICS

*The moment of betrayal is the worst, the moment when you
know beyond any doubt that you've been betrayed: that some
other human being has wished you that much evil.*

Margaret Atwood

An overview of the statistics pertaining to adoption
during the BSE shed considerable light on the populations,
situations and conditions involved, and of course, any
discussion about adoption must include statistics about
unmarried mothers. During this period, the stereotype of
the unmarried mother was someone who was "shiftless and
lazy, unwilling to work, sexually promiscuous, and
neglectful of her children. She is thought to spend her time
and her ADC check in the local bar, to have child after
child in order to obtain a larger assistance grant, and to
enjoy living on the public largesse." Overall, however, this
image was false, and statistics revealed that under three
percent of unmarried mothers had any of the above
characteristics (Greenleigh, 1961).

A North Carolina study conducted in 1959 showed that
just 18 percent of the illegitimate children in the state
received Aid to Dependent Children (Adams & Gallagher,
1962).

Conservative estimates placed the proportion of births to unmarried mothers at four percent of the total number of births in the United States in 1961, or 240,200. Comparatively, in 1938, there were 88,000 out of wedlock births (Pinson, 1964).

Between 1945 and 1959, the fertility rate for all women aged 15 to 44 years increased from 36 births per 1,000 women to 120 births per 1,000 women. At the same time, out-of-wedlock births among women of the same age group increased from ten per 1,000 to 22 per 1,000, indicating that the one-million-birth rise in births in 1959 included some 100,000 additional out-of-wedlock births (Adams & Gallagher, 1962).

Six thousand of the 193,500 young, unmarried women who became pregnant in 1956 turned to the Florence Crittenton homes (Hickey, 1958). According to reports from the Florence Crittenton Association of America and the Salvation Army, the facilities that represented 80 maternity homes and 50 percent of total capacity for unmarried mothers in the U.S., these homes served 14,400 unmarried mothers in 1961, and about 75 percent of the mothers surrendered their babies to adoption. The mothers in the homes were younger than those handled by child welfare agencies, with about 70 percent aged under 21, and about 33 percent under 18 (Adams & Gallagher, 1962).

In 1960, over 250,000 babies were born to unmarried mothers of all ages in the U.S. Over 91,700 "fatherless" infants were born to unmarried teenage mothers. In 1959, the Florence Crittenton Homes were able to handle 8,073 unmarried mothers, but a lack of space required the facilities to turn away about 1,700 who were looking for help. Of the unmarried mothers aided by the homes, 61 percent were between 11 and 20 years of age, and 91 percent of them were white, seven percent were black, and two percent were of other ethnicities (Allen, 1963).

According to Rose Bernstein:

> Many voluntary child-placing agencies… have tended to define their function in terms of adoption, and many maternity homes… tend to give priority to mothers who plan to relinquish their babies… Recent figures from a national association of maternity homes indicate that in 1961, 79 percent of the live babies born to their clients were released for adoption and 13 percent were kept by their mothers… Some maternity homes are frankly or indirectly discriminatory in their admission policies (Bernstein, 1962).

By 1963, although there were 150 maternity homes operating in the U.S. - 48 run by the Florence Crittenton League, 35 by the Salvation Army, and 38 run by various Catholic charities – these homes were only able to accommodate 10 percent of the population of unmarried mothers (Rinehart, 1963). Commissioner Ellen Winston of Welfare, Department of Health, Education and Welfare, provides a slightly different set of statistics:

> …there are approximately 190 maternity homes, located in 46 states and the District of Columbia, with a capacity of about 5,000 unmarried mothers. Forty-five are nonsectarian agencies affiliated with the

Florence Crittenton Association of America;
35 are operated by the Salvation Army; about
50 are operated under the Catholic auspices…
about 60 are operated by other religious
groups or are independent, nonsectarian
social agencies. With the full use of the
present capacity of 5,000 mothers and an
average of 70 days of care per mother, about
25,000 could be cared for in a year…
maternity homes care for well over 20,000 a
year, but for less than 1 out of 10 of the
240,200 mothers who had children born out
of wedlock in 1961 (Winston, 1963).

Data from the U.S. Public Health Service indicated that
in 1963, the illegitimate birth rate had reached an all-time
high, listing 240,200 out-of-wedlock births, with 41 percent
of these infants born to teenagers. (Bridges, 1964).

The percentage of non-relative adoptions arranged by
social agencies rose in 1966 to 71 percent, according to
Children's Bureau estimates:

[I]n 1966 a total of 152,000 children were
adopted in the United States. About 80,600
(53 percent) of the 152,000 children were
adopted by non-relatives and 71,400 (47
percent) by relatives. Over the five year period
1960-1965, the annual increase in the total
number of adoptions has remained at 6
percent… the proportion of non-relative
adoptions arranged by social agencies has
continued to rise, to 71 percent in 1966, at

57,200 out of 80,600 non-relative adoptions (Infausto, 1969).

Some 6.4 percent of all white babies and 41.6 percent of non-white babies (13.0 percent of all babies) were born out of wedlock in 1973. The principle source of children available to adoptive applicants are children born out of wedlock. In 1971 about 87 percent of all children adopted by nonrelatives were so born… the trend has been toward an increasingly large percentage of nonrelative adoptions being made under agency auspices (Turner, 1977).

There was 'a steady increase in the number of non-relative adoptions from 47,000 in 1957 to 89,000 in 1970' which had nearly doubled within thirteen years. Below is a statistical table outlining the number of stranger adoptions through agencies from 1945 through 1971 (Turner, 1977).

Children Adopted During Calendar Year By Unrelated Persons

Year	Total In thousands	Agency Placements In thousands
1945	28	14
1950	37	20
1951	38	20
1952	42	24
1953	46	25
1954	47	26

Year	Total	Agency Placements
	In thousands	In thousands
1955	48	27
1956	47	27
1957	47	28
1958	50	30
1959	52	32
1960	58	34
1961	62	38
1962	63	40
1963	67	45
1964	72	48
1965	77	53
1966	81	57
1967	84	62
1968	86	64
1969	89	67
1970	89	70
1971	83	65

(Turner, 1977)

By 1969, there was a decline in demand for the services of residential maternity homes.

> A slight decline in the demand for residential maternity services was first noted in the 1969 edition of Unwed Mothers; 8,724 unmarried mothers were served in that year, resulting in an 85 percent occupancy rate. By the following year, however, in some areas of the country - particularly the Northeast and Midwest, the drop in demand for maternity

home care was precipitous. Such a rapid
decline can be attributed to several social
changes of the 1960s. One of these was the
virtual revolution in contraceptive technology
and its impact on women's birth control…
'the pill' in 1960 and… the IUD,
contraception became almost 100 percent
effective... (McDonald & Dore, 1983).

Statistics show that racial differences in the rate of
relinquishment existed during the BSE. In 1955, 72 percent
of children surrendered for adoption to non-relatives were
born to unmarried mothers, another 150,000 women each
year gave birth to children out of wedlock; 54,000 of the
unmarried mothers were white, while 96,000 were non-
white (Thornhill, 1955). In 1960, there were a total of
224,300 out-of-wedlock births, with 63 percent to non-
white mothers and 37 percent to white mothers. (Adams &
Gallagher, 1962).

Alice Shiller, Managing Editor of The Public Affairs
Committee No. 440 pamphlet (a non-profit educational
organization founded in 1935), in *The Unmarried Mother,*
discussed how many white babies were born to white
unmarried mothers compared to the number of babies
born to nonwhite unmarried mothers. She claimed that:

[O]nly from 5 to 10 percent of nonwhite
children born to unmarried mothers are
placed… contrasted with slightly under 70 per
cent of white out-of-wedlock children… The
illegitimacy rate in the United States increased
steadily from 1940 to 1957… The national
rate, the number of illegitimate births per

1,000 unmarried women in the prime child-bearing years (15-44) was 7.1 in 1940... 21.0 in 1957, and 23.6 in 1966. However, the actual number of illegitimate births (due to increase in population) has more than tripled in 25 years... there were 89,500 illegitimate births in 1940 and 302,363 in 1966 (Shiller, 1969).

Between 1965 and 1972, approximately 20 percent of white babies and two percent of black babies were surrendered, but between 1973 and 1988, the percentage of white babies surrender dropped to eight percent, while the percentage of surrendered black babies fell to 0.2 percent; the percentage of white infants decreased again between 1982 and 1988, falling to three percent, while the percentage of black infants surrendered during this period totaled one percent (Luker, 1996).

Of the babies put up for adoption in 1964, 70 percent of white infants and just four percent of black infants were surrendered, with 42 percent of the unmarried mothers in that year being designated as white (although it was believed to be higher as many of these women did not register the births) (Poinsett, 1966). In 1963, approximately 70 percent of white infants born to unmarried mothers were adopted, but only about five percent of black infants were surrendered (Winston, 1963).

Studies in 1968 that relied on court files, police records, welfare agency information and data from "homes for wayward girls" showed that 45 percent of white unmarried mothers had contact with maternity homes, child care agencies, or both, while only six percent of black unmarried mothers had contact with the homes. Additionally:

> Eighty-one percent of the white mothers were known to some social agency within the community; only 11 percent of black mothers received such care. The 11 relationships described appear to be independent of age. At every age level, substantially fewer black than white women had contact with child care agencies and/or maternity homes...for those under twenty, over 50 percent of the white girls pregnant out of wedlock reported contacts with maternity homes, child care agencies, or both (Osofsky, 1968).

In 1961, Hannah Adams, Research Analyst, Division of Research, Children Bureau, in "Two Studies of Unmarried Mothers in New York City," shared some statistics regarding registered births of babies born to unmarried mothers in New York City:

TABLE I
Number of Illegitimate Live Births

Year	Births	Registered
1960	42,707	5.40
1961	48,490	5.98
1962	55,376	6.60
1963	59,104	6.92
1964	63,340	7.23
1965	66,249	7.67
1966	67,056	7.90

Of the girls under 17, 90% received some type of social agency service and 50% received services from agencies… adoption service, or specialized counseling for unmarried mothers (Adams, 1961).

Howard Osofsky provided the chart below that shows the number of live out-of-wedlock births and total live births in the U.S. in 1965.

TABLE II
Out-of-Wedlock Live Births in U.S.
by Age of Mother in 1965

Age	Births
Under Age 15	6,100
Age 15—19	123,000
Age 20—24	90,600
Age 25—29	36,800
Age 30—34	19,600

Abstracted from Department of Health, Education and Welfare Vital Statistics Reports (In Osofsky, 1968).

Alice Shiller shared that:

[O]ver 90 percent of the unmarried fathers in Denmark give them their names and some financial support. Although many American social service experts have studied the Danish programs and admire them enormously, none suggests that we simply import them… (Shiller, 1969).

In 1971, Robert Tod compared the number of illegitimate children born in the 1950s and surrendered in

Britain compared to the number of children born in the 1960s and surrendered in the United States:

> In 1965 in Britain 23 percent of the illegitimate children born in 1955-59 had been given up for adoption; in 1967 in the U.S.A. 67 percent of the illegitimate children of white parents born in 1966 were similarly relinquished (Tod, 1971).

In 1977, the treatment of unmarried mothers in Denmark and that in the U.S. was compared:

> [I]n America it is estimated that 67 percent of the illegitimate children of white parents were released for adoption (1969)... in Denmark the adoption rate among illegitimate children is 2-3 percent... I was often tempted to suggest to a single woman who wished to keep her baby that she should immigrate to Denmark. In that country facilities abound for the support of the unmarried mother and her child. The unmarried mother receives... preferential treatment in housing, the allocation of nursery school places and adequate financial support. Danish unmarried mothers have to 'pay' for these privileges in that they are required by law to state which man or men is or may be responsible for their condition. It then becomes the state's responsibility to extract financial payment from the man or men assumed to be responsible... This situation clearly demonstrates a more sympathetic and less

punitive attitude towards sexual behavior…
(Gill, 1977).

According to the Child Welfare League of America's Standards for Adoption Service, "In 1971, 87% of the children adopted by nonrelatives and 34% of the adoptions by relatives were born out of wedlock. In 1971, it was estimated that 18% of the white unmarried teenage mothers placed their first child for adoption" (Child Welfare League of America, 1978).

And according to social work associate professor Leroy Pelton (1988) at the University of South Carolina, independent adoptions predominated proportionately over private adoptions between 1951 and 1961, but private adoptions were dominate from 1962 to 1975, reaching a peak of 45 percent in 1970. External factors, including opposition from family, pressure from social workers or doctors, and financial constraints, were cited by 69 percent of those studied as the major reasons for surrendering a child.

CHAPTER 20

DECIMATING THE DYAD

The premeditated interference in the biological sequence of birth between mother and child for the benefit of others is a crime against humanity.

Dian Wellfare

During the Baby Scoop Era, adoption practices were not based on valid, long-term research or evidence. Many adoption workers continued to pressure mothers into surrendering their children even though they knew that separation was likely to be harmful to both. Adoption workers were aware of the severe, life-long adverse effects of separation, yet chose to ignore the evidence. Inez Baker, supervisor of the Children's Division of the Orleans Parish Department of Public Welfare, stated, "We know what separation means to children; that it is akin to death and carries with it anger, disillusionment, despair, and a deep sense of 'badness'." (Baker, 1948). If Baker knew this in 1948, others must also have known at that time and during the past six decades.

Social worker Inez Baker further stated:

The parent has a right to know where his child is, to visit him in accordance with established arrangements, and to maintain his

relationship with him, unless specifically
forbidden by a court. The latter restriction is
rarely placed on parents except in spectacular
situations where the child or the person caring
for him is physically endangered (Baker,
1948).

Psychology professionals were well aware of the impact
of mother-and-child separation early in the BSE,
recognizing that children surrendered to adopters at or
shortly after birth missed out on the "mutual and deeply
satisfying mother and child relationships, the roots of
which lie deep in the area of personality where the
psychological and physiological merged." They recognized
that for both the child and the mother, this period was an
integral part of the biological sequence, "and it is to be
doubted whether the relationship of the child to its
postpartum mother... can be replaced by even the best of
substitute mothers..." (Clothier, 1943).

Elizabeth Nicholds also informed adoption workers that
babies suffered trauma when separated from their natural
mothers after spending nine months in-utero:

> Even things that happened to the infant
> while he was still in his mother's womb have
> subsequent consequences...we do know that
> her health and, to a certain extent, her feelings
> about her pregnancy affect the baby's body...
> Extreme unhappiness or worry on the part of
> the mother will affect her health and with it
> the health of the unborn child...Everything
> that happens to an infant from the birth
> process itself, on through the handling he gets

after his arrival, brings from the baby a
response either of satisfaction or of
discomfort, pain, protest, fear, and anger
(Nicholds, 1966).

Jonathan Rinehart (1963) noted:

> [T]he girl whose baby is adopted has the
> formidable task of reintegrating herself in the
> society which cast her out… From the time
> she becomes pregnant until she is able to
> return to society the American unmarried
> mother travels a route of namelessness…
> [S]ays Charlotte Andress, the able director of
> Inwood House,… 'the girls are known only by
> their first names and last initials to preserve
> anonymity… our society isolates the offender
> and loses interest in her once she is out of her
> 'state of sin.' We spend paltry thousands on
> researching illegitimacy's causes and, as Clark
> Vincent says, 'Nobody even thinks to ask
> what the unmarried mother's problems are
> ten years later'…

Psychiatrist John Bowlby (1953) observed three phases
in a child's response to separation from the mother: protest
marked by crying and acute distress; despair exemplified by
greater and greater feelings of withdrawal, hopelessness;
and detachment. He noted depressive states arising from
early separation of child and mother were not suggested by
previous studies and believed this indicated something
profound: that the effects of such early separations can
hide only to emerge in later life. Perhaps, Bowlby

suggested, when another loss is experienced it "reactivates" the earlier loss.

Bowlby (1953) went on to say that removing a baby from a "foster mother" could also cause trauma, so it was reasonable to conclude that separating a baby from its own real, loving and willing natural mother could have even stronger repercussions. He cited a study by psychologist Marian Radke-Yarrow that showed a baby reared from birth by a foster mother suffered immediate "disturbances of behavior" when transferred to an adoptive mother. These included "blunted responsiveness to people, excessive clinging to the new mother, excessive crying, unusual apathy, disturbances in adaptation to routines, sleep and feeding, a drop in the measured IQ."

In 1953, recognizing that removing babies from their natural mothers continued in spite of the growing knowledge that such separation brought lasting and adverse effects on both the children and the mothers, and that this dynamic had received little attention, the Children's Bureau planned to launch a "quest of knowledge" and conduct a "small study" to test its own research. The study was to consider questions such as "How harmful is the separation of a child from his parents? At what ages, under what circumstances, in what ways, and to what extent is it damaging? By what means can the detrimental effects of separation from parents be overcome?" (Children's Bureau, 1953).

In spite of this effort, however, one is left to wonder, where are the answers to those very important questions?

While adoption workers assured unmarried mothers that they would "forget" their pregnancy and delivery experiences, that they would just go on with their lives "as if nothing had happened," social workers understood as early as 1954 that, "No girl, mature or immature, can at any time give up her baby without developing an inner void and sense of loss" (Edlin, 1954).

Adoption workers and social work professionals knew by the mid-1950s that babies removed from their natural mothers suffered emotional damage. Children old enough to put their feelings into words were less often victimized by the mistakes made by child placement workers dealing with infants, but according to child welfare author Jean Charnley (1955):

> The greatest mistake in social work with infants is crediting them with too little feeling... In any separation there is a wound... I know that the statement that a child's own parents, however inadequate, have particular values for him that even good foster parents rarely offer... My impulse is to say, 'look at all the good social workers who have written that this is so: Dorothy Hutchinson, Henrietta Gordon, John Bowlby, Leon Richman, and a hundred others.'

That was 1955. This is further confirmation that, they, too, knew that children of surrendering mothers would suffer from being separated from their real, loving and willing natural mothers.

As more and more adoption workers admitted to understanding the psychological and emotional damage inflicted on natural mothers and their babies due to separation, some professionals urged such separations be performed only as a last resort.

> The separation of child from parent is perhaps the most tragic occurrence in a child's life. Its unfavorable aftereffects are usually irreversible... The painful meaning of [the adopted child's] fate becomes crystallized into awareness... that he is different, and this leaves lasting wounds... child placement truly may be termed a matter of major surgery, an irrevocable operation from which the child never fully recovers... social workers from all agency settings should consider this treatment measure a last resort... (Glickman, 1957).

No one could be certain about situations of infant adoption and the separation of mother and child, but the authorities continued to believe that the uncertainties should be tolerated. "There can be only this certainty: that no certainty exists and that the task of ameliorating the separation of the natural mother and her child calls for the toleration of uncertainty, however great" (Gianakon, 1960).

Social workers began to discuss whether children's lives were better if they were adopted or if they stayed with their natural mothers. They began to question what happens to a child born out of wedlock once he or she grows up. Again, they had little to go on, since so few studies had been undertaken to study the effects of adoption on children. Research was hampered by the relative novelty of adoption in the 1950s and a tendency among professionals to want to protect the privacy of adopters and few adopters were willing to take part in any studies. Social workers, facing a lack of real research on the issue, could continue to tell themselves that the question of whether children were "happier" with their adopters or with their natural mothers remained open (Wimperis, 1960).

In 1960, sociologist Virginia Wimperis noted that "Adoption is an art that our society is only beginning to learn. No one can yet speak with confidence about how it is working, or how it compares... with a reasonably loving unmarried mother keeping her baby until very much further research has been undertaken."

Dr. L.W. Sontag (1960) described a study demonstrating that infants bond with their mothers during the nine months of gestation and that the natural mother is ideally and uniquely suited to providing care to her own infant:

> [E]lementary conditioned reflexes begin in utero... the baby's whole psycho-biological system must be learning how to adjust to the biological, hormonal, physiological rhythm of his mother, even before delivery. He is already beginning to build up a very primitive concept of the way she functions, the way she feels, and the way she regulates the tension and stress within her body... the infant's regulatory mechanisms are slowly and imperceptibly being tuned to the maternal vibrations which will be the basic foundation on which the relationship will grow after

delivery... ideally, the baby should be cared for
by the mother who has borne him.

Pointing out the lack of research about the effects of
adoption and separating an infant from his or her
unmarried natural mother at birth, training specialist Clark
Vincent noted that, in 1960, estimates placed the number
of people living in the United States who were born out of
wedlock at about 7,000,000, with another 225,000 such
individuals being born every year.

> What do we know about the childhood and
> adult experiences of illegitimates? How many
> of them are aware of or wonder about their
> illegitimacy? What emotional scars do they
> carry throughout life? What loss of dignity do
> they suffer? What material and social status
> deprivations do they experience? Such
> questions are unanswerable at the present
> time, having rarely been asked in systematic
> research, even though illegitimates pay an
> unknown and perhaps the greatest price for
> illegitimacy (Vincent, 1962).

Because there was a large gap between knowledge and
practice among adoption professionals, results of research
studies tended to go unnoticed and unimplemented for
some time (Zackler and Brandstadt, 1975).

More and more social work professionals were
bemoaning the lack of hard data to inform their case
decisions. Social worker Elizabeth Nicholds, who was
involved with in-service trainings, warned, "...before we try
to influence a client's way of life, we should be sure that we

really know what is best, and we almost never do"
(Nicholds, 1966).

As more research was conducted and as more adoption
studies were completed, it became clear that neither the
child nor the natural mother came out of a mother and
child separation and subsequent adoption experience
unchanged or undamaged. It became clear that it was
always difficult for a woman to separate from her infant
and that being "unmarried" had nothing to do with the
maternal instinct.

> [M]aternal feelings are not easily ignored. If
> she tries to deny or suppress them, she may
> become irritable, restless, and depressed...
> Although she may know realistically that it is a
> lost cause, nevertheless she needs the comfort
> of an 'as if' game that permits her to muse on
> what it might be like if 'something could be
> worked out' so she would not have to give the
> baby up... In reality, there is probably no
> such thing as total termination of the
> relationship with the baby... No doubt, some
> are left with scars (Bernstein, 1971).

In addition to the biological and psychological impacts
of surrendering a child, unmarried mothers faced
downward social mobility as a result of being dropped
from any aid she may have been given during her
pregnancy. Once a child was released for adoption:

> [T]he mother was usually dropped from
> service. There was no continuing follow-
> through to help her reintegrate into society...

rejected by family, isolated from peers,
ostracized by the school system, barely
tolerated by the medical establishment, and
mostly ignored by the social service system, it
is no wonder that young mothers showed up
so disproportionately in a negative way in
divorce, health, educational, employment, and
welfare statistics (Zackler and Brandstadt,
1975).

The grief of a mother upon being separated from her
infant was rarely considered if the mother was unmarried.
It was as if unmarried women were completely "different"
from other women experiencing pregnancy and childbirth.

The [natural] mother must be different, an
aberration; for if it were true that she had the
same degree of love for her child as all other
mothers, the good of adoption would be
overwhelmed by the tragedy of it… Neither
society nor the [adoptive] mother who holds
the child in her arms wants to confront the
agony of the mother from whose arms that
same child was taken. But that agony is real, as
we have come to learn through our experience
with reunions (Lawrence, 1979).

*[P]iled one upon the other are a series of difficult,
painful and shameful experiences for the unmarried
mother who is constrained to place her baby for
adoption by a society that does not make it easy for her
to keep the child…* If she chooses to look after
the baby herself, little in the way of support
will be offered… The unmarried mother who

chooses adoption will find herself at the end of a process *that will have made her the subject of a variety of social, moral and psychological definitions, almost always unflattering. Her position is not only unenviable but also a source of major psychological stress.* [emphasis added] (Howe, Sawbridge & Hinings, 1992).

But the surrendering mother's grief was real.

> Disenfranchised grief is grief that is not openly acknowledged, socially accepted or publicly mourned... the [natural] mother was not recognized as a legitimate mourner; the loss of her child was not considered real... she lives in a world in which some mothers are rewarded and others punished for their fertility; that most people failed her, that she failed herself; that she did the right thing; that she did the wrong thing; that she grieves, that grief is not appropriate; that she is unnatural in her ability to take such a course; that she is natural in thinking of her baby before herself or conversely of thinking of herself before the baby; that she was, and still is, isolated in her experience; that her grief cannot be resolved and must somehow be lived with alone (Rowland, 2000).

The feelings of loss experienced by a natural parent were never forgotten, contrary to the assurances of social workers. The experience always leaves a scar, and despite adoption workers who led unmarried teens to believe that adoption provided an easy "solution" to a "problem," it remained difficult for unmarried mothers to cope with the reality of relinquishment; babies placed for adoption were mourned nonetheless, and the guilt unmarried parents feel never goes away (Penny, 1988).

The long-term effects of parental separation were seen later in the high rates of adoptees who turned up in adolescent and young adult residential treatment centers and clinics.

> The number of adoptees in the adolescent and young-adult clinics and residential treatment centers is strikingly high. Doctors from the Yale Psychiatric Institute and other hospitals that take very sick adolescents, have told me they are discovering that from one-quarter to one-third of the patients are adopted… Too often, counselors of adopted children are not aware that special issues exist and they attempt to treat the least disturbing problem and thus they fail to get to the core issue of adoption. Parents who called me have taken their child, usually an adolescent adopted at birth, from therapist to therapist, without ever having come upon one who is knowledgeable about adoption. The child now has become what Kirschner calls a 'secondhand patient.' Therapists who do not see adoption as a core issue cannot reach the child. The adoptee remains isolated and continues to act out (Lifton, 1988).

Surrendering a baby for adoption can cause severe dysfunction as "…others have noted, grieving and mourning are components of the relinquishment experience that, if denied or repressed, can cause severe dysfunctioning later in life" (Cushman, Kalmuss, Namerow, 1993).

According to a 1999 study published in the *Journal of Obstetric, Gynecological and Neonatal Nursing*:

> A grief reaction specific to the relinquishing mother has been identified. This is accompanied by other long-term reactions to the experience of relinquishment and by the mother's efforts to resolve her grief. The relinquishing mother has experienced a life-changing event that may profoundly affect her mental and physical health and her relationships at the time of relinquishment and far into the future.

By 2014, adoption researchers criticized the past practices of "forced adoption," noting that studies showed mothers and adopted persons suffered lifelong consequences. Among adoption study participants, some of the more disturbing experiences offered included mothers who were sexually assaulted by medical professionals or who faced medical maltreatment or neglect (such as being tied to beds, forcibly held down, pillows put over their faces and having sheets placed to form a shield between them and a view of their newborn infants). Mothers were also:

> [A]dministered drugs that caused impaired judgment capacity to make informed decisions; mothers and fathers being informed

that their newborn son/daughter was deceased when they were not; the unethical and illegal obtaining of consent to adopt (or no consent obtained at all); adoptees as babies being used for medical experimentations; adoptees being placed with abusive adoptive parents; adoptees being lied to regarding the circumstances surrounding their adoption…The most common impacts of forced adoption were found to be psychological and emotional, and included mood disorders, grief and loss, PTSD, identity and attachment disorders and personality disorders… Mothers had a higher than average likelihood of suffering from a mental disorder… (Higgins, 2014).

CHAPTER 21

WHAT ADOPTERS KNEW AND WHEN

Song birds hatched by silent foster mothers can't sing.

Alfred Tomatis

During the BSE, adopters often held stereotypical and usually erroneous beliefs about unmarried mothers. The prevalent attitudes of social workers, medical and maternity home professionals, who were moving away from the aid model to the punishment model in handling out-of-wedlock pregnancies during these years tended to foster and promote the negative opinions of adopters toward natural mothers. Adopters wanted to view unmarried mothers as "different," although:

> [A]ccording to medical opinion, the biological and physiological changes that occur in child bearing are the same whether the mother is 'wed' or 'unwed' and it is generally agreed that the greatest emotional damage suffered by the woman who has a child out of wedlock is that of having to give up her baby... The public's picture of the unwed mother as a calloused wench who blithely gives away or 'sells' her baby is an erroneous one, judging by those who inhabit

> maternity homes. Most of them… are
> emotionally upset at the thought of giving up
> their babies – particularly as the date of birth
> draws near – that they can't discuss it
> (Browning, 1965).

Nor were adopters fond of going to the maternity home for their baby. They felt "uncomfortable" being confronted with an "acute awareness of the natural mother's pain;" it spoiled "the pleasure of the day" they had anticipated for so long, and workers were trained to expect to provide help to adopters who would have to "explain illegitimacy without slandering the parents or making the child feel ashamed, yet without condoning out of wedlock sex…" and allay their fears "that their child will follow the sexual patterns of the natural parent. It can be very difficult to change this sort of deep-seated attitude…" (Rowe, 1966).

The professionals recognized another dynamic among adopters, however. Adopters sometimes feel bad about taking a mother's child:

> Many take the political dimension of
> adoption very personally, and have trouble
> justifying it to themselves or to their adopted
> children. They cannot bear to think about the
> situation of the natural mother, or to explain
> it to the child. They may point to the youth of
> the natural mother, or to her emotional
> problems, with evidence that their particular
> adoption was not associated with inequality or
> social injustice… Indeed, the political
> dimension is usually ignored (Benet, 1976).

Some social workers thought it was a positive factor if adopters saw the natural mother in the act of surrendering her baby because they would be able to use that experience in explaining the adoption to the child later:

> From the adopters' point of view, besides giving them insight into the early life of their baby, this brief glimpse of the mother can be valuable years later when the child is curious about his origins. It will carry a great deal of weight with him if they can say, for example: 'We did see your mother for a few minutes. She was tall and slender, with straight dark hair and she had on a pretty red dress. She cried when she said 'goodbye' to you, but we told her how much we loved you already' (Pochin, 1969).

One adopter expressed her feelings by saying, "I felt a little uneasy about the natural mother parting with such a lovable baby and worried that she might be unhappy" (Kirk, 1984). In "feeling bad," adopters acknowledge that there is nothing natural about surrendering a baby to adoption, and they are forced to examine their motives:

> There are many would-be adoptive parents who would not consider open adoption because they have a need to own the children. With so few babies now available for adoption, social workers should only consider adoptive parents who are willing to enter into an open adoption where the natural mother has an equal right to share in the life of her

child… Adoptive parents must take a long
hard look at their motives for continuing to
keep the natural mothers of their children out
of sight and so out of mind. No one can take
happiness at someone else's expense...
(Shawyer, 1979).

It is easier for adopters to eliminate the image of the
natural parents altogether by avoiding any references to
them or through depersonalization by considering
themselves to be the "real" parents and referring to the
natural parents in conversations with the adoptee as "the
lady and the man who had you" (Kirk, 1984).

The subject of motivation among adopters became
more of a consideration as knowledge of the adoption
dynamic expanded. It could no longer be assumed that all
adopters decided to take in a child for healthy, child-
centered reasons:

The haste with which society, through its
doctors and others, proposed adoption as a
quick solution to infertility, or to compensate
for the loss of a child at childbirth, often
propelled grieving parents into application to
adopt before their anguish was resolved. Many
a prospective father was motivated by his
wife's need for a child, while he remained at
an emotional distance from the prospect, and
later, perhaps, from the child (Marshall &
McDonald, 2004).

A MOTHER'S STORY / *Priscilla*

I am a mother who lost my first born child to adoption.

I was 18 years old. It was in early 1964 I found myself pregnant. My boyfriend – the father – and I were from the same small town in New Jersey. He was in the Navy, and we had been casually long distance "dating" by correspondence and telephone calls for several years. When he asked me to join him for Thanksgiving Weekend 1963, and our physical attraction was as strong as the emotional commitment I had been feeling, I was deliriously happy. I was naïve and ignorant about sex and dating. I thought it meant he wanted to take our relationship to the next level, that it meant he wanted to make a commitment to me. But I was wrong. It turned out he just wanted sex. He was already engaged to another girl in California.

I was afraid to tell my family because I knew my strict, Polish-Catholic stepfather would make life unbearable for my mother, so I approached my employer to ask for guidance, and he immediately referred me to an adoption agency. No one ever gave me any hope that I could keep my baby. Not once was any suggestion other than adoption discussed. It was understood that I had to hide in shame and suffer for what I had done. It wasn't until years later that I realized I had done nothing but trust my boyfriend when he promised he would take care of me.

The agency found a place for me in a "wage home" in the next town over where I lived for six months as housekeeper, cook, and babysitter for $10 a week plus room and board. Other than friendship with two other unwed expectant mothers, I was alone and depressed and afraid. I had prenatal care, but nothing prepared me for what was to happen.

On the day I went into labor, I was unceremoniously dropped off at the front door of the hospital by my employer's boyfriend. I was stripped of my clothing and possessions, placed in a windowless, empty four bed ward being used as a storage room and told to stay put and not come out. How long I was there I have no idea. There was no clock, no phone, no radio, no visitors other than medical personnel who would come and check my progress. No words were spoken other than to the effect of, "Well, aren't you proud of yourself now? Look where your slutty ways have landed you!" I was given no pain medication nor any comfort whatsoever. When my water broke, I didn't know what was happening. I went to the door and called for help. The nurse (a nun) came running down the hall yelling at me to "Get back in there! There are 'decent' women here having babies!" Then angrily, "Look at this mess you've made!"

On the last visit, the medic (a doctor? nurse?) decided that I was dilated enough. I was given a shot, wheeled to the delivery room and immediately knocked out. I woke up in a dark private room. I had no idea what day it was, whether my baby was alive, healthy, was a boy or a girl. And I was told to not ask questions, that I had no right to know anything about my baby. Sometime a day or so later, the candy-striper brought a little pink bundle to me.

"Here," she said, "this is your baby." I thought I was
dreaming! I can still remember 50 years later all the
feelings that went through me then – joy, awe, relief,
sadness, fear – when all of a sudden the nun burst into my
room and literally snatched my beautiful daughter out of
my arms. "You were not supposed to see this baby!"

Thankfully, at that very moment my doctor walked in
(Dr. Barney Bowlin – I will bless his name forever) and
said, "Oh, for heaven's sake, sister, let her see her baby!
Let her 'count the fingers and toes.' She's not in any
condition to run away with her!" I am grateful for the time
I got to spend with my daughter. I was able to whisper in
her ear how much I loved her and the reasons society had
decreed we could not be together. I named her "Donna
Michelle" after her father. Then they took her away.

As I was being discharged, the nun began to lecture me.
"Now you must go home and get back to your life and
forget about this baby. You will marry and have more
children. Don't ever tell anyone, especially not a potential
husband, what you've done because no 'decent' man will
want to have anything to do with you."

When I protested and begged for some way to keep my
daughter, I was told I was being selfish and inconsiderate.
There were married couples who could not have children,
good, "worthy" people who would love my baby and
provide her with everything I could not – a good home,
care, and education. With an 'illegitimate child' I would not
be able to find a job. "You won't be able to take care of
yourself, let alone a baby! You'll have to become a barmaid
or 'walk the streets!' What kind of life is that for a child?!"
She made me feel like I was unworthy to breathe, let alone

raise my own child. Further, I was told if I wanted to keep her, I would have to pay our entire hospital bill before I could take her from the hospital, and the charges would increase by $5 a day for every day I could not pay. If I kept my part and gave her up, the agency would pay the bill. (In fact, I did pay the agency back every penny. It took me over a year, and I paid my own doctor bill, too. I never wanted anyone to think that I had benefitted in any way by giving my baby up for adoption!)

Three days later, I signed the papers in the agency office. I could not see what I was signing because my eyes were filled with tears. I was never given copies of anything I signed, but I do remember seeing or being told that I would face criminal charges if I ever tried to find my daughter or interfere in her new life. I remember begging the social worker for some assurance that, if she wanted to know me, she would be given information about me and be able to find me. (I found out later that many other mothers were promised the same thing, and even advised to keep a phone listing in our maiden names, but we came to find out it was all lies – the records were sealed forever in all states but Kansas and Alaska – and adoptees would never be legally entitled to know our identities or their own, for that matter.)

I did try to go on with my life, but it was impossible to forget about my baby. I moved 2,500 miles away because everywhere I went in my hometown I would see happy women with babies, and I would wonder if it was my daughter they were mothering and lovingly cooing over. My heart was broken. I was bereft. There wasn't a day that went by that I didn't think about her. Even five years later, thoughts about my lost daughter tainted the joy I felt when

I gave birth to my precious second daughter. Every moment of happiness was followed by many moments of questions. I wonder where/how Donna is. Did she look/act the same at this age? Will we ever see her again?

I'm sure unconsciously I clung to my second child a little too much, was too protective and hysterical for fear I would lose her, too. I also had a nagging sense of insecurity, low self-esteem and self-loathing. I was a bad person. I was not worthy of anyone loving me or being a mother because of the terrible thing I had done. It has taken many years of self-analyzing, praying, studying, and enlightenment to realize none of that was true. In fact, I've probably gone overboard now and become a super-achiever to prove them all false. Still I mourn the loss of my daughter – what might have been - and future generations. I was deprived of being her mother and a grandmother to her children and perhaps even great-grandma.

Yet, I am here to testify that, although we have been deprived of the mother-child relationship, physically and genetically, in my heart, I am her mother. I always was and will be into eternity, and no piece of paper or claim of custody or "possession" will ever change that. There is an invisible, invincible "golden thread" that binds us forever. I am not a "birthmother", a "first mother", "natural mother" or "tummy mommy" or any other qualification. I am a mother who lost her child to adoption.

In the process of dealing with my loss over the years, I have come to understand how wrong infant adoption is. Adoption is a fake family built on tragedy. Separating mothers and babies should be a last resort and we, as families, churches, and communities, should instead be working to help these young women become better mothers and insisting that fathers step up to their responsibility, as well. We need to understand the terrible damage it will potentially cause both the mothers and babies, and that adoption is a permanent solution to a temporary predicament.

I also work to draw attention to the fact that millions of adult adoptees are still subjected to archaic, ridiculous laws that deny them from accessing their original birth certificates. Adopted persons in all but ten or so states in the U.S. are barred from knowing their original identity, their family history, heritage, genetics, health information. People 50, 60, 70+ years old are cruelly denied the most basic information about their existence and told by nasty bureaucrats and politicians that they can never know who they are or the identities of those to whom they are blood related.

These laws were passed instigated back in the 1930s by the infamous Georgia Tann, the woman who was charged with snatching and selling thousands of babies and whose criminal behavior has controlled adoption for over 75 years. These laws were designed solely to protect the adoptive families, cover up the criminal activities of the baby brokers, and hide the adoptee from the stigma of illegitimacy. Today we are coming face to face with the awful ramifications these decades of secrecy and lies have wrecked upon our families and society.

Through my advocacy for mothers of loss to adoption, I also hope to reach out to other mothers of loss who have been hiding in fear and shame, who perhaps never told5their families, or who are waiting in silence, too timid to come forward and proclaim their motherhood. We understand. We know the experience and the remaining years after have been painful, with terrible damage to our emotional and physical wellbeing. There are many who are afraid their sons and daughters are angry and resentful. "Why did you abandon me?" These adoptees don't understand why or how they were "given up" and assume it must have been because we didn't want them. There is a great deal of educating that needs to be done about the way life was for pregnant, single girls. There are many mothers who are afraid of "opening old wounds" and reliving the past, but we are here as testament that it must be done for healing to begin. There are thousands of us here to support and love them through it.

Finally, as a free, voluntary Search Angel, I have helped countless hundreds of families reunite over the past seven years. Here is what one of the mothers I found wrote to me:

> I just wanted to say thank you to you for finding me! ...My love for and my bonding with [my son], I believe, started at that conversation. Then I received a picture of him and his wife and I was just thrilled! I recently met him in person and am very proud to claim him as mine! The Christmas of 2010, I received the best present I've ever received; the gift of a son! Not only a son, but I have two wonderful grandchildren! So, when I say thank you, it seems woefully inadequate. You've changed my life! I've never been happier. Thank you for finding me!

Fortunately, this woman is typical of mothers-of-loss-in-waiting. More than 95% are delighted to be found, giving proof that the adoption industry is lying when they claim that we mothers want to remain in anonymity and privacy.

It's time to blow the lid of secrecy and lies off of the adoption industry and free people from the oppression of "closed" adoption.

Please join us.
www.priscillasharp.org
Mothers of Loss (to Adoption) on Facebook

PART III
PENANCE PAID

CHAPTER 22

A FAILED SOCIAL EXPERIMENT

The fact that an opinion has been widely held is no evidence whatever that it is not utterly absurd.

Bertrand Russell

The Nuremberg Code is a set of research ethics principles for human experimentation resulting from the Subsequent Nuremberg Trials at the end of the Second World War. Some aspects of the Code's ten points could arguably pertain to the procedures and policies common in the surrender by unprotected unmarried mothers to adoption during the BSE, including the "absolutely essential" voluntary consent of the person involved and that person's "free power of choice" in any experimental situation (See Appendix E).

Psychiatrist John Bowlby (1953) admitted that the problems inherent in adoptions were not fully understood, acknowledging that "very little serious study" had focused on these problems and that "it is only gradually becoming recognized as a process requiring scientific understanding and professional skill." Too often, Bowlby said, the future of a baby is considered only by a "well-meaning amateur" or a physician or other health care worker who typically focused only on the baby's physical condition.

In effect, much of the adoption process during the BSE could be termed "experimentation." According to social worker Sara Edlin (1954), "...we *experimented* with permitting the girl to make her own choice in the matter of seeing or not seeing her baby..." [emphasis added]. Typically, mothers were not allowed to decide whether or not to see their babies and it was common practice for caseworkers to discourage or prohibit mothers from seeing or holding their babies as they wanted to ensure a mother would go through with the adoption.

Even more bluntly, social worker Esther Glickman (1957) said, "I believe that such experimental work is vital for increasing our knowledge and for developing new skills…"

Lillian Bye (1959), executive director of the Crittenton Hastings House, noted the advantage that a private social agency has due to its flexibility. Bye even quotes Margaret Millar, case supervisor with the Family Welfare Association in Baltimore, Maryland, who stated that "the private agency is usually in a position to experiment and this gives it an opportunity to emphasize quality of casework." Bye concurred and described the operations of her maternity home, which was under the direction of the Florence Crittenton League of Compassion in Boston, that "we have permitted ourselves the privilege of experimentation."

Because social work was still a relatively new profession at the beginning of the 1960s, agencies either were not interested in or lacked the resources to research critical issues and tended to make assumptions about the cost of serving their clients, methods for evaluating case records, how to determine if a client had really been helped, or "testing of fundamental assumptions in counseling..." (Stroup, 1960).

As a result, little was known about the future impact of adoption on mothers and their children or its consequences during the BSE. Organized and professionalized adoption had only recently been implemented to any degree, and adoption societies were unwilling to open their operations to researchers, citing a need to protect the privacy of adopters, "a large number of adopters, although grateful for the help they have received, prefer to fade out of the picture once the legal process had ended. For this reason it is impossible to collect reliable statistics of adoption success or failure" (Wimperis, 1960).

No one knew what effect surrender would have on the baby.

> There is no timetable by which all woman can be expected to have resolved their post-separation problems. We do not know what psychological effects the seemingly voluntary nature of the surrender of the baby may have as compared with situations in death or a medical condition. These important areas in the unmarried mother's experiences merit a good deal more attention in research than they have been receiving (Bernstein, 1971).

Clark Vincent (1962), sociologist and training specialist at the National Institute of Mental Health, explained how a woman's need for care during her pregnancy and delivery:

...make her available for study and identifiable for censure; his [father of the baby] biological role ends at conception, and society's protection of him via disinterest enables him to remain anonymous and at large in the general population where he is unavailable for study... social attitudes and practices tend to preclude research on unmarried fathers... social attitudes which compartmentalize cause (illicit coition) and result (illicit pregnancy) have permeated research efforts to such a degree that studies of unwed mothers are rarely conducted within the larger context of all females who engage in pre- or extra-marital coition... the research focuses on only those who 'got caught.'

In the 1930s, social worker Mary Brisley spoke of the experimental nature of infant adoption practices, as well as the trauma experienced by both the mother and her child due to separation. Brisley encouraged a three month nursing period, noting "the necessity for research on the subject, since *not enough was known* about the results of keeping or relinquishing" [emphasis added] (Brisley, in Costigan, 1964).

In the mid Sixties, social work professionals continued to promote the idea that adoption practices should be examined, tested and explored:

Let us continue to examine and test customs, to be courageous in trying modified methods... In adoptive placement agencies, let us encourage ourselves to do more joint

relative *experimentation…* in the joint
recruitment by groups of agencies and sharing
of adoptive home for any child… [emphasis
added] (Canada, 1964).

Adoption workers continued to believe that more
research was needed to help them learn the effects of
separation on mothers and their children. Some workers
called for more experimentation. "More study should be
done experimenting with powerful assertive intervention
with one type of service, i.e., casework, comparing those
cases with others receiving less intensive service or other
services" (Bedger, 1969).

Experts at the Child Welfare Bureau noted the
experimental nature of child placement agency, stating that
the voluntary agency "has the freedom to engage in
experimentation…" (Child Welfare Bureau, 1971).

Many adoption workers were well aware of the many
uncertainties associated with adoption for everyone
involved. Unmarried mothers lacked support when they
needed it most, and "the facts and uncertainties of
adoption highlight the heavy responsibilities of balancing
the happiness and interests of one person against another"
(Cheetham, 1977). There were no assurances that any of
the decisions made would be good for both mothers and
children, while it seemed likely that a good decision for one
could be a bad decision for the mother.

Vance Packard, an American journalist and social critic,
provided a detailed discussion about experimentation on
captive subjects. Arguably, his conclusions could be applied
to unmarried mothers, especially young minors who were

hidden away in maternity homes or sent to live in the homes of strangers.

> *Modern Medicine* reported that most doctors favor experimentation on humans, even on prisoners, children, the mentally retarded, and other captive subjects…peer review committees consist overwhelmingly of fellow staff members. Few include, lawyers, ethicists, ministers, or scientists…Today there is general agreement on the principle that human subjects of experimentation must give this 'informed consent.' This concept came largely out of the Nuremberg trials... The June 1973 Report of the Institute of Society, Ethics and the Life Sciences states: '…less than twenty-five percent of the studies in our files claim that consent was obtained from the participants' and not a single paper documented the form in which the consent was given (Packard, 1977).

The voices of parents who experienced the loss of their children through surrendering them to adoption went unheard until the 1970s, when there arose a "renewed realization of the irrevocable losses associated with the surrender of a child. Whatever were the unstated concerns of some adoption workers and others in the community, the belief in the value of adoption went pretty much unchallenged until the late 1970s, when questioning voices were heard" (Marshall & McDonald, 2001).

CHAPTER 23

STICKS & STONES

The old rhyme was wrong, words hurt. Names matter, labels stick. The stigma isn't always patent; inherent in our lexicon are modifiers and morphemes that convey status with just the addition of a mere suffix. Too often those bearing the brunt of the verbal assault inherent in the institution that is language are the disenfranchised, the marginalized, the minorities. The words we choose to express our thoughts and feelings, explicitly and implicitly – they are a reflection of our attitudes and the wrong words can disaffect others, particularly those on the margins.

Juliah

In 1954, Sara Edlin wrote, "My experience... at Lakeview has shown me time and time again that there is a deep emotional upset, a kind of emotional sickness... in each girl's relationship to her parents which drives her... to have reckless sexual relations with a man who is usually not likely to marry her."

According to Jean Pochin:

Immature and neurotic girls will often make desperate efforts to find a painless way out of their dilemma... there is no solution which will spare them all suffering, and all that they can choose is what kind of suffering they will have... the anguish of parting with their baby or the pains and penalties of bringing him up themselves. The caseworker needs patience as well as skill and understanding to help her client to make a choice of painful remedies, and must strengthen her to stand by her decision once made (Pochin, 1969).

Parents... were viewed originally as sinful and immoral, a threat to family structure... the unwed mother was ostracized by family and community, unless she was black (Turner, J. (Ed.), 1977).

The way unmarried mothers were described by adoption professionals has a strong impact on the way these women are perceived by society at large. In an attempt to address the reality of words being used as weapons with a strong effect on how we think, feel, and treat others, Minnesota adoption employee Marietta Spencer (1979) developed Positive Adoption Language or Respectful Adoption Language (RAL) in the United States in 1979. Spencer proposed that adoption professionals and people who adopt take the lead in adoption related discourse and terminology. The new terminology was designed to place adoption in a more favorable light, however, and to disguise aspects of adoption practices that the public might find uncomfortable and begin to question.

Sociology professor Edwin Schur addressed the way negative labeling stigmatizes women and acts as a form of social control:

Women's vulnerability to stigmatization rests on their…relatively poor power position… when women are effectively stigmatized, that reinforces their overall subordination…This is part of what labeling analysts' mean when they note that stigmatization can become self-propelling or snowballing in its impact (Schur, 1983).

Schur also noted the devaluation of unmarried mothers inherent in describing them in any other way than experiencing "single motherhood:"

When we consider 'unmarried' or 'unwed' motherhood… the very fact that the situation usually is described in this way… is significant. It underscores the devaluation of single mothers, and shows that their perceived offense lies partly in a violation of marital norms… Perceived violations of these norms include at least the following major 'offenses': intentional non-motherhood, 'unwed' motherhood, and 'unfit' motherhood… just about any female behavior which diverges from general prescriptions is likely to be interpreted in mental illness terms… (Schur, 1983).

There are stark differences in the social attitudes reflected in the terms used to describe married and therefore "normal" mothers and unmarried mothers. Societal norms included the words "marital" and "maternity," while typical "offence" and "deviance" labels included "unmarried," "unwed" mothers and "unwed, unfit mothers" who were "unmaternal" (Schur, 1983).

In the 1950s and 1960s, few social workers were concerned about disguising how they felt about unmarried mothers. An unmarried mother was frequently described with labels and terminology meant to marginalize her for the "sin" and "crime" of unmarried motherhood.

Unmarried mothers were viewed as criminals in some cases, described as "defective culprits" or "welfare dependents" or "welfare cheats" or even as the cause of violence against their children, "… guilty of having failed to stop the abuse, or to protect their children; or of failing to provide the children with adequate surroundings and clothing on the inadequate doled out resources" (Armstrong, 1995).

As the profession of social work evolved, it became a common practice to describe unmarried mothers in psychiatric terms. The unmarried mother was no longer viewed as having "bad blood," but instead as a criminal needing correction or as a "girl" needing "a cure" for her neurosis. In other words, the mother as sick, but her soon-to-be-born baby was not. Once unmarried mothers were no longer viewed as having genetic deficiencies - the "bad blood" that could be passed on to their children - their babies became highly adoptable.

Hastings Hornell Hart, an ordained pastor with a national reputation in penology and prison reform, described the standard procedure for admitting an unmarried mother to a maternity home and referring to her and the home's "inmates" as "homeless and wayward white girls and women" who came from any part of the United States, who required physical examinations to detect the presence of venereal disease, who could be used to do the chores and thus save money for the institution, which was maintained for the care of "inmates" by public monies from the District Board of Charities (Hart, 1924).

Continuing into the 1970s, at least one sociologist described how the "inmates" of maternity homes differed from those of other "deviant housing institutions" in that the "girls" at the home did not "encounter rules which expressed a specific regard for the shameful aspects of their situation" (Rains, 1970).

In the 1940s and early 1950s, the psychological and psychiatric behavior theories emphasized emotional disturbance as a cause for "illegitimacy" and colored the descriptions of the unmarried mothers in maternity homes, welfare agencies and out-patient clinics who were studied by clinical psychologies, psychotherapists and psychiatric social workers (Vincent, 1962). Unmarried mothers were viewed as lacking the strength to make their own decisions and needing the "strength" and "clarity" of others, presumably social workers, if they were not to "remain hopelessly adrift" or bringing "down upon her head the disastrous consequences of daydreams which have lost their grounding" (L. Young, 1954).

In fact, in the opinion of social worker Leontine Young, unmarried mothers had feelings for their babies that were different than those felt by a "normal" mother:

> Young dismissed the unwed mother's relation to her child in no uncertain terms. 'The caseworker has to clarify for herself the differences between the feelings of the normal

[married] woman for her baby and the fantasy use of the child by the neurotic unmarried mother.' Professionals belittled the meaning of the relation, as they actively engaged in separating the one from the other on an every case basis (In Solinger, 1990).

The language of pathology was ingrained in the views of some of the social workers, psychiatrists, and sociologists who worked with unmarried mothers. Beginning with the idea that illegitimacy was taboo, these mothers were considered "social outcasts" or "irresponsible sexual delinquents" who had to be "forced into seclusion as punishment for (the) flagrant violation of our most sacred principles." Social workers, psychiatrists and sociologists believed that most unmarried mothers were "emotionally disturbed" and that:

> The vast majority... have a neurotic and unconscious urge for motherhood...There is increasing belief that unmarried mothers are suffering from a neurosis...They almost *will* themselves to become pregnant...Experts feel that any hope of prevention of the tragedy of unwed motherhood must take the *neurotic* urge theory into account [emphasis added] (Erichson, 1955).

Some social workers warned about this approach, including Jean Charnley who noted, "That we don't know just what to do is not the only danger of labelling. Parents are often labelled 'psychopathic,' 'paranoid' or 'not able to respond to casework'" (Charnley, 1955).

The idea that unmarried mothers suffered from neurosis held for some time. Throughout the 50s, social workers and other adoption professionals labeled the woman's relationship with her baby's father as neurotic.

> ...a *neurotic* and/or psychotic disturbance of a female, the expression of an intra-psychic conflict... a conflict with her environment, the near one: her family, and the wider one: the cultural setting in which she lives and it is the responsibility of the social worker to clarify for herself the differences between the feelings of the normal woman for her baby and the fantasy use of the child by the *neurotic* unmarried mother [emphasis added] (Heiman, 1960).

The information handbook issued by the Salvation Army cautioned that "the more immature or neurotic the personality of the unmarried mother was, the less likely she was to view her child as an individual and the greater her need to keep the baby," viewing him/her as "one more pawn in her search to meet her own needs" (Salvation Army, 1962).

Adoption workers apparently felt that single mothers should not raise their own children whether they were willing and able to or not. Mothers who wanted to keep them were considered immature, deviant and neurotic. They believed that separating an unmarried mother from her baby was the best "treatment" for the neurotic woman and in the "best interests" of her child:

Social workers began interpreting the 'best interests of the child' as consistent with separating parents and child rather than keeping them together... Because the child was portrayed as a symptom of unwed mothers' *neurotic* drives, social workers believed that, with rare exceptions, unmarried mothers were incapable of providing sustained care and security for their babies... The inescapable conclusion social workers drew from the professional social work literature was that the best treatment was to separate unmarried mother from her child... [emphasis added] (Carp, 1998).

Is it any wonder that so many unmarried mothers had their babies removed from them? They were labeled sick, unadjusted, immature, neurotic, sinning and infected culprits. How could any of these unprotected, vulnerable and defenseless mothers stand a chance of keeping and raising their own children in such a climate? The goal of caseworkers was to break down the natural defenses of mothers who wanted to keep their babies. Social workers followed psychology professionals, believing psychiatrists like Helene Deutsch and her observation that:

[T]he least mature among unmarried mothers are the very ones who often *fight to keep their children... the best solution* for the majority of unwed mothers was to *give the baby up…* the unmarried mother's resistance to placing the child for adoption should be understood in 'terms of the dynamics of defense and

symptom formation' [emphasis added] (Deutsch, 1945).

The caseworker's job was to assist the client to recognize her defenses and help her work through them, and by "working through her defenses," it was meant that social workers would convince the new unmarried mother that she could not possibly keep or raise her own child; if she wanted to do this, it was evidence of neurosis (Carp, 1995).

By "working through her defenses," Carp appeared to suggest that social workers help the unmarried mother make a decision and to find help from psychiatrists who would diagnose the mother with a character disorder, such as displaying hysterical features.

Echoing earlier descriptions of unmarried mothers as lacking sufficient strength to make their own decisions, an adoption social worker claimed that a "neurotic mother who dithers endlessly will specially need the strength and conviction of her caseworker's decisive attitudes." Because a mother often changes her mind about the birth of her child and wants to keep it rather than surrender it for adoption, it is the "neurotically needy" mothers who declare that they will keep their children regardless of any problems. Cognizant of how it could appear to characterize unmarried mothers as mentally defective, social workers were counseled to avoid using words like "insane," "defective," or "immoral" when describing natural mothers, noting that the same information could be conveyed in "much less threatening ways" (Rowe, 1966).

As late as 1966, S.R. Slavson, the founder and president emeritus of the American Group Psychotherapy

Association, continued to promote the idea that unmarried mothers "by and large have inadequate ego development," said his impression was that a "predominant majority" of Protestant, white girls have "character disorders," including among these was a small number of neurotics, a negligible number of psychotics and no full blown psycho neurotics (Slavson, 1966).

In the 1990s, social worker and adoption caseworkers took on the job of "disciplining" females such as lesbians, delinquents and single mothers:

> Historians of 'deviant' populations - including prostitutes, lesbians and gay men, 'delinquents,' and those judged insane, as well as single mothers - have had to wrestle with the methodological quandaries presented in sources composed by those who were also responsible for surveying, analyzing, and often disciplining those subjects... Key to the professionalizing project of social workers, casework used a step-by-step procedure of collecting information about a person's experiences and background, followed by 'diagnosis' and 'treatment' of their problem (Kunzel, 1995).

Any young woman who was sexually active, especially if she was not married and when intercourse resulted in an out-of-wedlock birth, was labeled deviant and unfit. As debate surrounded whether such women should be punished or rehabilitated, the focus of psychologists was to practice "scientific management of the 'unadjusted girl'" (Luker, 1996).

The professionals who worked with white, unmarried mothers followed the general beliefs of society, tending to view their clients as "deviant" unless they decided to surrender their babies for adoption:

> If the young mother is unmarried, white, and gives the baby up for adoption, white society tends to view this as a small problem despite the fact that it may be very traumatic to the mother...[S]he has contributed to the currently inadequate pool of white babies available for adoption (Klerman & Jekel, 1973).

Adoption terminology also reflected gender bias. Lillian Bye, executive director of the Crittenton Hastings House in Boston, Massachusetts, contrasted the perceptions of social workers and society at large of the unmarried mother and the unmarried father, stating that:

> ...we as social workers have...over stressed the sociological shame factor...The social caseworkers as a group are predominantly women and almost exclusively so in the problem area of the unwed mother. They are consciously or unconsciously... reacting with fear to their society's concept in relation to words like 'out of wedlock,' 'unlawful,' 'bastard,' 'promiscuous,' 'prostitute,' 'sinful.' If we examine these words closely we find that they have distressingly disastrous meaning for our cultural image of the 'good' woman in a society where the male represents the master

group. None of these words affect the social position of the 'good' man in the same society as he is the participating agent in the moment of conception (Bye, 1959).

Social workers would actively encourage unmarried mothers to surrender their babies, arguing that "sex delinquents were unfit to be mothers, and neurotic unmarried mothers were considered no more competent to care for their children..." Social workers also tended to assign unmarried mothers to various categories or "types" (Kunzel, 1993) that further dehumanized them. The categorization involved both "moral and physical segregation of these mothers" from general society as there was a lack of public money to care for them in institutions and a lack of professional staff assigned to their care. This constituted additional punishment for the "sexual misconduct," with "sexual deviance" even outweighing class differences (Morton, 1993).

By the mid-1960s, some adoption professionals used language that brought a hint of sin to the conversation, describing unmarried mothers as transgressors who impose their needs for concealment as the responsibilities of already burdened social workers:

> Social work most frequently encounters the problem of the unmarried mother in the person of the illegitimately pregnant woman who needs shelter, concealment, economic support through pregnancy and childbirth, medical care, and planning for the disposition of the child once it is born... The professional functions of social work, then,

become those of inventing and providing
such services and resources by which the
problems' consequences may be confined,
curtailed, or ameliorated… [S]ocial work is
charged with the responsibilities of providing
for the woman who is clearly the
transgressor… (Perlman, 1964).

Or unmarried, pregnant women were considered
"objects of shame and scorn" and required to submit to
strict training meant to change them from "immoral fallen
girls" into chaste and prudent women" (Cheetham, 1977).

By 1970, the language applied to unmarried parents
shifted to a more sociological perspective: these parents
were "unsocialized" and had little ability to fulfill the
parental role no matter how many resources and how much
aid was available. Children left in the hands of such parents
would be harmed, were in danger of being abused or
neglected, and therefore it was necessary to "interrupt the
cycle." According to McBroom, "treatment is based on a
judgment and *prediction* that parents will be actively harmful
to children" [emphasis added] (McBroom, 1970).

In 1977, Derek Gill shared that some who dealt with
unmarried, pregnant females often referred to them as a
"patient" or just "girls:"

The influence of the medical setting is also
apparent in the labeling of clients. The
medical social workers sometimes used the
word 'patient' to refer to the women who
came into contact with them. These women
were also referred to as 'girls' (Gill, 1977).

There was a serious impact on the unmarried mother when, as time went on, instead of being called an "unwed" mother, she began to be treated as simply a vessel to carry and give birth to a baby ("birth" mother) meant for a married couple and denied the right to her own motherhood.

> Even if the law did work for the natural mother, she won't find a lawyer who will take her case and battle for her right to get the baby back. They all feel 'sorry' for the adoptive parents and angry with her for upsetting the social order... no matter how difficult society makes the lives of single mothers who refuse to relinquish their children, those women who gave into the pressures suffer in a way the others will (mercifully) never know. For the saddest and most horrifying aspect of adoption is the amount of emotional damage inflicted upon the natural mother. To call her the 'birth mother' instead of the 'natural mother' allows her only the physical birth and denies her those feelings she wasn't supposed to have. By implication this makes the adoptive parents unnatural, but secret adoption cannot be considered natural when the real mother, the victim of this hit and run, is left battered shocked and damaged. Nothing could be more unnatural (Shawyer, 1979).

When describing the terminology applied to the mother of adoption loss, it was suggested that if the birth prefix was to be used at all, that all women who create life should be called "birth" mothers regardless of whether they gave birth while married or not, acknowledging that:

> We have no word for the woman who surrenders her child for adoption... The absence of a name is further evidence that once the child is adopted, the mother is expected to do the decent thing and disappear from the picture. Her silence is required... 'Natural mother' was used for a while but adopters objected... with the added suspicion that a woman who did not look after her own child had no right to call herself a 'natural' mother, the act of surrendering an infant being a wholly 'unnatural' thing for a mother to do. The current fashion is to call the relinquishing parent the child's 'birth' mother. This does not have a particularly distinctive ring, for all women who have had a child are birth mothers (Howe, 1992).

In addition, adoption workers apparently felt that the phrase, "best interests of the child" meant that single mothers should not raise their own children whether they were willing and able to or not.

In the early 1970s in Australia, efforts began to redefine and counteract the language traditionally applied to these women:

> T]he efforts of second wave feminists and of organisations such as the National Council for the Single Mother and Her Child were by

the early 1970s yielding demonstrable results. 'Coming together in self-help groups, single mothers sought to redefine their conditions and appropriating rather than avoiding *labels which in the past had been used to brand them as sinful*... They fought to be recognised as mothers rather than condemned as unmarried and to be supported in their parenting role rather than separated from their children as unwanted' [emphasis added] (Marshall & McDonald, 2001).

However, it is telling that one adopter discussed the natural mother of the boy he was raising by "indignantly denying any relevance of the birth mother in his son's life. "I don't call her a mother. I call her the *'conceiver'* [emphasis added] (Marshall & McDonald, 2001).

In Ireland, there was a move to reject the stigmatizing, marginalizing prefix of "birth" for mothers whose babies were taken for adoption:

> The label 'birthmother' was rejected by Natural Parents Network as stigmatizing and imposed by professionals who lacked knowledge and compassion about their situations. They suggested that the name 'natural parent' should be used to describe their position and status. Using an anti-discriminatory perspective, which recognizes the oppressive components of labeling and the importance of empowering users to define their reality by choosing the discourse, the researchers decided to use their appellation…

The application of a feminist perspective to the research allowed for the deconstruction of the taken-for-granted knowledge of the time when the adoption placements were made which had labeled the 'unmarried mother' as a social deviant (Wilson, Lordan & Mullender, 2002).

Into the 21st century, a deep bias existed regarding the issue of what to call a "resourceless" unmarried mother who had surrendered her baby for adoption, and more marginalizing efforts began to apply a new term to these unprotected mothers:

> One coin: two sides. What is a mother? I know what the word means to me, but I'm hardly neutral on the question. A couple of weeks ago, Jo and I were discussing the language of adoption: birthmother (this itself a p.c. improvement on real mother or natural mother); adoptive mother. We both allowed as how we find all the modifiers deficient. 'You're just my mom.' She thinks her sci-fi books have it right. 'They invest language for precision – maybe a word like *birther...*' [emphasis added] (Brennan, 2007).

CHAPTER 24

WHAT SHOULD HAVE BEEN

Sadly, during social work's history, some practitioners have crossed the line and caused great harm.

Frederic G. Reamer

It is difficult for young women of today to imagine the extent of the social, emotional and financial crises that surrounded families faced with unmarried pregnancies during the BSE years. Looking back from the present, it is almost impossible to understand how natural mothers could surrender their children against their will. It may also be difficult to understand that the exiled mother who has been through this experience often punishes herself because she did not stand up to her parents or to the social workers or to society, even if, in reality, there was no way she could do so. "[I]t is time to examine the role of the 'helping professionals' in this aspect of adoption... What is gradually becoming more widely understood... is that bottling up grief, anger or guilt can be harmful to people's mental - and indeed physical - health." (Howe, Sawbridge & Hinings, 1992)

The United States Children's Bureau and the Child Welfare League of America issued guidelines regarding adoptions. The guidelines specified the proper treatment practices regarding unmarried mothers and their children.

Contrasting these practices with those of Sweden in 1961, Dr. Hunter Comly, the director of the Children's Center of Wayne County in Detroit, Michigan, described how the "relatively stable, homogeneous and mature culture" of Sweden handled its unmarried mothers without stereotyping them and noting that it "clearly extends more consideration to the unwed mother and more protection to their babies. Laws are non-punitive to the parents and the infant. Unwed mothers' pre and post-natal medical care is guaranteed. The illegitimate child may inherit. The relative absence of shame and punishment obviously safeguard the mental and physical health of both mother and child" (Comly, 1961).

The findings of research conducted at an adoption agency in the United States in 1964 showed that the dire situations predicted for unmarried mothers who decided to keep their children rather than surrender them did not occur frequently. The research also provided an interesting side note: parents wished that the casework services offered to them by their adoption workers had also been available to them during their initial period of adjustment to being parents. "How obvious it seems," wrote adoption worker Ruth Canada, "that help in the initial parenting adjustment has been given only if the placement were with adoptive parents?" She went on to say that her agency's practices were changing to extend casework aid to include natural mothers (Canada, 1964).

After the BSE years, in 1978, the Child Welfare League of America established its standards of practice for dealing with unwed pregnancies. The standards called for the preservation of the natural family and stated specifically that "No child should be deprived of care by his natural parents… No children should be deprived of care by their parents solely because of their economic need, or their need for other forms of community assistance to reinforce their efforts to maintain a home for them" (CWLA, 1978).

Actually, even before 1978, the CWLA's guidelines for adoption services recommended preserving the natural family "whenever possible" and that children should not be "deprived of their natural parents until other assistance has been tried and found wanting." The standards also recommended making services available to unmarried fathers, particularly teen fathers, and that natural parents – married or not – should "fully understand" what it meant to surrender their child. If the natural parent(s) decides to keep the child, the CWLA standards required that "help should be available" if she decides to keep it. "Relinquishment should not be accepted before the child is born and the mother has recovered from the effects of the delivery, nor before the mother is emotionally ready to relinquish him…" (Ford, 1978).

Counselors recognized the fact that surrendering babies for adoption hurt the mothers. When they suggest adoption, counselors feared that the mothers would no long view them as trustworthy or unbiased and will suspect there are "hidden motives – perhaps financial – for encouraging mothers to 'give away' their babies."

Curtis Young advised:

> A consistent, national message directed toward the next generation could help permanently change the value this culture places on adoption…a long window of opportunity is available to reach these women

with messages that will motivate them to consider adoption… There must also be *solid counsel and encouragement of adoption… Counselors must be trained to give women sound reasons that will counter the desire to keep their babies* [Emphasis added] (C. Young, 2000).

The real nature of the "decision" to surrender a child to adoption was known to social workers as evidenced by the ways they used their influence to steer natural mothers toward adoption as the only appropriate solution. As Mary Block Jones explained upon looking back at her experience:

What 'decision?' There was no decision. The word decision doesn't apply to relinquishing a child. In fact, the word reflects the prejudice of society toward birth mothers. We are supposed to be unfeeling, inhuman trash, who decide to give up our children because life would be more fun, less expensive, and easier without them. That's hogwash. No mother in the world, human or animal, would decide to give up her baby. It isn't normal or natural. It wouldn't happen if mothers had the power to decide. It only happens when they don't (Jones, 1993).

In 1971, the United Nations issued a report on the discrimination faced by individuals who were born out of wedlock, an important official recognition that such discrimination existed and that included recommendations about what could – and should – be done to help unmarried mothers. In reviewing the family law status of women in four regions of the world between the years

1961 and 1964, the UN found that "discrimination against unmarried mothers still existed in law" and that in a large majority of nations, the general approach was "social discrimination against the unmarried mother." The UN report went on to state:

> [O]wing to her status and the inadequacy
> of measures of social protection in her favor,
> the unmarried mother and her child are still
> the subject of discrimination in many
> countries…the number of unmarried mothers
> is continually increasing in certain countries
> and they are often subject to legal and social
> discrimination in violation of the principles
> of equality and non-discrimination… (United
> Nations, 1971)

As more women experienced reunions with the children they surrendered to adoption, the effects of both the natural mothers and their surrendered children became known. For many of these women, the reunion triggered years of repressed grief and guilt as they felt they should have fought harder to keep their children. Adoption agencies are still frightening for natural mothers as their last dealings with such agencies left them with wounds that never completed healed. "It is not surprising, therefore, that many birth mothers feel 'put out,' if not resentful, towards mandatory or 'highly recommended' counseling sessions at the agency where their child was originally taken from them" (McColm, 1993).

Frequently, natural mothers had not considered adoption before coming into an adoption agency, and the counselors knew it. In such cases, it was recommended that unmarried pregnant females be "trained" by a counselor who developed a "rapport" with her in order to facilitate the adoption process. When asked why adoption was not considered in a specific case, adoption workers said because the client was "closed" to adoption.

> The challenge for centers committed to the fair consideration of adoption will be to educate *counselors that maintaining rapport with the mother* and providing for her immediate welfare must not pre-empt consideration of the long-term good of the child... a new understanding of adoption and integration of adoption in both services and training are required... One counselor wanted to suggest adoption but thought that the client 'wouldn't want to go there.' This experience is common, and it frustrates counselors. Another counselor summed up her experience with a client: 'I did not talk about adoption with her because she came in with her mind made up. I did not feel she would read the brochure...' [emphasis added] (Curtis, 2000).

In 2002, Douglas Henderson made this claim:

> The mental health community may desire to see adoption as professional problem-solving and as a 'favor' done to all involved. Problems in adoption thus represent both a failure on the part of those professionals and a favor gone bad. Fear that discussing adoption-related problems will lead to adoption itself being labeled as pathological is

also likely operating to support the silence (Henderson, 2002).

In 2012, veteran journalist and reporter Dan Rather devoted one of his "Dan Rather Reports" cable television news programs to mothers who shared some of their heartbreaking experiences of life in "wage homes," living in a "maternity home" and being separated from their newborns. After the show aired, which was entitled "Adopted or Abducted," on AXS, representatives from Catholic Charities, the Salvation Army, the National [Florence] Crittenton Foundation and the National Association of Social Workers issued their responses.

Larry Snyder, President of Catholic Charities, stated, "While some of the personal experiences reported by birth mothers in the 1950s and 1960s are heartbreaking, as the social stigma of being an unwed mother has changed, so have adoption practices" (Snyder, 2012).

Major George Hood of the Salvation Army's National Community Relations and Development unit, said:

> In the middle of the last century, the Salvation Army operated a number of homes for unwed mothers in the United States. These homes were operational during a time when significant social pressures were placed upon pregnant, unmarried girls, and a majority of the young girls came to the homes after being guided by their own families... Certainly, society's treatment of unwed mothers has changed dramatically during the

past 40 to 50 years and our operations have similarly adjusted (Hood, 2012).

Jeannette Pai-Espinosa, President of the National Florence Crittenton Foundation, commented that:

> [T]here is no doubt that the attitude of American society to single and young mothers and their children was and remains a complicated issue rooted in our views on race, gender and class. In the late 1940s and fifties in response to shifting social mores, a dramatic increase in middle class young women seeking admission to Crittenton homes and changes in the field of social work practices at homes began to change. Although adoption had not traditionally been part of the Crittenton care philosophy, homes began to turn more and more to adoption. TNCF and the Crittenton agencies that are still in operation today are aware of, saddened by, and regret the experience of mothers 'forced or coerced' into placing their children in adoptive homes and the impact on their children…These practices were not required, supported or endorsed by any National Crittenton directive and as independent agencies or homes each had the ability to determine its own priorities and operating policies… not a week goes by that we don't hear from someone searching for a family member and we are acutely aware of the pain and damage done by the past practices…(Pai-Espinosa, 2012).

Gail Woods Waller, Director of the National Association of Social Workers, responded by saying, "All professions have historical practices that were negatively shaped by the mores, politics, and prejudices of previous eras… Social work and its members have made mistakes as the profession matured from its founding in the late 19th century to the present" (Waller, 2012).

It is important to keep in mind when considering how appropriate it was for social workers to operate within the field of adoption. Brian Berry offers this explanation of social justice:

> Social Justice is generally equated with the notion of equality or equal opportunity in society. Although equality is undeniably part of social justice the meaning of social justice is actually much broader. Further, 'equal opportunity' and similar phrases such as 'personal responsibility' have been used to diminish the prospective for realizing social justice by justifying enormous inequalities in modern society (Berry, 2005).

As the social work profession matured, it recognized that its representatives can do good or cause harm. The workers were cautioned to pay attention to clients who engaged in harmful or self-destructive behavior and consider what drove them to it, which in most cases was either desperation, greed, or impairment. According to Frederic G. Reamer, "[S]ocial workers must pay keen attention to signs of unethical conduct and impairment within ourselves and our colleagues… social workers must bring their concerns to the attention of people and organizations that are in a position to support social workers and hold them accountable" (Reamer, 2002).

CHAPTER 25

POST-TRAUMATIC STRESS DISORDER
IN MOTHERS OF THE BABY SCOOP ERA

*Post-Traumatic Stress Disorder is defined as being a
disorder linked to having experienced a traumatic event, and
characterized by symptoms such as hyper vigilance, flashbacks,
emotional numbness, avoidance of stimuli associated with the
trauma, difficulty sleeping, concentrating, persistent anxiety, etc.*

DSM-IV-TR (468)

Suicides related to mother and child separation are rarely
reported as such. Therefore, it would be very difficult to
report statistics regarding mothers or their removed
children. We can rely only on historical references.

What emotional after-effects did these mothers suffer
following the surrender of their babies to adoption? How
did they fare during the ensuing years; for decades
afterwards?

During the BSE, many of the hundreds of thousands of
unmarried mothers in the United States, Canada, New
Zealand, Australia, Ireland, and the United Kingdom were
separated from their infants against their will. They were
targeted by a system whose purpose was to obtain healthy
newborn infants for adoption (United Nations, 1971).

Many mothers who experienced the loss of a child to adoption have gone on to describe these symptoms. Even though the current Criteria A (1) of PTSD mandates that the person must have "experienced, witnessed, or was confronted with an event or events that involved actual or threatened death or serious injury, or a threat to the physical integrity of self or others," there is a rationale for researchers to examine the impact of other potentially traumatic events:

> Clearly more studies are needed in which a wide variety of stressors is examined with respect to their ability to elicit PTSD symptoms. Regardless of how Criterion A is officially defined, investigators can and should empirically evaluate the impact of alternative definitions on the prevalence of trauma exposure and PTSD, if they include explicit operational definitions such that others can critique or attempt to replicate their findings (Weathers and Keane, 2007).

Unmarried mothers began their journey as pregnant, "unwed" women in America. They were usually between 16 and 18 years of age. During the BSE, as stated earlier, contraception was difficult for single women to access; and young women's natural fertility predictably took its course. Learning of their pregnancy, they ignored their changing bodies as long as possible although eventually they were unable to hide their socially unsanctioned sexuality. They were mothers without wedding rings but in all other aspects, no different than any other mother in their era. During this period women were "forging new standards of sexual behavior" and this became known as "the girl problem" (Kunzel, 1993; Solinger, 2000; Osofsky, 1968).

The 'problem girl' tells the child's father she is pregnant. He leaves town, goes off to college, marries another woman or joins the armed services and is dispatched to Vietnam to avoid having to marry her. He totally rejects her. She seeks help from her parents. When the parents have recovered from the news of this unwelcome, unwed pregnancy they seek counsel from "experts" on what can be done with their daughter. Doctors and pastors advise the parents to commit their daughter to a maternity home and put the baby up for adoption.

Incarceration

An historical shift whereby the pre-WWII mentoring foster homes that supported mothers in raising their babies changed to become wage homes for expectant mothers before their transfer to maternity homes and an inevitable adoption. Adoption workers who controlled the maternity home movement and used it to create an adoption industry promoted this change. Wage and maternity homes worked together with adoption agencies and their lawyers to complete the net that snagged unsupported unmarried mothers. The net closed tightly around them. The catch was her baby (Kunzel, 1993).

The conditions of confinement of a pregnant girl in the United States maternity homes were determined by the meaning of "illegitimacy," which simply means "wrong" (Vincent, 1962).

Until the girl was seven months pregnant, she was often placed by her parents, guided by adoption workers, into a "wage" home (the private home of a married couple) to hide her away while she earned her keep with chores and childcare. These wage home positions were a short-term solution until her admittance into a residential maternity home. Ironically, seldom were any wages paid. The expectation was that the expectant mother should feel indebted for her room and board for which she worked extremely hard. She was expected to be grateful for an anonymous place to hide so as to not embarrass her parents. This practice was widespread across western nations including the United States, Canada, the United Kingdom, Australia and New Zealand. It was the social policy of the day, commonly known as housekeeping positions (CWLA, 1978).

The role of the host woman in the private wage home was not that of a motherly type mentor. Rather she was a "decent" woman, that is, a married woman who expected free (or low cost) live-in servitude provided by the unwed, pregnant girl for a few months in return for providing the disgraced girl a place to hide her pregnancy until she was qualified to enter a maternity home for the birth and subsequent adoption (Pinson, 1964).

Wage homes were connected with maternity homes. The wage and maternity homes worked hand-in-hand with adoption agencies. There were no childcare centers associated with these maternity homes, and there were no longer any religious women offering the mother support to keep her baby. There were no kindly maternity home workers providing money, food or clothing to the mother living independently with her baby. The focus during the BSE was no longer on the mother/child bond. The focus was on the needs, wants and demands of married couples (infertile or otherwise) with a self-perceived need for children, and on the newborn that adoption social workers decreed would fulfill those needs. The focus was also on enriching the budding professionalism of social work as a child welfare field that related specifically to adoption and the adoption worker's need to be viewed and respected as an "expert in unwed motherhood." Again, it was as growing field of professional expertise. Careers were built on adoption loss strategies that depended upon separation of mother and baby (Kunzel, 1993).

The Child Welfare League of America warned against the use of unregulated wage homes, which it defined as one in which board and lodging are provided in return for services. "Work homes and... wage homes... should be used only in exceptional situations. Such homes should be carefully studied, selected and closely supervised. Such homes should conform to minimum age and Social Security requirements" (Child Welfare League of America, 1978). Wage homes were exploitive to expectant mothers who were forced into them because they had nowhere else to go.

Decades later, natural mothers from other countries have also disclosed that they were not usually paid a wage for their live-in services providing housecleaning, cooking and childcare. It is interesting to note that girls were deemed capable and worthy of caring for the children of the wage home couple, but not considered capable or worthy of taking care of their own babies.

Commonly at the seventh month of pregnancy, the girl entered the maternity home. It generally was a place many miles from home, where no one knew her name or would recognize her face. Solinger (2000) cites Ruth Pagan,

Salvation Army maternity home worker, who in 1947 wrote in a letter to Maud Morlock (Children's Bureau Consultant on Services to Unmarried Mothers) stating "maternity homes were springing up in the West for the sole purpose of getting control of the babies."

Not all unwed mothers were sent to maternity homes. Some were sequestered in their own family homes for the duration of their pregnancy, often times hiding in the basement or an attic, or sent to live with relatives until they gave birth and then returned home without their baby. A few lived independently in a town far from home. But during the BSE most white unmarried expectant mothers encountered social workers and their brainwashing practices during the course of their pregnancy that resulted in an inevitable encounter with the adoption system (Marshall & McDonald, 2001; Carp, 1998).

The pregnant girl sees the book where she will sign herself in and out of the maternity home for her chaperoned outings of two hours a week she may have after her orientation period. She is to follow a strict schedule of when to get up in the morning, when to eat her meals, and when to go to bed. There will be bed checks every night. No food is allowed in, nor visitors or phone calls, made or received, that are not on an approved list. She is not allowed in her own room during the day without a note from the nurse. She is to have a chore assigned to her while an "inmate" of the home. She sees the locks on the door. She sees the faces of her peers behind the fence. She is now on the inside.

Behind the fence, and in essence incarcerated in a maternity prison, she is truly cut off from the world, from family and friends and, most importantly, from the father of her gestating child. Note: but he has already abandoned her. The boyfriends who were not sent away by family were blocked from contacting the pregnant girl. No phone calls, visits, letters or any form of contact with the father was allowed. Even if she had wanted contact, she didn't know where she had been sent. How to call? How to write? She had simply disappeared.

Manipulation and Grooming

What effect did the environment of a maternity home have on the pregnant girl? Could brainwashing, more commonly known today as thought reform, have played a part in the surrender of her baby to adoption? There is more than adequate proof that it did. Brainwashing, or thought reform, was an accepted and applied method of separating women from their babies so those babies could be adopted.

Social workers were trained to hold judgmental social work "values" of the profession and trained to impart to clients "what he knows and thinks to be good" (Perlman, 1957). Clearly, the concept of non-judgmental counseling did not exist during that time. Professional social workers were trained to be agents of social control. Reid (1956) clarifies the rigid instruction given to social workers to justify the mind control/brain washing psychological methods implemented by adoption supply recruiters to each mother and baby under the guise of "casework."

> The third service the agency can render, and one which no one else is in a position to render is to make certain that the child is really relinquished, that the adoptive parents are protected against intervention by the

natural parents. Her work with unmarried mothers or other natural parents is the key. Making sure that the child is relinquished is by no means just a legal matter. It is essentially a psychological one that requires the professional help of casework (Reid, 1956).

Her days are punctuated with admonitions from staff and social workers about the meaning of her pregnancy. The meaning they impose upon the pregnant girl is a newly created psychoanalytic theory that casts unwed mothers as sexual delinquents, neurotics, deviants and sinners, with surrender of the child for adoption as the only possible path to health, salvation and rehabilitation.

In her dissertation, Costigan (1964) identifies how social work literature supported the role of the social worker in making the adoption decision and clarifies how the decision was not the mother's decision to make stating that social work professional opinion in 1964 favored relinquishment by the unwed mother. In addition, she adds that a three month residence in a maternity home is associated with surrendering and that "... longer agency contact, continuity of interviews and frequency of interviews would be associated with the decision to relinquish."

From the pregnant girl's entry into the maternity home up until the moment she signs parental termination papers, she will be subjected to interviews that stress her unfitness as a mother and the pressing need to surrender *The Baby* (workers being careful not to use the phrase "her baby") for adoption. Great care will be taken to subvert her strengthening maternal instinct in order to serve the needs of the agency's adoption plan that required an early adoption. Her isolation behind the walls of the institution is the first step in that process (Costin, 1972; Heiman, 1960; and Costigan, 1964).

The pregnant girl is then repeatedly "counseled" by other workers, that because she is unmarried, she will be an incompetent mother. She becomes the object of their self-serving theories that paint her as a delinquent, neurotic and therefore an unfit and unworthy parent. They will relentlessly apply this minimizing theory to her as she waits along, behind the fence, for the birth of her firstborn: "*The Baby*" (Luker, 1996 and Chesler, 1986).

Day in and out she is relentlessly given the same message - surrendering The Baby is the only path to her redemption. If during her meetings with her adoption worker, she asks about public assistance and other resources available to unmarried mothers, she will be kept ignorant (assuming she even knows about those resources, which most did not). It will be repeated over and over that her child will be called a bastard, will be handicapped by illegitimacy and grow to hate her as the cause of this misery. It will be emphasized that The Baby needs two parents who are able to afford things without needing public assistance, who can give The Baby material advantages unattainable by a pregnant girl who has only love to offer. She will guided, cajoled, coerced, shamed, diagnosed, pushed, guilt-tripped and if she resists, even threatened into surrendering her child to these adoption workers who have The Baby earmarked for married (paying) strangers to parent. She learns that wealth is preferable to love (Chambers, 2006).

Costigan concluded that her research showed that the social worker is deeply involved in manipulating the adoption decision:

T]he closeness of worker-client relationship is

associated with the decision to relinquish the baby is strongly supported by the findings of this study...with a close or moderately close relationship with the caseworker, the unmarried mother was more likely to relinquish her baby than if the relationship was moderately distant...These differences were statistically highly significant (Costigan, 1964).

Missing from this scenario is the concept of nondirective counseling. Instead, adoption workers direct (brainwash, manipulate, groom) her to the resolution they seek which is the decision they have previously determined to be the proper outcome for her and *The Baby*.

As pregnancy advances, the intensity of the directive counseling increases, emphasizing what an adoptive couple is able to give to The Baby that she is not. She is not advised of resources available to her as a single mother. Government assistance (Aid to Families with Dependent Children) to unmarried mothers is not mentioned. She is not advised to seek independent legal guidance. She is not told about child support from the father of her soon to be born baby. In fact, these resources and all of this information, is withheld from her. If she asks, her thoughts are redirected to the adoption workers' suppositions of pathology about unwed mothers. This creative theory is substituted for accurate information (Costin, 1972; and Bernstein, 1962).

Some mothers were drugged so heavily that they were denied the birth experience. Some were given no pain relief at all. All of these tactics were meant to be punitive, intended to break down any sense of self she may, by some miracle, still have (Rickarby, 1998).

The pregnant girl progresses towards delivery. The institution does little, if anything, to prepare her for childbirth. She is not given information that may help her to understand what is happening to her body while pregnant, much less for the labor ahead.

Some new mothers were allowed to see, hold and even feed their babies for a few days following the birth. Many never even saw the children they birthed. But the application of the brainwashing/mind control methods worked with the majority of the babies of unwed, unprotected white mothers being taken for adoption. Many mothers do not remember the actual event of signing their "consent" to the adoption. This is a result of the seriousness of the trauma induced by their experience (Rickarby, 1998).

When the time comes, the girl labors alone; no family member is present, no maternity home staff, no friend, and especially not the father of her baby. She has no one to provide her with emotional support.

The tactics of a thought reform (brainwashing) program are organized to destabilize individuals' sense of self by getting them to drastically reinterpret their life's history, radically alter their worldview, accept a new version of reality and causality, and develop dependency on the organization, thereby being turned into a deployable agent of the organization...(Singer & Ofshe, 1990).

A major background fundamental regarding the advice provided to unmarried, pregnant women during the BSE was that they would "forget" about their pregnancies and their babies and return to their "normal" lives as if nothing had happened. But did the so-called experts and professionals involved with adoption during this time period, many of whom felt that the "sin" of unwed pregnancy needed to be "punished," believe this to be true?

For example, it was known as early as 1960 that unmarried mothers were subjected to physical and legal punishment, as well as being ostracized by society. Because of the actual or expected cruelty imposed on unmarried mothers-to-be, many concealed the pregnancy which often had serious ramifications. These consequences included lack of physical health care, death during delivery, suicide, or abandoning the child. Even if efforts were made to change or mitigate such treatment, the unmarried mother would frequently lose her social ties to family, friends, and community. She was expected to forgo a normal life; in short, "she is expected to wear the 'scarlet letter'" (Wimperis, 1960).

The woman pregnant out of wedlock suffers despair and loneliness. A feeling of helplessness, coupled with that of severe guilt, sometimes leads to suicide. Denial and a desire for concealment are frequent first reactions; this is dangerous because a lack of proper care may be the consequence (Pinson, 1964).

Societal pressures became too much and unmarried mothers succumbed to anxiety and depression. Sometimes suicide seemed the only answer. Many mothers under custodial siege became anxious, depressed, and insomniac. Some attempted suicide or began drinking. Some had 'nervous breakdowns.' Each mother blamed herself for 'breaking down.' Each mother was terrified that such information would be used against her in court. (Chesler, 1986).

In a study conducted in 1991, 49 of 64 women had considered suicide, while 14 had made actual attempts. All of the attempts were directly related to "the birthmother issue." One of the women in the study tried to kill herself 12 times and stopped only when she discovered it was possible to search for her surrendered child with hope for a reunion. (Stiffler, 1991).

According to research that involved interviews with mothers who surrendered babies for adoption, the impact of the 'decision' never ended.

> Surrendering a child for adoption has been described by many of the women I interviewed as the event that defined their identity and therefore influenced every major decision they made thereafter. Since most of these girls surrendered when they were between the ages of sixteen and twenty-three, the event shaped their entire adult lives (Fessler, 2006).

What long term physical and emotional consequences could surrender have had on "unwed" mothers? What about the effects it had on the babies they gave birth to, who were subsequently removed from them and offered for adoption? Adoptees also considered suicide, illustrating the long-term effects of mother-child separation.

Later research on how children responded to negative

events in their formative years found:

> [L]ong-term consequences on health … is a concept that has gained strength in the past decade as experts have revisited a pivotal study [Study: American Journal of Preventive Medicine 1998] on adults that linked chronic illnesses, substance abuse and other health problems to stress experience during childhood… they did a long study with the Centers for Disease Control and Prevention with about 17,000 people the first time…the study's official title is 'Relationship of Childhood Abuse and Household Dysfunction to Many of the Leading Causes of Death in Adults'… The study asked about their life experiences before they turned age 18… we know that [adults] have significant links to things like heart disease, diabetes, obesity, psychological issues and substance abuse… The mechanism for the injury focuses on how trauma affects a developing brain… you have stress hormones coursing through the bloodstream of these children, which then starts a cascade of the production of very negative neurotransmitters within the brain…that's how adverse childhood events affect the wiring of the brain… you have a mis-wired brain, and what you have is an individual who does engage in risky behavior…problems with attention span…problems with impulse control… you cannot really make decisions that are the best for you (Smith, 2015).

Legal and Civil Rights

Maternity homes that previously supported mother and infant had become institutionalized and punitive adoption clearinghouses. Court appointed judges, who presided over adoption proceedings, approved adoptions based on mothers' signatures without concerning themselves with the process by which those signatures were obtained. During the BSE, practices around obtaining infants for adoption in western countries were systematically based on unethical, immoral and improper adoption practices by all parties directly involved and supported by families and communities who colluded and approved even when they did not actively participate. They were passive conspirators who, even today, shy away from accepting responsibility for their role in what was a sinister conspiracy. The victims of these systemic abuses continued their lives after adoption loss being forced to carry enormous burdens of irresolvable grief compounded by the huge burden of guilt imposed upon them by the adoption industry (Condon, 1986; and Chesler, 1986).

Many adoption workers disregarded the constitutional, civil and legal rights of the unwed mother. She lived for the balance of her pregnancy not as a United States citizen, but as the subject of a man-made social experiment whose end was not "rehabilitation," that is, a socially sanctioned, serene return to respectable society as promised, but instead the beginning of a decades-long nightmare of loss and mental and physical health issues.

When the girl arrives at the maternity home, she is divested of her personal possessions, money and clothing. She is often provided clothing by the maternity home. Since identifying information such as names and addresses are forbidden, she is told to choose a pseudonym and given a list of names from which to choose. Alternatively, she may use her first name and family name initial. This is how she will be referred to throughout her stay. Her incoming and outgoing mail, which will be censored by staff must be addressed in this manner. Her ability to make phone calls is restricted. She must use a pay phone controlled by the administrative office. She no longer is allowed money of her own. If she has money there is a risk she will run away (Rains, 1970).

She is shown around the facility by one of her peers. She sees the common room with its black and white TV, pay phone booth and institutional furniture. Shortly after admittance, she will be able to use the pay phone for fifteen minutes a week for one call with coins provided by the office staff.

Evidence of Traumatic Stress

Many self-help books, memoirs, and articles have been published on the subject of the long-term consequences of having surrendered an infant to adoption. Research published in peer reviewed journals as well as theses, reports, and dissertations, has often commented on the fact that the psychological consequences are both long term and often debilitating. These long-term consequences include symptoms that closely resemble those of Post-Traumatic Stress Disorder.

Symptoms of PTSD can include flashbacks, disturbing thoughts and memories that are often intensified when people are exposed to happenings that remind them of the event. Anniversaries of the event can also trigger symptoms. People suffering from PTSD can experience emotional numbness, sleep disturbances, depression, anxiety, irritability, anger and intense guilt. Natural mothers of adoption loss commonly experience a range of PTSD. Soll, a New York psychotherapist and adoption educator explains that, "There are... psychological parallels between the exiled mother and someone who has been sexually, physically or emotionally abused. Post Traumatic Stress disorder is the inevitable result of her tragic loss, leading to anxiety, depression, insomnia, and issues with her sexuality..." (Soll, 2003).

Askren and Bloom offered that:

> A grief reaction specific to the relinquishing mother has been identified. This is accompanied by other long-term reactions to the experience of relinquishment and by the mother's efforts to resolve her grief. The relinquishing mother has experienced a life-changing event that may profoundly affect her mental and physical health and her relationships at the time of relinquishment and far into the future (Askren & Bloom, 1998).

Stiffler describes the emotional condition of a post-surrender mother:

> She experiences her loss as an emptiness, a freezing, a wound that never stops bleeding, as arms eternally aching to hold the lost baby, or as a limbo loss similar to that felt by families of soldiers missing in action. Her experience of grief is inhibited and

prolonged... She has spent a lot of psychic energy keeping a secret of this magnitude and repressing her feelings, which are variably manifested in guilt, anger and unconscious fear of sex, tenseness and uneasiness around children, a vague fear of discovery, depression, social anxiety agoraphobia, chemical dependence, eating disorders and other anxiety/phobic states (Stiffler, 1991).

The same process and outcomes were recorded as happening in New Zealand during the same period (Shawyer, 1979). The state of New South Wales, in Australia held a Parliamentary Inquiry into adoption practice perpetrated against mothers in Australia during the BSE (Standing Committee on Social Issues, 2000).

During testimony, Australian psychiatrist Rickarby stated to the Standing Committee that PTSD was "a central issue for mothers who have lost a child to adoption." He states that major depression, dissociative disorder and other forms of psychopathology as "almost universal" in his experience of working with mothers who had surrendered children to adoption (Social Issues Committee, 1998).

Bloch Jones (1993) recognizes common symptoms such as flashbacks, nightmares, anxiety, avoidance and phobias among the natural mothers with whom she had corresponded (272). Kelly (1999) states that findings from her survey of seventy-nine mothers, 99% indicated that relinquishing their child was "extremely, very or somewhat true."

Wells surveyed three hundred mothers who had surrendered babies to adoption and found that close to half of the mothers felt that the trauma of surrendering "affected their physical health and almost all of their mental health," as well as their "interpersonal relationships with family, partners and their parenting of subsequent children." She offers symptoms such as avoidance, psychogenic amnesia, psychic numbing, lack of positive image, recurrent dreams and nightmares, triggering from being exposed to similar situations, depression and anxiety (Wells, 1993).

The following mothers of the BSE speak for themselves regarding their symptoms of Post Traumatic Stress Disorder following the surrender of their babies to adoption:

> For the first several years afterwards, I was just numb, unable to understand what was being said to me, unable to feel anything at all. I was like a lobotomized beast... I dropped out of college...I barely existed. Eventually I married and had more children, but still, on holidays and special days, and especially around her birthday and Christmas, I experienced a pain and a heaviness that would put me in my bed for most of the month. The nights were the worst. I would experience a pain that was like being in the middle of a whirlwind. The whirlwind threatened to destroy me. I remember pushing the pain down, pushing it down into a place like a steel pipe inside of me, and welding on a steel cap so the pain could never overtake me again. In

December 1987, I gave birth to my last child, a girl. Within a year of her birth, I was experiencing a complete inability to deal with life, my kids, and my job. I laid in bed. That's what I did. I went through weeks of having to choose minute by minute not to end my own life... (Barb).

The loss of my child will haunt me the rest of my life. It has made parts of my life unbearable. It led to bouts of serious depression. It led to repeated attempts at therapy, which, oddly enough, never really addressed the grief I was trying to deal with. So great a part did my daughter continue to play in my life that I went into premature labour with my only other child, a son, on her tenth birthday. Somehow, after his birth, I became incomplete. One baby cannot take another's place. I don't think that I will ever feel 'whole' (Elizabeth).

In the ensuing decades it has become obvious that I suffer from post-traumatic stress disorder. I have a very pronounced startle response, screaming and adopting a physical posture of self-defense. When I am suddenly awakened from sleep I also scream. I have nightmares about being pregnant and being locked up; these vary in frequency from monthly to yearly. I have been unable to plan a career because I fear having my life suddenly disastrously interrupted again; I have worked at a variety of jobs, sometimes for years, but I have no sense of a future or control over my future. (For many years I regarded my life as just waiting to die.) I struggle daily with deep feelings of worthlessness and guilt over having 'knuckled under' and given my daughter up for adoption. I have flashbacks of my incarceration several times each day; coping strategies for these such as gripping ice cubes in my hand are partially successful in cutting them short. I take medication for clinical depression...I avoid the city where I was incarcerated and people who remind me of that horrible experience, especially family members. (Mary, personal communication, September 11, 2009).

Conclusion

It has been estimated that more than a million and one half unmarried mothers in the United States may have had children taken by pressured adoptions during the BSE. By the evidence provided by social work and historical literature and by testimony of the mothers themselves, it is clear that they were treated more commonly as criminals. The sentence imposed upon these mothers has caused them to suffer a lifetime of loss, grief and ill health induced by the actions of the adoption industry and its "professional" workforce.

The assumption of pre-existing pathology in pregnant girls was the star by which adoption social workers of the BSE steered their ship. Because of their unfounded theories of pre-existing emotional damage in young pregnant girls it is likely that many hundreds of thousands of young American mothers lost their children to adoption. Regardless of the mounting evidence that adoption is damaging to mothers, the fishing net for adoption supply continues to be cast wide as the supply of adoptable infants in the United States continually dissipates.

Other nations recognize PTSD as a consequence and strongly recommend that pre-surrender PTSD counseling with pregnant girls should be included. The New South Wales Law Reform Commission cites Wells' 1993 study in Footnote 59 of its final report. The report states that their pamphlet should "…place more emphasis on the psychological effects… Serious attention is now being given to the link between relinquishment and the development of post-traumatic stress disorder in birth mothers" (New South Wales Law Reform Commission, 1997).

Today, as senior mothers of adoption loss are entering the winter of their lives, it is imperative, and certainly long past due, that extensive research be quickly undertaken in order to explore the incidence and extent of their suffering from symptoms of Post Traumatic Stress Disorder, some for over five decades.

CHAPTER 26

ADMISSIONS & APOLOGIES

...adoption healing is wonderful, but the better path is not to contract the disease.

Hal Aigner

A speaker at an adoption conference held in 1948 stated that an adoption agency can only meet its goals for serving parents and children if it recognizes the right of the parent to make the decision about whether or not she wants to surrender her child for adoption without being pressured or persuaded or threatened by adoption workers. However, according to the speaker, Inez Baker, social workers sometimes focus on the advantages of adoption in the hope that a mother will be satisfied with a decision that is not really hers.

> The fact that a parent brings his problem *to an agency does not give the agency authority or license to determine the course of a child's life...* If I labor the point that children's agencies do not have the authority... to control the lives of children... it is *because of the widespread misconception in this area* [emphasis added] (Baker, 1948).

It is interesting to note that Baker refers to "parent" instead of "mother" in terms of the woman who is directly involved with the pregnancy and childbirth.

Psychiatrists in the 1950s recognized the common practice of maternity homes in western societies that separated mothers and children as "astonishing" and an "aberration" that would hopefully not be copied by developing nations (Bowlby, 1952). Author Pearl Buck described how insecure and inadequate social work professionals felt and how this caused them to resent any criticisms or suggestions, stating "They fly to defend themselves as only the insecure feel it necessary to do" (Buck, 1956).

Virginia Wimperis (1960) expressed the view that often parents do not make their choice freely, sharing that, "One must recognize that the fate of illegitimate children is not just a matter of chance, and that it *does not always represent the free choice of the parents*" [emphasis added].

According to Viola Bernard, J.D., clinical professor of psychiatry and director of the Division of Community Psychiatry at Columbia University (1964), "Shouldn't agencies make every effort to encourage natural parents, both married couples and unwed mothers, to keep their children in order to prevent psychic trauma from permanent separation?" (Bermard. 1964).

Jean Pochin noted:

> It is as important for an illegitimate child to know his real mother as it is for an adopted child to know that he is adopted... Social workers also knew that a pregnant woman would almost certainly receive less criticism

and more encouragement if she had a ring on her finger… *social workers are acutely conscious that the unmarried mother who has decided to keep her baby is preparing to bring up a socially handicapped child* [emphasis added] (Pochin, 1969).

Sally Headsten questioned prevalent attitudes to adoption, writing:

Maternity home…residents wonder if surrendering their child for adoption is an entrance requirement. Do we…wish this were so? Do we feel that the giving away of one's baby is the best solution for every girl, enabling her to return to single life as though nothing has happened? I believe that our attitudes towards adoption need stiff examination…Ruth Chaskell (1967)…says that 'more and more we are developing …homemaker and day care service to buttress the faltering family. *Why then…are we so ready to accept the natural mother's precarious environmental circumstances as indicators of adoption as the best interest for separation of mother from child?* (Wright, 1965) And my question is, 'Why so early?' …*it seems likely that there may be far wider acceptance of unmarried motherhood in society than in in the social work profession!* [emphasis added] (Headsten, 1969).

Discussions of the "problem" of unmarried mothers in the mid-1960s noted that the public's understanding of their plight was inaccurate, distorted, ignorant, confused and marked with misunderstanding. It was believed not enough was known about illegitimacy and what was known was probably wrong due to the stereotyping of unmarried mothers as "from the other side of the tracks" and different from respectable society, both physically and behaviorally. The public had convinced itself that the "problem" only applied to "tramps, loafers and members of minority groups" for which it had no direct responsibility. The instinctive response of the public to an unmarried mother was to ostracize her and if she was young enough to be in school, to expel her immediately; however, "such swift action is not meted out to the unmarried schoolboy father..." (Reinhart, 1963).

If too many women decided to raise their children rather than surrender them for adoption, social workers felt like failures. These workers viewed adoptive parents as their primary focus, which kept them from addressing the real issues related to adoption and to perpetuate the myths surrounding it and compounding its negative psychological effects (Pannor, 1987).

According to Patricia Roles, adoption had been considered the price an unmarried mother paid for the shame of her situation. In the past, unmarried mothers were to get on with their lives, that they could have other children in the future, that they would forget the surrender of their baby, because, according to Roles, to "acknowledge and encourage the grief reaction might jeopardize the signing of the adoption papers, and might risk disproving the assumption that adoption was the 'best' alternative for everyone..." (Roles, 1989).

Natural mothers felt that any choice they had in regard to their child had been taken away because of pressures imposed by their families, friends and the adoption workers handling their cases. Unmarried teens or young adults trying to decide what to do about the impending birth of a child were naturally intimidated and pressured by anyone in a position of authority over them; of course, they would be influenced by the opinions of someone with power over them (Roles, 1989).

By 1990, some adoption workers could admit that wrongs had been committed in the past. Annet Baran and Rueben Pannor acknowledged that adoption practice has "never" reflected the idea that surrender was to be a last resort. All efforts were focused on adoption as the only solution:

> [W]e are now embarked on a world of 'how to' books, video tapes and seminars to teach couples methods and ruses of locating and convincing pregnant women to give up their babies. We are a heavy presence in the high school classroom, and the advertising columns luring vulnerable and economically deprived pregnant teenagers... (Baran & Pannor, 1990).

Baran and Pannor asked of the social work professionals: What have we been doing for the last 20 years?

> It seems to us that…we must admit that we have been co-opted into supporting a system that causes pain and lifelong suffering to the parties involved…What have we done to underwrite

and support keeping babies and helping the family stay together? ... Knowing the agony and lifelong pain that would result from an unplanned pregnancy and subsequent relinquishment, why have we not made prevention a major issue? ...Open adoption, which we helped pioneer, is not a solution to the problems inherent in adoption. Without enforcement, *open adoption is an unenforceable agreement at the whim of the adoptive parents...* The struggle to open records and address the wrongs of the past must continue [emphasis added] (Baran & Pannor, 1990).

Adoption research findings published in a 1966 study by Iris Goodacre, did not even include unmarried parents, and yet it concluded that, quoting Goodacre:

'[C]hildren should be protected from unnecessary separation from their parents' and 'natural parents must be protected from hurried or panic decisions to give up their child, and from being persuaded to place them unsuitably.' The law endeavors to protect mothers from hasty action by requiring them to wait until their baby is six weeks old before they can give a valid consent to adoption... Although natural mothers who relinquished their babies were not interviewed, records and other sources suggested that few had been able to explore the alternatives to adoption...' (Howe, Sawbridge, Hinings, 1992).

The 1990s brought many apologies from adoption workers and social workers who had a part in the adoption process during the BSE. Social worker Murray Ryburn wrote, "I am desperately saddened by, and sorry for the things that I as a social worker have done, as a member of that profession, to them. I apologize as a social worker for my neglect, my acts of coercion, my failures as someone with a moral, ethical, legal and paid duty to care, who did not always do so" (Ryburn, 1994).

Patricia Dorner of Catholic Charities wrote:

> There will be situations where…untruths were told at the time of the adoption…those who were given correct information and those who received false information. There seemed to be no rhyme or reason for which birth parents were blessed with truth and which were to receive falsehoods. When the practice orientation changed and post-adoption services were extended, discovery about the untruths traumatized and angered the deceived birth parents…There is no way to justify the deception. Perhaps one can look at the secretive nature of the closed adoption practice and frame it from that standpoint. It is not indicated to…try to justify what happened…the most constructive path is to tell the truth, acknowledging the errors of past thinking and cover ups…It does mean providing support and empathy to the person who again feels robbed of yet another part of her child… (Dorner, 1997).

The National Association of Social Workers (NASW) addressed past adoption practices by stating:

> [T]he need to address impairment among some social workers and the ways in which *blurred or confused boundaries between social workers and clients* can compromise the quality of services… Social work historically has given particular attention to the needs and empowerment of people who are *vulnerable, oppressed...* standards pertain to social workers' competence, *obligation to avoid any behavior that discriminates against others, private conduct, honesty, personal impairment and solicitation of clients...* acting *to prevent and eliminate domination, exploitation and discrimination against any person, group or class of people* [emphasis added] (NASW, 1999).

Tim O'Shaughnessy noted that there is no "triad" in adoptions because not all parties are represented. Other parties, other "actors," are involved. Social workers, adopters, adoptees (the babies) and the surrendering parents are four parties, not three. This is not a "triangle." (In addition, lawyers and judges play a part in the "transaction.")

> *Triangularization removes a range of institutions and actors (including social workers) from the primary picture of adoption*, encouraging the misrecognition of adoptions as a private consensual transaction between, and in the interests of, members of the *triangle. Important dimensions of the social location and function of*

adoption are thereby denied or blended out of analysis
[emphasis added] (O'Shaughnessy, 1994)

In 2014, the Australian Parliament undertook an Inquiry of Forced Adoption Practices. Many mothers who were "unwed" mostly during the Baby Scoop Era testified. These experiences of the unmarried Australian mothers were similar to those of unmarried mothers in the U.S.

Many working in adoption activism suggest that infant adoption is not a "triad" or "constellation" or "circle." Instead infant adoption is a "transaction" involving four parties: two with all of the power (facilitators and adopters) and two with little to none (vulnerable, mostly single, mothers and their infants).

> [T]his House recognizes the suffering that forced child adoptions during the 1950s, 1960s and 1970s caused, which took place owing to social pressures on women who had children outside marriage; notes the unacceptable adoption and care practices of the past, such as not giving information about welfare services including housing and financial help which were available at the time, and not questioning whether women putting their children up for adoption had given informed consent; further recognizes the negligence of previous governments... resulting in many women suffering traumatizing pre and post-natal experiences and children being denied contact with their birth parents; further notes that the Australian Prime Minister has in 2014 apologized to the

victims of forced adoptions in Australia; and therefore calls on the Government to apologize in order to go some way towards helping the parents and children who were victims of these practices (Australian Parliament, Inquiry of Forced Adoption Practices, 2014).

It is clear that more of apologies and admissions are necessary so natural mothers can find validation and healing. These apologies and admissions should be issued by the United States' federal and state governments and other countries who also practiced forced adoptions.

CHAPTER 27

EUGENICS, SOCIAL ENGINEERING & CHILD TRAFFICKING

*Such good blood of our own kind as there may be among the
nations we shall acquire for ourselves, if necessary by taking
away the children and bringing them up among us.*

*Heinrich Himmler, Speech to SS Officers, Poznan,
Poland, 1943*

It is not too much of a stretch to characterize the BSE as
an experiment in social engineering. The so-called
professionals and experts in adoption were well-aware that
they were changing lives by taking babies away from their
natural mothers and families and giving them to other
people. That was the whole point, whether adoption
workers had benign or positive motivations ("best interest
of the child") or darker motives involving a desire to
punish unmarried mothers. Along the way, the adoption
world became associated with issues of heredity and
eugenics. In some cases, the actions of adoption authorities
even veered into the child-trafficking lane.

In 1984, *Time* magazine quoted a family court judge in
South Carolina as saying, "Even if baby selling does exist,
what's so horrible about that? If the child is going to a
home with good parents who can give it all the love and
security it will ever need, why should we care if the parents

313

paid $50,000 for the privilege? The child is happy, the parents are happy, so what is the harm?" The terms "good parents" and "happy parents" appear to have left out the perspective of the natural parents in this judge's view, however.

The idea that when money is paid for something, the return on investment of that money becomes an issue, and whatever has been paid for becomes thought of as a commodity. This happened among adoption professionals and adopting parents, who began to question whether they had "gotten a good one" for their money. This, in turn, gave rise to questions about heredity.

While child welfare workers recognized the importance for every child of having a permanent home of his own, there was at one time so much fear about the possible effects of heredity on the child that it was very difficult to find adoptive homes for even the most attractive babies. As knowledge about the influences of environment in the development of children became more generally known, the idea of adoption became more acceptable, eventually growing into an overwhelming demand for healthy white infants (Mayo, 1962).

With the professionalization of social work, the training of adoption workers included courses providing information about eugenics.

Hundreds of colleges and universities in the United States and Europe introduced eugenics into their curricula in the areas of biology, social work, public health and medicine, and 'sex hygiene'…feeble-mindedness was inherited largely through the mother. 'It seems certain that from this class come...illegitimate children'...supported contentions that 'defectives breed defectives' and was responsible for the growing burden on the taxpayer... From the chorus of complaints against 'incompetent' and 'immoral' parents emerged a consensus that the modern state must serve as the ultimate guardian of children's health and future... The term of confinement was too short to successfully retrain 'mentally deficient sex-delinquent' women... 'having borne illegitimate children'... The 1930 White House Conference on Child Health and Protection... had condemned social workers' past practice of breaking up families for 'reasons of poverty alone'... Yet in 1931... the sanction against breaking up families applied to 'all family homes worthy of the name home' and exempted families with 'unfit mothers'... Instead of suppressing the history of past eugenics work in Vermont, DPW social workers exploited the Eugenics Survey records in the 1940s to promote their own agendas (Gallagher, 1999).

In the social sciences, social engineering refers to efforts by governments, private groups, or media to influence attitudes and behaviors in society so that certain desired characteristics are produced in a specific population. The efforts of public and private adoption workers meet these criteria. Efforts by an adoption agency to place a child in an adoptive home that was wealthier and more socially "secure" than the home of the natural parent was seen as bringing benefits to the agency itself.

> [A]gencies considered adoptive parents suitable if they were desirable citizens of the community without consideration of what they were as people… other agencies considered their responsibility for the child fulfilled if the child was placed in a home offering financially or socially glamorous security for the child, a placement that would reward the agency also with greater, financially and socially glamorous, security. The emotional demands of adoptive parents were the essential criteria. Material or more superficial and socially significant needs of the child were the yardstick by which to measure the anticipated gains to the child (Shapiro, 1955).

By 1992, social critics acknowledged the real motivation for many adoptions.

> Adoption has been attacked as a practice that encourages promiscuity because it allows unmarried women to 'get away' with the consequences of their immoral behavior. It has also been condemned as an activity that allows rich, middle-class, childless couples to appropriate the children of the poor. All the fancy psychological theorizing to justify the practice is no more than an excuse to transfer the children of the weak and disadvantaged to the strong and prosperous (Howe, 1992).

In 2001, Audrey Marshall and Margaret McDonald, discussed the issue of "bad blood" and how it played into the adoption of infants:

> …not many people wanted to take a chance on a baby whose 'bad blood' might show up…added to these ideas, among the general public, were ill-informed notions about 'bad blood', the idea that the child carried within him or her the mark of the parents' 'sin'…Fears about 'bad blood' were still prevalent.

> [T]he popularity of adoption declined…due to the rhetoric deployed by the child welfare agencies and experts who justified the mass removal of children from morally and mentally unfit parents. As explained in 1955 by Justice Wise Polier (New York City's Children's Court)… 'Adoption was a rare and unusual thing, risked only with a brand new, beautiful and perfect baby known to have an excellent family history.' During the baby boom, the penance for a single mother's moral failing… was to surrender her child to a loving home inhabited by an… infertile married couple… courts could, and did, terminate her parental ties based on her out-of-wedlock status… the private maternity homes that had once counseled women to keep their children during the Eugenic Era… again changed tactics to convince women to

give up their children at birth (Marshall & McDonald, 2001).

Fears associated with adoption and so-called "bad seeds" provided a fertile ground for an interest in eugenics. Gena Cora in her study of the eugenics movement (1977) noted that, although doctors were not the only professionals promoting eugenics, they, together with university professors, provided the concept with a scientific validity. Early on, birth control proponent Margaret Sanger was an advocate of eugenics, outlining a plan to give "the unfit a choice of segregation or sterilization." By "unfit," she meant 'morons, mental defectives, epileptics, illiterates, paupers, unemployables, criminals, prostitutes, and dope fiends' who chose segregation would be put on farm lands and taught to work 'for the period of their entire lives.'

Corea went on to discuss the writings of doctors, professors, business people and others "among the most respected members of society" as setting forth:

> ... putting as yet nonexistent fertility control agents in the drinking water, would affect everyone equally but others would mainly afflict the poor: sterilization of unwed mothers, compulsory abortion of all out-of-wedlock pregnancies, elimination of welfare payments for mothers with more than two children, imposition of a 'child tax,' payments for those who undergo sterilizations and abortions. Planned Parenthood, the direct descendant of Sanger's birth control groups (which had themselves been involved in the

eugenics movement) joined the population control forces in 1962 (Corea, 1977).

Corea also quoted Herman J. Juller of Indiana University, an early worker in the field of genetics:

> 'The means exist right now of achieving a much greater, speedier and more significant genetic improvement of the population, by the use of selection, than could be effected by the most sophisticated methods of treatment of the genetic material that might be available in the twenty-first century.' Eugenics is sometimes regarded as divided into 'negative eugenics' and 'positive eugenics' ...eugenics must be a hit and miss business...it might be advantageous to a country, or any large group of people, to encourage selection...there are some who believe that it is currently deteriorating and that the people with poorer heredity are procreating more numerously than those with good heredity (Corea, 1977).

By 1991, the tendency of society to associate genetics and reproductive technology with the "inevitability" of genetics was recognized. "It is thus the social context and not just the availability of reproductive technology that gives some credence to the fear that reproductive technology may ultimately produce unsavory consequences. (Greil, 1991).

Some of the factors and processes contributing to the continued influence of eugenics on American society in the 1950s had a regional component. For example, "Few sterilizations occurred in the 1930s in North Carolina (and some of the other southern states) because the Great Depression resulted in funding crises that didn't allow for sterilization to occur in full force in the South. Sterilization picked up pace after WWII, especially during the 1950s" (Woolridge, 1997).

> Women that were deemed 'subnormal' intellectually were also likely to be forcibly sterilized… Women, including wives, daughters, sisters and unwed mothers, were over-represented. They were labeled as either 'promiscuous, lazy, or unfit'… Women that were social workers were strong supporters for the eugenics movement… women were often coerced and that many social workers provided sterilization as an opportunity to save money from future drains on society… eugenics was a key element of progressive reform and was indicative of the new mentality surrounding sexuality and the standard gender roles of the time' [emphasis added] (Woolridge, 1997).

Having read the above, one can argue easily that this "new mentality" had a deep and pervasive influence on how social workers and society viewed and treated "unwed" mothers throughout the 50s and 60s, in other words, throughout the entire Baby Scoop Era, especially where saving the "drains on society," not to mention the severe and unforgiving view of sexual morality, were concerned.

In 2012, Charissa Keup shared in Girls in Trouble: a History of Female Adolescent Sexuality in the Midwest, 1946-1964 that a "…boy's crimes were 'primarily against property,' the court system thought girls usually posed a sexual or eugenic threat to the individual offender or to society" (Rembis, 2011).

A MOTHER'S STORY / *Carla*

I was so busy with my college studies at the University of Kansas. I had gotten pregnant on a night out during a play practice of "Gypsy" and didn't get an excuse from the director when rehearsal ran late. A carful of older theater students waited while I rang the bell of my dormitory and no one was sitting there as they should have been. It was mid-October and starting to get chilly. They invited me back to this communal house and played cards, and when I got sleepy, I asked where I should sleep. I had already had some dates with one of the guys, so the woman I asked where I should sleep took me to his bed, but I didn't actually realize it was his bed.

I truly had never slept with a guy before....was a virgin. My parents hadn't told me anything about sex. My mom just said stay out of the bushes, or something like that. I never had any counseling on sex, and for that matter, no one counseled me at the hospital or sent me any social workers, just nurses telling me that if I didn't want my baby Catholic, then she should go to a "Christian Protestant" couple...it was like a kind of religious "bait and switch"....it happened so fast...it felt like a kidnapping.

I hadn't even considered adoption at all; the word never entered my mind as I went to give birth in the Leavenworth hospital. It was a scheme planned behind my back by the woman I was staying with in a room at her house and a friend of hers. I learned about it after I woke up from anesthesia. My baby was not in the window, and I demanded to know why. I yelled and screamed for a few days, and they wouldn't tell me where my baby was. I hadn't told my parents or anyone. The doctor wouldn't even tell me anything.

This woman Donna who worked at my job in the advertising dept. was renting the house in the town where I'd gotten a summer job. In hindsight, I had made the big mistake of saying yes when she asked if I was "P.G." She brought me to this doctor in the weeks leading up to my giving birth. My water broke in the morning and she drove me to the Catholic hospital. I wasn't even Catholic. I wasn't told anything about delivery, what giving birth was like. At one of my appointments, I asked the doctor what it would be like and Dr. Snow, there in Leavenworth, Kansas, in the summer of 1968, said, "Don't worry, I'll take care of everything!" I trusted him (unfortunately for me).

Donna came to see me in the hospital and asked me if I liked Betty and her husband, who worked at the local penitentiary in Leavenworth. Betty was the bookkeeper at my job and interestingly enough had quit her job the day before I gave birth. I asked, "Why, is Betty trying to take my baby away from me? They won't bring my baby to me." Donna started explaining that Betty arranged with Doctor Snow to have him adopt my baby girl and that she knew about all my appointments and everything. It was like this conspiracy behind my back!

I was so angry and demanded my baby!!! In hindsight, I wish I'd called the police and made a report on the four of them, including the doctor, the lady I was staying with who I thought was so nice and the bookkeeper at the newspaper and her husband!! I didn't know any better and still didn't call my family on the farm about four hours away. They were busy with wheat harvest while I was having this crisis, and I was thinking I shouldn't "bother" them, that people would know that I had had sex this one time (in my little religious community) and how mixed up people's minds were back then. I should have told ANYONE but a Protestant minister in Leavenworth.

I was able to hold my baby finally, nurse her with a bottle as they took away my ability to breast-feed without telling me at Saint John Catholic Hospital. They only gave me minutes with her before taking my precious baby away, I called her Rene Marie.

I believe it was the minister who sent a stranger into my room. The stranger turned out to be a lawyer for a different couple. I have no memory how this lawyer was able to get my baby away from me. I feel in hindsight I was drugged and traumatized and shamed for having a baby and not being married. I told the nurses the name of the father of my baby. I told them my parents, but the father, Harley, was not contacted, nor were my parents.

Mr. Cochran said things like the minister sent him to "help" me. I remember the word "help..." Their only "help" was manipulating my baby away from me. The lawyer (who I didn't know was a lawyer, was just told by the Protestant minister. I said I wasn't even Catholic and what was I doing in a Catholic hospital!!!? Betty and her husband, who started this whole baby-napping scheme behind my back, were Catholic and perhaps also Dr. Snow). You can't trust anyone when you keep your pregnancy a secret and delay what to do.

I sent over the years requests for documents from that hospital and from the doctor (telling him off on the phone for what he did to me)...the doctor never even came back to see me in the hospital after I nixed his planned adoption (I always wondered if they were going to tell me my baby died...I think in hindsight my mind was foggy from being put under anesthesia after hearing a nurse yell "it's a girl!" plus "calming medication" after I was demanding to see my baby after waking up groggy from the anesthesia (which was never discussed with me or whether I wanted my ability to breast-feed taken from me, which would have bonded me to my newborn!!). It was horrendous the way I was treated. Outrageous.

I told my mother after I went back to my summer job in Leavenworth. She and my father continued to try to get my baby back, to no avail. The county social work department had determined this was a good home.

Years later, after having a talk with the adoptive father, he said no one ever came to their home, that they had seen a little baby in the arms of another couple at church and they wanted a little baby girl also. They asked how to get a baby girl. They were given the name of Mr. Cochran, who specialized in "Christian adoptions." Two weeks later, Mr. Cochran and his secretary handed them my baby girl. The lawyer charged a fee to my daughter's parents.

He got my child through his slick-talking, asking me a series of questions: How can you afford this big hospital bill? How can you take care of her, you're still in college, etc. He told me the baby needs an experienced mother, the adoptive already had an adopted boy a year older, the woman was a homemaker and the man had good job as an engineer. My needs were not considered at all. All manipulation. No mention that I had parents, aunts and uncles, my child's father's parents, aunts and uncles, etc. There was no mention that their politics were not the same as mine. The "engineer" I learned later worked for a company in Kansas City that made atomic bombs, completely different than my Mennonite upbringing. Contacting them years later (my mother and father helped a lot and my brother and his wife), I learned they wanted nothing to do with me or my subsequent son seven years later, that they don't consider me a friend. "We don't want to be friends with you!"

I am treated completely as an exiled mother. There was a period that my daughter and I wrote letters to each other between the time she was 18 and 23, but she couldn't meet because she said that "would hurt" her "adoptive parents." My hurt is unimportant. She stopped writing letters when she got married. Her adoptive mother once told my son on the phone, "Your mother bothered us for 14 years." So now I haven't "bothered" them (inquiring how things are going and saying hello) for the past 14 years. Her adoptive father David was on a mission to convert anyone, asking me on the phone once years ago, "If you died right now, do you know if you are going to heaven or hell?" It was a helluva situation loving a child and her being taken before I could even recover from giving birth back in what is now called the Baby Scoop Era. I still love my child, now grown-up. I am in exile.

IN CLOSING

Ethical: Being in accordance with the accepted principals of right and wrong that govern the conduct of a profession

The Free Dictionary

Every time a newborn was removed from an unmarried but willing mother whose civil, human and legal rights were ignored, could be deemed an illegal act. The surrender of children by unmarried mothers was accepted by state and federal governments, by adoption agencies, by society, and by the parents of the unmarried mothers.

Society believed that those surrenders involved unmarried mothers who had their civil, human and legal rights fully enforced and protected. However, as the contents herein reveal, in many cases, they were not. Some still might believe that these mothers were offered choices. That they were offered information. That they were offered help and support. But often they were not. Many were not offered the choice to parent their own children. In order to make an informed decision, to have a real choice, these mothers would have had to be offered at least two fully discussed options from which to choose. Many were only given only one...surrender.

Adoption workers in agencies and in maternity homes know this to be true. The adoption industry knows this to be true. Generally, the public does not. Why? Because those who make money from infant adoption do not want The Truth to be known. The multi-billion-dollar annual profit generated by the adoption industry relies upon the removal of babies from young, unprotected, unsupported, vulnerable, mostly minor, unmarried mothers. Where else would potential adopters (the ones viewed as "more worthy," i.e., wealthier) get children to raise if not from frightened single mothers with few, if any, resources and protections?

In 2000, adoption industry profits totaled more than more than $1.5 billion dollars annually. Many thousands of people depend upon income and other benefits derived from the surrender of children for adoption; adoption workers, lawyers, judges, legislators - all of whom collect paychecks in some way from infant adoptions. The old saying goes, "Money corrupts... and it corrupts absolutely." There was a great deal of money to be made from mother and child separation during the Baby Scoop Era, and there even more so today.

Adoption workers are appointed the task of helping American citizens. They exist to help all, regardless of age, gender, income or martial status. They should help single mothers obtain child support. They should help them keep their infants, obtain child care and learn parenting skills. They should help them obtain job training, secure employment and housing. This is their duty as social agents. This is how our tax dollars are supposed to be used - to help not to hurt.

"Adoption" workers should be removed from the pregnancy, labor and delivery of single mothers. "Adoption" workers are inherently biased towards adoption. It could be claimed that having an "adoption" worker involved in an unmarried female's pregnancy is a conflict of interest.

Infant adoption is all about money. Who has it and who doesn't. Who makes a living from the separation of mother and child? Are these issues not of serious concern? Isn't this social engineering? The money comes from potential adopters in the form of fees and/or donations. Either way, money is money. Payment is payment. Donation is payment.

This arrangement is not questioned by society because the general public trusts that adoption workers do their jobs properly. That they will live by the high standards of their profession and help all citizens. That they will properly serve the public and do their socially entrusted duty.

Who made motherhood illegal? It certainly appeared to be during the Baby Scoop Era when money entered the picture; when playing God became a profession, when punishing a white, teenage, mostly middle-class white female became a "cure" for her "sins," "neurosis" and "deviancy;" and when the enormous demand for white infants by white potential adopters created such a lucrative market.

Why did so many adopters work in adoption agencies, adoption organizations, and legislative entities? The inclusion of adopters into these arenas could be viewed as a conflict of interest and ultimately dangerous to unmarried mothers and their at risk infants.

Based on twenty years of research regarding the Baby Scoop Era and the surrendering mother experience, I contend that what occurred during the Baby Scoop Era was highly unethical, improper and probably even illegal.

Could the removal of a baby from a loving and willing single mother during the Baby Scoop Era be considered legalized kidnapping? Could these mothers, who were pressured and coerced, have been unwilling accomplices to the legalized theft of their own babies? In most cases, those mothers could do nothing to stop the adoption mandate. In fact, some single mothers who did try to keep their babies found themselves, like criminals, in front of judges who threatened them with lock-up in a mental ward or juvenile detention facility until their signatures were obtained. Some were threatened with steep medical, foster and maternity home bills to reimburse before their baby would be released to them.

Were these methods of operation legal? Were these practices moral and ethical? Were mothers really given a choice? Did these mothers really make a decision, much less a fully informed one?

A United States Government Investigation into Baby Scoop Era adoption practices is in order to learn the answers to these critically important, and long overdue, questions. These mothers deserve answers.

APPENDICES

APPENDIX A

TERMINOLOGY: THE NAME GAME

The terminology set known as "Positive or Respectful Adoption Language" (RAL) has proven to be a useful tool for the Adoption Industry and people who adopt to reframe adoption in such a way as to make it more socially palatable to the public. However, this "redefining" also renders invisible some inconvenient truths which should be held under greater social scrutiny, and dismisses the experiences of many who have been affected by this industry, particularly mothers who have been separated from children by infant adoption. How does the use of language contribute to the industrialization of adoption and the marginalization and objectification of mothers who have been, and continue to be, separated from their children by domestic infant adoption? This terminology set has since spread to other English-speaking nations as well.

In the United States, Minnesota adoption employee Marietta Spencer is generally credited with developing this terminology set, first presented in 1979 in Child Welfare. She proposed that the industry and adoptive parents take leadership of adoption-related discourse and terminology:

> Social service professionals and adoptive parents should take responsibility for providing informed and sensitive leadership in the use of words. For adoptive parents, a

> positive use of vocabulary may encourage
> open communication within their families.
> For professionals, the choice of vocabulary
> helps shape service content... (Spencer, 1979).

This statement serves to approve and normalize the ownership of adoption-related discourse by adopters and adoption agencies, with the potential consequence of removing from "approved discourse," and thereby silencing, the words and experiences of those separated by these adoption: natural parents and adopted persons.

RAL, now the official terminology used by the adoption industry in the United States and elsewhere, redefines adoption in two ways. First, it portrays adoption as equivalent to having given birth to a child. In order to accomplish this, RAL employs two tools: using birth terms to define some mothers and fathers as being former mothers and fathers after the reproductive process is complete, and using the term meeting to replace the term adoption reunion.

In the second way, it redefines adoption to cover an inconvenient truth: the possibility that the mother may have wanted to keep her baby, and perhaps did not willingly surrender. In order to eliminate these questions, RAL again uses two tools: labelling the surrender of a child for adoption as voluntarily placing, and removing attention from the role of the adoption industry worker by defining adoption as being a 3-party triad.

Creating Ex-Mothers Through the Use of Birth Terms

The earliest confirmed usage of the term birth mother was in an article by Pearl S. Buck: "When we wanted to adopt her, however, the birth mother took her back again"

(Buck, 1955). Buck again used both birth mother and birth parent: "If it is better for the child born out of wedlock to stay with his birth mother, what can be done to change social attitudes ..." (Buck, 1956, p. 63) and "...a family of the same religion as the birth parents professed" (Buck, 1955, p. 65). And finally, Buck said "Her birth mother was a girl in a small town in Germany" (Buck, 1972).

In 1974, the terms birth mother and birth parent began to appear in social work journals (e.g. Pannor et al., 1974; Sorosky et al., 1974; Sorosky et al., 1975). Prior to this, natural parents and relinquishing parents were the social and industry standard terms.

Buck's intentions for the term are unclear, but in RAL, "birth mother" denotes a woman who ceases to be a mother to her child after the reproductive act, with the adopting parents possessing exclusive parenthood from that point onwards.

Social worker Marietta Spencer (1979) defines a "birth parent" as being a "non-parent" by using numerous examples in her article which validate the sole parenthood of adopters after the adoption of a child, implying that no emotional or familial connections remain between members of the pre-existing family:

> An adoptive mother becomes the child's parent through the transfer of parental rights. Although she can never become the child's birth or biological parent, socially, functionally, and finally she does the permanent mothering of the child. In terms of the time continuum, she is the successor to the biological mother (Spencer, 1980).

Granting exclusive motherhood to the female adopter as the child's sole female parent (opposite sex adopters) eliminates the natural mother from any claim, either singular or joint, to this title. The result of this exclusion of the natural mother whose infant is adopted is that she thereby defaults to having served a solely physical reproductive purpose, becoming no more than a "breeder."

In fact, evidence of the adoption industry's treatment of some mothers as "breeders" is seen early in its own literature. Adoption worker Leontine Young stated, "The tendency growing out of the demand for babies is to regard unmarried mothers as *breeding machines*... [by people intent] upon securing babies for quick adoptions" [emphasis added] (L. Young, 1953). Perlman follows with "Sometimes social workers in adoption agencies have facetiously suggested setting up social provisions for more '*baby breeding*'" (Perlman, 1965). The objectification of women which results from the semantic construction of woman-as-uterus illustrates the irony of the term "Respectful Adoption Language." This concept of an ex-mother is also specific to adoption. Divorced mothers are not defined as being former mothers even if the father has sole custody. Mothers who have died in childbirth are not considered to be ex-mothers, nor are mothers whose infants have died at birth.

Policy analyst Joss Shawyer remarked how the term "birth mother" denies the existence of any post-birth bond, emotions, or relationship between mother and child: "To call her the 'birth mother' instead of the 'natural mother' allows her only the physical birth and denies her those feelings she wasn't supposed to have" (Shawyer, 1979, 62). However, numerous studies have shown that mothers separated from their children by adoption still experience an intense maternal connection to their children and prolonged grief resulting from the separation. The dynamics of adoption reunion show evidence that a strong emotional bond between mother and child can survive despite decades of separation.

Oppressed groups often discover dignity and empowerment in choosing words to define themselves. As a means of resisting repression, marginalization, oppression, and degradation, they begin to recognize their power and right to self-definition.

For this reason, many mothers who are separated from children by adoption are choosing alternatives to the term birth mother, rejecting terms which define them as being non-mothers, and choosing instead to use terms which reflect the continuity of motherhood and a mother's love for her child, e.g. mother, natural mother, mother of adoption loss or exiled mother.

Exiled mother is defined as:

> A natural mother whose child was lost to, or taken for, adoption solely because of her age and income vulnerabilities and lack of information and resources -- not because of negligence or abuse. She is an unrecognized mother who has been thrown away, banished and discarded by her parents, social workers, the adoption industry and society, who deemed her unworthy to raise her own child (Wilson-Buterbaugh, 2001).

Erasing Reunions

A second tool that is used in RAL to linguistically extinguish recognition of a relationship between mother and child is the renaming of a common event known as adoption reunion, which occurs when family members who were separated from each other reconnect once again. Instead of reunion, RAL prescribes the term meeting as being the proper term for the re-entry of mother and child into one another's lives. Johnston (2004) illustrates this with: "Frequently news stories refer to reunions between people who are related genetically but have not been raised in the same family… The more objective descriptor for a meeting between a child and the birthparents... is meeting." The use of the adjective "objective" implies that the term reunion is subjective, emotionally derived, and thereby questionable.

The term meeting has many uses in everyday language, including a business function, contact between strangers, and sporting events. In an adoption related context, meeting denies the physical and emotional connectedness of pregnancy. It excludes shared genetics and emotional connection. The term reunion is thus an appropriate descriptor when the adoptee reunites with his or her natural parents. Mother and child were united until separation occurred, as Chamberlain (1995) describes: "Few things can compare with the oneness between mother and baby during gestation. The connections are total and holistic, embracing mind, emotion, and sensation." In addition, family reunion is the term used for a common event where many members of an extended family gather, with many possibly not having prior contact, but all recognizing a shared genetic connection and shared family history.

By deliberate replacement in adoption-related discourse of terms such as "relinquish," surrender," "give up" and "lose" by terms such as "decision," "place," "choice," "adoption plan," as the universal description in all cases, the issue of coercion no longer becomes part of the discourse. No matter what the circumstances of the surrender were, the separation of mother from child automatically has become a "decision" that the mother has made, implying free will, implying multiple options available to her, and implying informed consent. This assumption of the mother's sole responsibility for the "placement" of her child has far reaching consequences.

Hiding the Broker: The Adoption Triad

In the 1970s, the adoption industry introduced the model of the adoption "triad" to describe the parties who have been affected by adoption. Books such as *The Adoption Triangle* (Baran, Sorosky & Pannor, 1978) popularised the image of adoption as a 3-party event.

However, O'Shaughnessy states in his ground-breaking work *Adoption, Social Work, and Social Theory: Making the Connections*:

> Triangularization removes a range of institutions and actors (including social workers) from the primary picture of adoption, encouraging the misrecognition of adoptions as a private consensual transaction between, and in the interests of, members of the triangle. Important dimensions of the social location and function of adoption are thereby denied or blended out of analysis (O'Shaughnessy, 1994).

If the woman has not made the decision about adoption of her own free will, then which party made the decision to influence her? How were methods of influence chosen, or not chosen? What was the intention behind the application of these methods? Was there a profit motive involved, or there a perception by the worker that any child is better off with married parents than with a single mother? These questions cannot be asked if adoption is solely conceptualized as being a triad or triangle with no external agent.

A decision obviously has been made in each case of adoption. However, the question remains: Were these decisions made by mothers themselves or by professionals who could structure the adoption agency counselling and the maternity "home" and hospital experiences to insure the outcome desired by the professional? Social historian Solinger wrote:

> While motherhood as a state-of-being was apotheosized by the culture at large in the post war years, only 'good' and properly married mothers were inviolate. For the others, 'mother' was an honorific that could be bestowed or denied by the judgments of professionals (Solinger, 1990).

These "professionals" who had the power to bestow or deny motherhood on a woman, these gatekeepers who held the ability to enable a mother to keep her baby or not, were for the most part social workers, and hence exist the ethical issues that must be dealt with by the social work profession. However, the role of "gatekeeper" was not limited to the social work profession. Clergy, nuns, nurses, physicians, lawyers, judges or laypeople employed, contracted, or enlisted by adoption agencies all may have a role to play in either supporting or denying the mother's presence in the life of her child. In the role of providing post-adoption counselling services, domestic social workers may also become aware of the role of these 4th parties in an international context, be it families created by unscrupulous international adoption agencies which may have engaged in "child laundering" (Smolin, 2005; Allen, 2009), or former inmates of institutions such as the Magdalene Laundries whose babies may have been transferred overseas (Justice for Magdalenes, 2011; Millotte, 2011).

The adoption worker and her agency's role and influence as the "4th party" in the adoption transaction also continues past the surrender in the form of promises made to clients, such as "an adoptive family is the same as any other family," and "adoptive parents will be the only parents." Again, these concepts are embodied in the RAL terminology set. Some adoption agencies attempt to protect these promises through "post-adoption services" that attempt to maintain the separation of natural parent from child, even upon reunion. Spencer describes how an agency can try to ensure continuation of the separation through directive counseling for the natural family: "Through preparation before the meeting, Eric's birthparents learned that he would never 'rejoin' their own family unit as a 10th child, but is wholly tied in with his parents and the family who adopted him 35 years ago" (Spencer, 1998). But adoptive parents are sometimes shocked when these agency promises are shattered upon reunion, when an adoptee searches for his/her natural family, when the natural family searches for the adopted person, or when the reunited family members work to restore their emotional/social family relationship once reunited. As described by Redmond and Sleightholm:

> Adoptive parents often feel betrayed by the prospect of government sanctioned reunion registries… The moment the infant was placed in their arms, he or she belonged to them alone: hence the rationale behind altering the birth certificate and retaining the original in a sealed file (Sleightholm, 1982).

The question should be asked whether responsibility for this disappointment lies with adoption agencies that have mislead prospective adoptive parents into believing that adoption is "just like giving birth" and will provide them with "a child all their own." Is it fair to the child being adopted when an agency makes a lifetime guarantee of "loyalty" on behalf of the child, without the knowledge or consent of that child? The role of RAL in affirming the "sole parenthood" of adoptive parents, relegation of the natural mother to being solely a birth-giver, and erasure of any remaining connection or bond between the separated mother and her child, should be examined.

Perhaps a better term to replace adoption triad would be adoption transaction, recognizing adoption as involving 4 parties (agency, customer, mother, and child) each holding differing degrees of financial and social power, decision-making ability, and freedom of choice. It has been suggested that the power dynamics in the adoption transaction can be viewed as an imbalance of power and decision-making ability: On one hand the mother and baby lack the social support, financial power, and choice to remain together. On the other hand, the "broker" (agency, facilitator, or lawyer) and the paying customer hold greater power and choice; i.e., the broker having the power to separate mother and baby, to offer the baby to a client for adoption, and to financially profit from this separation; and the customer having the choice whether or not to adopt and financial ability to obtain the baby from the broker. On the basis of extensive research, Solinger describes this lack of choice on the part of a mother who loses her child: "Almost everybody believes that on some level, [mothers] made a choice to give their babies away. Here, I argue that adoption is rarely about mothers' choices; it is, instead, about the abject choicelessness of some resourceless women" (Solinger, 2001).

Discussion

The rise in for-profit adoption, both domestic and international has produced a new commercialisation of the adoption process and an accompanying risk of exploitation for vulnerable families. RAL was defined and created by this industry to play a distinct role in redefining adoption. It has proven to be an effective tool: selling adoption as a "service" while profiting from each transaction, camouflaging those aspects which might be "distasteful" to the public, objectifying mothers as being biological "producers" of babies, and reducing public recognition of the role of industry workers in the separation of mother and child.

However, is RAL accurate in its definition and portrayal of mothers who have not made a willful choice -- free of all pressure or manipulation -- to be separated from their babies? Its ubiquity and acceptance in adoption discourse should not prevent it from being scrutinized in terms of both its accuracy in portraying adoption and the ethics of defining and objectifying a vulnerable social class. In essence, RAL may play a role in normalizing the dehumanizing and exploitation of these mothers, and this very fact should provide reason for it to be questioned.

APPENDIX B

LEGAL PROTECTIONS, DEFINITIONS & OTHER RELEVANT ISSUES

The Baby Scoop Era was a collaborative campaign of doctors, attorneys, adoption agencies and associated adoption social workers to isolate traumatized, single, white females and new mothers. Some legal protections that would pertain to unmarried mothers are provided below for consideration.

Mother and child separation, without proven abuse and/or neglect, constitutes an abridgement of privilege. Of course we don't like to think of our own children as "property," but anything that "belongs" to a person, such as family could well fit under the definition of this Amendment. Therefore the removal of newborns or infants from an untested, not abusing or neglecting mother simply because she is unmarried and without resources, appear to be a violation of Article 7 under Amendment XIV of the United States Constitution, which declares that:

> No State shall make or enforce any law which shall abridge the privileges or immunities of citizens of the United States; nor shall any State deprive any person, life, liberty, or property, without due process of

law; nor deny to any person within its jurisdiction the equal protection of the laws.

In addition, no United States citizen should ever be punished for a crime for which they have not be duly convicted declares Amendment XIII, Sections (1) and (2) of the United States Constitution:

> Section 1. Neither slavery nor involuntary servitude, except as a punishment for crime whereof the party shall have been duty convicted, shall exist within the United States, or any place subject to their jurisdiction; Section 2. Congress shall have power to enforce this article by appropriate legislation.

Most of the following definitions come from *Black's Law Dictionary*.

BAD FAITH. The opposite of "good faith," general implying or involving actual or constructive fraud, or a design to mislead or deceive another, or a neglect or refusal to fulfill some duty or some contractual obligation, not prompted by an honest mistake as to one's rights or duties, but by some interested or sinister motive. The term bad faith is not simply bad judgment or negligence, but rather it implies the conscious doing of a wrong because of dishonest purpose... it is different from the negative idea of negligence in that it contemplates a state of mind affirmatively operating with furtive design or ill will.

BREACH OF DUTY. Any violation or omission of a legal or moral duty... the neglect or failure to fulfill, in a just and proper manner, the duties of an office or...

employment... whether willful and fraudulent, or done
through negligence or arising through mere oversight or
forgetfulness, is a breach of duty.

BRIBERY. The act of giving money, goods or other
forms of recompense to a recipient in exchange for an
alteration of their behavior (to the benefit/interest of the
giver) that the recipient would otherwise not alter. Bribery
is defined by Black's Law Dictionary as the offering, giving,
receiving, or soliciting of any item of value to influence the
actions of an official or other person in charge of a public
or legal duty.

BULLYING Uses superior strength or influence to
intimidate (someone), typically to force him or her to do
what one wants.

CAMPAIGN Work in an organized and active way
toward a particular goal, typically a political or social one.

CHOICE. The act of choosing; the act of picking or
deciding between two or more possibilities; the opportunity
or power to choose between two or more possibilities; the
opportunity or power to make a decision; a range of things
that can be chosen.

COERCE AND COERCION. Compelled to
compliance; constrained to obedience, or submission...
compelling by force... as where [she would be]
constrained... to do what [her] free will would refuse.

COERCIVE ORGANIZATION. Uses force to create
a strict environment of rules and regulations. Once you

enter a coercive organization, you are not allowed to leave unless under special circumstances. Membership is usually involuntary. There are strict rules that you must follow once you enter, and individuals usually go through the process of resocialization, being stripped of their former status as an individual and given a new identity.

COLLECTIVE TRAUMA. Trauma that happens to large groups of individuals... symptoms of collective trauma include rage, depression, denial, survivor guilt, and internalized oppression, as well as physiological changes in the brain and body which can bring on chronic disease (Garrigues, 2013).

COLLUSION. Secret or illegal cooperation or conspiracy, especially in order to cheat or deceive others; illegal cooperation or conspiracy, especially between ostensible opponents in a lawsuit.

COMPLEX POST-TRAUMATIC STRESS DISORDER (C-PSTD). Psychological injury that results from protracted exposure to prolonged social and/or interpersonal trauma in the context of dependence, captivity or entrapment (a situation lacking a viable escape route for the victim), which results in the lack or loss of control, helplessness and deformations of identity and sense of self... traumas in which there is an actual or perceived inability for the victim to escape... elements include captivity, psychological fragmentation the loss of a sense of safety, trust and self-worth, as well as the tendency to be revictimized... there is a loss of a coherent sense of self.

CONFLICT OF INTEREST. Refers to a clash between public interest and a private, direct interest related to money in an action or case.

CRIMINAL CONSPIRACY. An agreement between two or more people to commit a crime or to perpetrate an illegal act… While intent is key in any federal conspiracy case, only 'general intent' to violate the law is necessary; proof of the defendants' specific intent to violate the law is not needed, only an agreement to engage in an illegal act. The end may be legal, but the planned means are illegal

CRIMINAL INTENT. The intent to commit a crime: malice, as evidenced by a criminal act; an intent to deprive or defraud the true owner of his property. People v. Moore. 3 N. Y. Cr. R. 458/

CRUEL AND UNUSUAL PUNISHMENT. The Eighth Amendment to the United States Constitution forbids some punishments entirely, and forbids some other punishments that are excessive when compared to the crime, or compared to the competence of the perpetrator.

DUE PROCESS. The Fifth and Fourteenth Amendments to the United States Constitution each contain a due process clause. Due process deals with the administration of justice and thus the due process clause acts as a safeguard from arbitrary denial of life, liberty, or property by the Government outside the sanction of law.

DURESS. Coercion used by a person to induce another to act (or refrain from acting) in a manner [she] otherwise would not (or would); subjecting a person to improper pressure which overcomes [her] will and coerces [her] to comply with demand to which [she] would not yield if acting as a free agent.

ECONOMIC DURESS. Arises where one individual, acting upon another's fear of impending financial injury, unlawfully coerces the latter to perform an act in circumstances which prevent [her] exercise of free will.

EXTORTION. The practice of obtaining something, especially money, through force or threats.

EXTRINSIC FRAUD. Fraudulent acts which keep a person from obtaining information about his/her rights to enforce a contract or getting evidence to defend against a lawsuit. This could include destroying evidence or misleading an ignorant person about the right to sue. Extrinsic fraud is distinguished from "intrinsic fraud," which is the fraud that is the subject of a lawsuit

FALSE CONSENSUS EFFECT. Popular social phenomena where an individual believes that own beliefs, ideals, concepts, opinions, values and attitudes are held more widely within a certain population than they actually are.

FRAUD IN THE INDUCEMENT. The use of deceit or trick to cause someone to act to his/her disadvantage, such as signing an agreement or deeding away real property. The heart of this type of fraud is misleading the other party as to the facts upon which he/she will base his/her decision to act.

FRAUD. An intentional perversion of the truth for the purpose of inducing another in reliance upon it to part with some valuable thing belonging to [her] or to surrender a legal right; a false representation of matter of fact, whether by words or by conduct by false or misleading allegations, or by concealment of that which should have been disclosed, which deceives and is intended to deceive so that [she] shall act upon it to [her] legal injury; anything calculated to deceive by suppression of the truth. Generated from Clause 39 of the Magna Carta, "No free man shall be seized or imprisoned, or stripped of his rights or possessions, or outlawed or exiled, or deprived of his standing in any other way, nor will we proceed with force against him, or send others to do so, except by the lawful judgement of his equals or by the law of the land."

GRAFT. The acquisition of money, gain, or advantage by dishonest, unfair, or illegal means, especially through the abuse of one's position or influence in politics, business, etc. 2. a particular instance, method, or means of thus acquiring gain or advantage.

INFORMED CONSENT. A person's agreement to allow something to happen that is based on a full disclosure of facts needed to make the decision intelligently.

INJUSTICE. Lack of justice and equity; violation of the rights of another; wrong; an unjust act or deed; a crime.

INTENT TO DEFRAUD. An intention to deceive another person, and to induce such other person, in reliance upon such deception, to assume, create, transfer, alter, or terminate a right, obligation, or power with reference to property.

INVOLUNTARY. Without will or power of choice; opposed to... desire; an involuntary act is that which is performed with constraint, or with repugnance, or without the will to do it; an action is involuntary which is performed under duress, force, or coercion... [if] it was arbitrary, if it offended society's sense of justice, or if it was not more effective than a less severe penalty.'

LATERAL VIOLENCE. Includes gossip, shaming, blaming, putting down of others...when violence is aimed at one's own people.

MARGINALIZATION. The process of according less importance to something or someone moved away from the inner workings of the group. A social phenomenon of excluding a minority, subgroup, or undesirables by ignoring their needs, desires, and expectations.

PATERNALISM. The policy or practice on the part of people in positions of authority of restricting the freedom and responsibilities of those subordinate to them.

TRAUMATIC GRIEF or COMPLICATED MOURNING. Both trauma and grief coincide...If a traumatic event was life threatening, but did not result in death, then it is more likely that the survivor will experience post-traumatic stress symptoms. If a person dies, and the survivor was close to the person who died, then it is more likely that symptoms of grief will also develop. When the death is of a loved one, and was sudden or violent, then both symptoms often coincide...for C-PTSD to manifest,

the violence would occur under conditions of captivity, loss
of control and disempowerment (Bradshaw, 2011).

UNDUE INFLUENCE. Persuasion, pressure, or
influence short of actual force, but stronger than mere
advice, that so overpowers [her] free will or judgment that
[she] cannot act intelligently and voluntarily, but acts,
instead, subject to the will or purposes of the dominating
party... urgency of persuasion whereby [she] is
overpowered and [she] is induced to do or forbear an act
which [she] would not do if left to act freely... Misuse of
position of confidence or taking advantage of [her]
weakness, infirmity, or distress to change improperly [her]
actions or decisions.

APPENDIX C

CHILD WELFARE LEAGUE
ADOPTION PRACTICE STANDARDS

The Child Welfare League of America (CWLA) is the oldest child welfare organization in the United States. Its goal was to make issues related to children a national priority. It is the only national organization that includes members from both private and public entitles.

The CWLA, originally located in New York City, was founded in 1921 as a federation of some 70 service providers. It later moved to Washington, D.C.

In 1978, the CWLA issued guidelines for appropriate adoption practice standards, as follows:

> *Services to enable parents to carry or resume their responsibilities* ...These services should include family services, financial assistance, day care, protective and homemaker services, and other social casework and treatment *services to children in their own homes*... The parents are given information about the agency's services, policies and procedures; *their legal rights* and responsibilities...

To preserve the child-parent relationship to the fullest extent possible... To enable parents to perform the parental role as fully as they can... To *insure parent's exercise of their legal rights...* Unnecessary *limitation of parent rights may weaken family ties...* the agency...should operate consistently within the framework of the rights it has assumed and *the rights that the child's parents retain...*

...any action to limit or terminate parent's rights must be taken by *proper legal procedure and in a court* of competent jurisdiction... All social workers must have professional training. The casework director should have had at least five years of experience as a casework supervisor... *Special requirements for caseworkers include: Conviction about the child's need to belong to his own family and about parental rights.*

Services to children in their own homes are needed *to strengthen and maintain families, to preserve for the child the values in his own home,* and *to prevent the need for placement.* These *services include financial assistance, particularly Aid to Families with Dependent Children, family service;* homemaker service, *day care service, protective service, public health services;* media and *psychiatric services;* recreational and *group work services; school* and social work.... enactment or improvement of legislation pertaining to... the custody and guardianship of children, *parental rights...* public assistance, and other provisions *to promote and safeguard the welfare and rights of children and parents.*

No children should be deprived of care by their parents solely because of their economic need, or their need for other forms of community assistance to reinforce their efforts to maintain a home for them. Services for natural parents should...*include services and resources required to meet their physical, emotional, and material needs, and to protect their rights... Services provided for unmarried parents should not be contingent on a decision to place the child for adoption.*

Such a decision should be regarded as the right of the parent. It should be made without pressure and with full consideration of alternative plans... If they decide to keep their child, and services needed by them are not available within the agency, *they should be helped to obtain them from appropriate community services.* These may include...*temporary foster family care, and financial assistance.*

...under our law, *the natural parents...*have the *right to custody and control of children born to them... parents including an unmarried parent, may not be deprived of these rights...*

Work homes (in which board and lodging are provided in return for services) and wage homes (in which a small salary is paid in addition to board and lodging) *should be used only in exceptional situations...*

A relinquishment should not be taken... until after the child is born and the mother has recovered from the effects of the delivery.

The decision about whether the mother should see her baby after should be made on an individual basis *by the mother* and the social worker... *It should not be assumed that conflicts are minimized and relinquishment made easier when the mother does not see her child;* in some cases, guilt and later *emotional disturbance may be intensified under such circumstances.*

Infants... should be placed in the adoptive home at as early an age as possible, preferably in the first weeks of life, except...*the mother (or parents) have not had sufficient time or help to become fully ready to relinquish the child.*

Direct placement should be considered under the following conditions ...*the natural parents* have had casework help for a sufficient period of time prior to the child's birth *to consider alternative plans to understand what permanent relinquishment and direct placement would mean to them and to the child...* the natural parents have *had the opportunity to reconsider the plan after the child has been born and to reach a final decision...* The agency *has foster homes available to allow for a delay or change in plans if the natural parents need more time before making a final decision...* The natural parents and the adoptive parents *have had legal advice to protect them against acting under duress.*

It is not appropriate for the agency's counsel to represent all the parties to the adoption, in relation to their respective legal rights, duties, and responsibilities.

Under no circumstances should services to be contingent upon a decision to relinquish the child for adoption...

An adoption service should operate within a framework of law *to protect the rights* and *interests of all parties...* Legal protections required in adoption should assure that: *The best interests of the child are paramount; parental rights and responsibilities are safeguarded. The child will not be deprived unnecessarily neither of his own...*

No child should be considered legally free for adoption until parental rights have been terminated *through proper legal procedures...* the *mother, if they are not married* to each other, *have the right to custody and control of children born to them... guardianship belongs to* parents in the first instance. *The right of the parents must be exercised for the child's benefit...* The *termination of parental rights* is as important as the establishment of new parental ties through adoption, *and should be as securely safeguarded.*

Termination of parental rights and relationships involves and alters basic human and property rights.

The full protection of those rights ideally requires court approval. The legal presumptions against fraud and duress created by court approval make judicial procedures clearly superior... Agencies ... should however, be fully aware that the *adoption procedures may be attacked by the natural parents for alleged fraud or duress...*

A relinquishment... should be permanently binding and should be set aside only on *proof of fraud or duress...* A relinquishment to an authorized *agency should not be subject to revocation by reason of minor age of the parents.*

APPENDIX D

THE CHILDREN'S BUREAU

The Children's Bureau was a part of the Department of Labor until 1946 when it was moved to the Social Security Administration. In 1962, it became part of the Department of Health, Education, and Welfare along with the Social Security Administration.

In 1968, the Children's Bureau became part of the Social Rehabilitation Service, and in 1970 it was drawn into the Office of Child Development of the Public Health Service. Today it is a part of the Department of Health and Human Services' Administration for Children and Families.

What information did the Children's Bureau release about infant adoptions in the United States? What guidelines did they suggest for adoption practices?

In 1920, Emma Lundberg and Katharine Lenroot of the Children's Bureau shared that the natural mother is best for the child, not a substitute, and they suggested that unmarried mothers and their babies have been separated from each other when they should not have been. They said:

> Separation from the mother at a very early
> age is a common experience among children

born out of wedlock… In the case of a child of illegitimate birth the chances of being separated from the mother during early infancy are great (Lundberg & Lenroot, 1920).

Maud Morlock, of the Children's Bureau, was against the labeling of unmarried mothers. She also discussed how foster care for mother and child should be utilized:

> The service offered should…*not 'label' the mothers or set them apart…* Many social agencies, particularly the child-placing group, have become interested in the use of foster homes, but because of limited funds only a relatively small number of *agencies have developed programs of foster home care for unmarried mothers…* The use of *foster homes for unmarried mothers* is not an altogether new development…the foster mother who has boarded children successfully is asked by the agency to care for an unmarried mother…. *A minor unwed mother must be protected from making a hasty and improvident decision regarding her child* [emphasis added] (Morlock, 1935).

> The sooner the mother receives such help, the more satisfactory is *the protection given the baby.* She especially needs this help in making her decision whether to keep the baby… At present, *when people are clamoring for babies and will go to almost any extreme to obtain one for adoption…* Some *State laws try to protect the baby by refusing to recognize as legal any relinquishment of parental rights without court sanction.* In one State

a relinquishment by an unmarried mother *is voidable at any time within 120 days after it is signed*....Every effort should be made to have the original birth certificate accurate, and to preserve it, *for every person has a right to know who he is and who his people were [emphasis added]* (Morlock, 1946).

In 1953, the Children's Bureau issued a publication, "To Better Children's Chances," claiming that "Child welfare services are social services for children. They are usually provided by social workers who have some special training or experience in child welfare... *The first effort of a child welfare worker is to keep the family together"* [emphasis added] (Children Bureau, 1955).

In 1955, a report presented at a Children's Bureau conference stated that social agencies, since they have a monopoly on adoptions in some areas, should make sure that their practices are based on scientific evidence and that their practices are sound.

Because social agencies do have at least a partial monopoly on adoptions... *they have all the more responsibility to make certain that their practices are based upon known scientific evidence*... they have a *deep obligation to make certain that their practices are sound, that they are above suspicion,* and that *none of the common allegations that are made against adoption agencies (and many of them are true at least in some agencies)* do take place... Every area of adoption practice is being exposed to scrutiny. Obviously *grave deficiencies exist in many aspects of social agency practice...*

They should be identified. They should be exposed. They should be corrected [emphasis added] (Children Bureau, 1955).

The same report made clear that a mother should not be pressured by financial stress to surrender her child and that professionals must be certain to meet the needs of the mother so that the decision she makes can be one that she can live with.

> *This is an ethical question…Protections for children begin with protections for natural parents…medical, legal, and social services for the unmarried mother are the first line of defense…*The problems that arise in adoptions often have their origins in areas that seem far removed: *professional ethics…parental rights…* (Children Bureau, 1955).

The same year, 1955, Margaret Thornhill, Special Consultant, Division of Social Service, wrote that there was a demand for white babies and expressed the concern that supply has not kept up with demand:

> *…the demand for babies exceeds the supply.* A frequent estimate by social agencies is 10 requests to 1 placement [emphasis added] (Thornhill, 1955).

Thornhill shared the view of some that help (medical or otherwise) could make an unmarried mother's life easier, should not be offered because it could encourage illegitimacy. She also issued a warning that some couples will pay whatever necessary costs in order to obtain a baby:

Medical *or any other kind of help*, some *people believe, should not be made easy for these girls*, lest it encourage illegitimacy.... The unmarried mother may be directed to a doctor known to welcome such patients because he has found that *adoptive couples are more than willing to pay whatever professional fee is asked in order to get a baby* [emphasis added].

Thornhill's warnings, too important not to share and stress here, ultimately appeared to go unnoticed and unheeded:

Some of the most vicious cases that have come to light from the black market are those in which a girl has been *frightened or coerced into signing a relinquishment before or immediately after delivery*... The adoptive couple takes the baby and is extremely happy with him. It is the girl who changes her mind....and if she knows where her child is, she may contest the adoption, with tragic results for everyone concerned... One of *the most frequently reported characteristics of individuals who arrange adoptive placements is their lack of concern with the future of the natural mother* [emphasis added] (Thornhill, 1955).

In 1957, Mildred Arnold of the Division of Social Services, Department of HEW representing the Children's Bureau at a national adoption conference, issued warnings about the common approach to unmarried mothers of quickly "placing" their babies without any thought to their emotional needs. She claimed that:

> We are confronted with girls who are repeatedly giving birth out of wedlock because *our only approach to their problem has been quickly to place their babies for adoption with no thought as to the mother's own deep-seated needs... separation of parents and children proves to be along step toward permanent family disintegration. The great motive to do better often goes out the window when the child goes out the door...* child welfare agencies must assume greater responsibility *for preventing family breakdown and for helping parents in their task of child rearing* [emphasis added].

Arnold claimed that because of the increased demand by potential adopters to increase the number of adopted children in their families, unmarried mothers became a real concern because of the lack of public assistance provided to them in the United States. She said:

> Not only are childless couples eager to obtain someone else's children, but many who can have only one or two of their own wish to enlarge their family... The picture is complicated further by the fact that so much of this problem centers around the unmarried mother...In what other situation do we find such extremes in feelings and so much conflict? *Perhaps the best evidence of this lies in our ambivalence as a country in providing public assistance for unmarried mothers...* [emphasis added] (Arnold, 1957).

In 1961, Hannah Adams, Research Analyst, Division of Research for the Children's Bureau, suggested that social services expand to include help for unmarried mothers to keep their children. She said:

> ...a girl may go to see a hospital social worker ... *but if she says she is going to keep her baby she may be offered no further counseling* ... extension of counseling to every unwed mother would not be possible without the enlargement of present social service staffs... Part of this new demand could require expansion of shelters and adoption agencies because more unmarried mothers might wish these services as they learned about them. Part of it might require *specially developed programs of supportive services for unmarried mothers who keep their children* [emphasis added] (Adams, 1961).

Were those "supportive services for unmarried mothers who keep their children" ever created or promoted? No evidence of this had been found prior to the end of the BSE.

The same year, 1961, Annie Sandusky, Consultant on Children in Their Own Homes at the Children's Bureau, shared that there was concern about the increase in the number of illegitimate children and the costs involved in the child welfare program. According to Sandusky:

> ...unique study of the aid to dependent children program which has significance for

the entire public welfare field and particularly for child welfare, has been completed in Cook County, Ill. The study grew out of the concern of the board of county commissioners over the *mounting costs* and criticisms of the program. The commissioners... *were concerned because the number of illegitimate children on the rolls was increasing...* [emphasis added] (Sandusky, 1961).

In 1962, Hannah Adams, Research Analyst, Child Welfare Studies Branch, Division of Research, and Ursula M. Gallagher, Specialist on Unprotected Adoptions and Services to Unmarried Mothers Division of Social Services, Children's Bureau, described the common attitude of the time regarding unmarried mothers and their children as either forgiving of a punitive outrage:

The widespread interest in this subject... takes many forms, ranging from genuine concern about alleviating the *problem to a punitive sense of outrage...* Attitudes toward unmarried mothers range from the *extremely punitive* to the forgiving... Too often the idea of helping a person in trouble is confused with condoning what she did [emphasis added] (Adams, 1962).

In 1962, the same year, Sanford Katz (Associate Professor, School of Law, The Catholic University of America), in "Legal Protections for the Unmarried Mother and her Child," shared the view that any person wishing to transfer custody from the natural mother has the legal burden to prove why and that a teenage unmarried mother should be protected from a "hasty decision." He said that her minor status means that the doctrine of "the best interests of the child" should not only protect her but her child as well:

> A *mother is the natural guardian of her illegitimate child*, and as such has the *legal right to his custody*, care, and control, superior to the right of the father or any other person... *The presumption in the law that the illegitimate child's best interests require him to be in the mother's custody...* the burden is upon the person disputing the mother's custody to show why the general rule should not apply... *The teenage unwed mother, then, is protected from the results of a hasty decision to transfer custody of her illegitimate child.* If she does make a decision to transfer custody, she can change her mind later and void the contract... *The hope is that 'the best interests of the child' doctrine will work to protect and benefit not only the illegitimate child but also his mother who, as another child, also deserves special consideration* [emphasis added].

Muriel Brown of the Department of Health, Education, and Welfare, admitted that not enough was known about sexual deviation (i.e. unmarried motherhood) and therefore they (those who work in infant adoption) operate in ignorance:

> As for the babies born to unmarried parents, who knows that story better than you

who are members of, or work with, the Florence Crittenton Association? These problems persist, I think chiefly because so much of what we do in the name of prevention *we do in ignorance*. Until our methods of studying human behavior and its origins are much more highly developed than they are at present, it is not likely that we will know enough about the causes of *sexual deviation* to be in a position to deal with them systematically [emphasis added] (Brown, 1962).

In 1964, Ursula Gallagher, Specialist on Adoption and Services to Unmarried Mothers, Children's Bureau, described the view of a newspaper columnist who believed unwed mothers should be imprisoned:

A columnist for a newspaper in a western state recently presented his answer to the question of what should be done about the unmarried mother and suggested a new use for a recently abandoned facility that had been operated by the Federal Government. '*House unwed mothers in Alcatraz,*' he urged...Other deterrents to service have included *emphasis upon the child to the exclusion of the mother's needs,* acceptance for service of a mother only if her child might be considered *in the group of babies in demand... Agencies that provide adoption service are often inclined to cease service to the unmarried mother who decides to keep her baby* [emphasis added] (Gallagher, 1964).

In 1965, Katherine Oettinger, Chief of the Children's Bureau, suggested that providing better health in this country should be free of coercion. Who else would have been the target of such coercion if not the unmarried mother?

> Many of us are working together at a new rapid pace… for reaching the goal of providing better health for the mothers and children of this Nation. If family planning is a useful tool in achieving this goal, *then it should be available on a universal basis as a right of parents, without coercion…* (Oettinger, 1965).

In 1969, Alice Shiller (Public Affairs Committee) indicated that the federal government was providing "resources" to state public agencies:

> The Crittenton Comprehensive Care Center in Chicago, Illinois is…an example of what can be accomplished when the *resources of federal*, state, and local public agencies, and a national voluntary organization work together. The Chicago Board of Health contracted with the Florence Crittenton Association to administer the Center. *The major portion of its funds are derived from the Maternal and Infant Care Program of the United States Children's Bureau, which allocates money to the Illinois Chicago Board of Health* which also contributes its own funds to the Center's financing [emphasis added] (Shiller, 1969).

It is frequently claimed today that adoption is a state matter, not a federal matter. However, in light of the information stated above, is that a valid claim?

APPENDIX E

THOUGHT REFORM, PERSUASIVE COERCION, BRAINWASHING, DISENFRANCHISED GRIEF, AND OTHER ISSUES

In 1977, Vance Packard raised the issue of brainwashing, reprogramming and personality transforming, noting the "Three Ds" three states of mind at play: debilitation, dread and dependency that prepare an individual for conversion via brainwashing when applied to someone like an unmarried, captive mother.

It is possible to reprogram people's personalities and beliefs, even when they resist if coercive techniques can be employed. Brainwashing is not as mysterious as it once seemed... In true brainwashing there is also relatively little use of excruciating torture... The brainwashers were less interested in obtaining information than in obtaining converts. The latter could be used for propaganda purposes... For the personality-transformers a major early objective is to destroy the prisoner's identity, disorganize [her] self-concept. Three states of mind or body, sometimes called the Three D's, contribute to the destruction of identity and readiness for conversion:

1) Debilitation...interrogated night and day...isolation can dramatically alter mental functioning within a few days.

2) Dread...treated roughly...comes to dread humiliation or degradation...

3)] Dependency...led to realize that [her] fate is at the whim of [her] captors...helplessly dependent...for sleep or food...[her] identity is in disarray...when prisoner's personality starts collapsing [she] is welcomed as a convert...

Such methods that may well have been applied to unmarried mothers by adoption social workers, adoption agencies, lawyers and others to obtain babies such as Thought Reform (aka Brainwashing) and Persuasive Coercion.

[I]n coercion the victim's 'will' is 'overthrown'...or 'destroyed,' or 'neutralized'...

The gun-at-the-head situation...typically includes some kind of psychological turmoil or even mental trauma in the victim...What is necessary for coercion is that the victims keep their wits about them, that they pay attention to what the coercer says and...obey.

[T]he coerced person does have a real choice in the obvious sense…it is appropriate to describe the victim as someone who literally does make a choice... what we are getting at here is the absence of a 'reasonable' choice.

[In] 'coercive persuasion'... one who is coerced must be rational in order to be coerced.

[One must ask] "...how gross was the wrong done the victim?

[A]bsence of any will at all is…not what is at issue here... when we say the will is overcome, we do not mean that the person acts without will.

Margaret Thayler Singer and Richard Ofshe, psychologists and longtime experts, made the statement that "...the effectiveness of thought reform programs did not depend on prison settings, physical abuse or death threats. Programs used the application of intense guilt, shame, and anxiety manipulation with the production of strong emotional arousal in settings where people did not leave because of social and psychological pressures or because of enforced confinement."

In "Not By Choice," Buterbaugh shared how these conditions applied to the "unwed" mother experience, especially for those interred in maternity homes.

Singer and Ofshe provided six conditions (in italics below) that are required to put a system of thought reform into place. Let's compare these six conditions of thought reform and coercive persuasion to the maternity home experience:

1. Keep person unaware: Girls were not instructed about pregnancy, labor, delivery; were left totally alone during labor and delivery; were not allowed contact with new mothers; not provided information about welfare and Aid to Families with Dependent Children (AFDC), child support and other government programs.

2. Control their environment and time: Girls forced to live in maternity "homes"; made to use fictitious names or first names and last initials only; allowed no contact with friends and boyfriends by letter, phone or in person; kept away from everything familiar; made to follow strict daily routines.

3. Create a sense of powerlessness: Took away their money (pay phones only); no personal (familiar) clothing; not allowed freedom to come and go; removed everything that would remind us of who we were.

4. Rewards and punishments to inhibit behavior reflecting former identity: Called "neurotic" if they said no to "relinquishing"; told they were "out of touch with reality" and "selfish" if they kept their babies; told our pregnancy was "proof of unfitness."

5. Rewards and punishments promoting group's beliefs or behaviors: Allowed no television, phone, visitation or radio privileges if not following rules; scolding and demeaning lectures for disagreeing; harangued when speaking up against "counseling" (reasons why we should "choose" adoption); praised for agreeing to surrender.

6. Use logic and authority which permits no feedback: Director, caseworkers and housemothers enforced strict rules and rigid schedule such as when to wake up, bedtime, meals and chores. They approved visitation and censored mail (both incoming and outgoing). No legal counsel and no support system (Buterbaugh, 2001).

It seems clear that all of the thought reform conditions were present during the many months expectant and new unmarried mothers were forced to hide away in maternity homes. Some or all could even apply also to those expectant and new unmarried mothers who were not incarcerated in maternity homes.

Of interest, and relevant to this discussion, is Professor and Psychiatrist Robert Lifton's (1989) list of eight criteria used to identify thought reform and brainwashing:

> 1. Milieu Control: Control of communication within group …resulting in... significant degree of isolation from... society.
>
> 2. Mystical Manipulation: ...allows the leader to reinterpret events... or pronouncements at will for purpose of controlling group members.
>
> 3. Demand for Purity: ...guilt and shame... powerful control devices.
>
> 4. Cult of Confession: …demand that one confess to crimes… not committed, to sinfulness …in the name of a cure that is arbitrarily imposed.

5. Sacred Silence: ...doctrine of group is considered the Ultimate Truth, beyond all ...disputing... leader of... above criticism.

6. Loading the Language: ... develops jargon... unique to itself... words and phrases which the members understand... but...act to dull one's ability to engage in critical thinking.

7. Doctrine over Person: ... experiences of group members are subordinated to the 'truth' held by group... doctrine is more important than individual.

8. Dispensing of Existence: ... converted to ideas of group or they will be lost ... drawn to conversion...as the only means of existence for the future   (Lifton, 1989).

Psychological Manipulation, according to Preston Ni, has also been described as "the exercise of undue influence through mental distortion and emotional exploitation, with the intention to seize power, control, benefits, and privileges at the victim's expense" (Ni, 2014).

Further, Preston Ni stated that a psychological manipulator can become a bully when "he or she intimidates or harms another person." Bullies pick on those who they perceive as weaker.

APPENDIX F

CODES, DECLARATIONS & LAWS GOVERNING
HUMAN EXPERIMENTATION

The Nuremburg Code states:

> The person involved should have the legal
> capacity to give consent; should be so situated
> as to be able to exercise free power of choice,
> without the intervention of any element of
> force, fraud, deceit, duress, overreaching, or
> other ulterior form of constraint or coercion;
> and should have sufficient knowledge and
> comprehension of the elements of the
> subject matter involved as to enable him to
> make an understanding and enlightened
> decision. This latter element requires that
> before the acceptance of an affirmative
> decision by the experimental subject, there
> should be made known to him the nature,
> duration, and purpose of the experiment; the
> method and means by which it is to be
> conducted; all inconveniences and hazards
> reasonable to be expected; and the effects
> upon his health and person which may
> possibly come from his participation in the
> experiments. (Trials of War Criminals before

the Nuremberg Military Tribunals under
Control Council Law, 1949).

THE BABY SCOOP ERA

REFERENCES

Adams, H., & Gallagher, U. (1962). Some facts and observations about illegitimacy. *Children, 10*(2), 43-48.

Adams, H. (1961). Two studies of unmarried mothers in New York City. *Children, 8*(5), 186-188.

Aigner, H. (1992). *Adoption in America.* Boulder, CO: Paradigm Press.

Allen, K. M. (2009. August-September). The price we all pay: Human trafficking in international adoption. *Conducive.* Retrieved from http://www.conducivemag.com/2009/10/the-price-we-all-pay-human-trafficking-in-international-adoption.

Allen, M. (1963, November 1). What can we do about America's unwed teen-age mothers? *McCalls*, pp. 42, 51.

Ariely, D. (2012). *The (honest) truth about dishonesty how we lie to everyone - especially ourselves.* (p. 232) New York, NY: HarperCollins.

Armstrong, L. (1995). *Of 'sluts' and 'bastards': A feminist decodes the child welfare debate* (pp. 10, 11). Monroe, ME: Common Courage Press.

Arnold, M. (1955, June 27). Protecting children in adoption. Lecture presented at U.S Department of Health Education and Welfare, Social Security Administration, Washington, D.C.

Arnold, M. (1957, May 19). Techniques and methods in child welfare. Lecture presented at 84th Annual Forum, National Conference on Social Welfare, Philadelphia, PA.

Arnold, M. (1959, May 24). New Trends in Adoption Practice. Lecture presented at 86th Annual Forum, National Conference on Social Welfare, San Francisco, CA.

Ashe, N. (2001). Big Business: Adoption Services Valued At $1.4 Billion. Retrieved March 3, 2016, from http://exiledmothers.com/adoption_facts/adoption_industry.html

Askren H., Bloom, K.C. (1999, July-August). Postadoptive reactions of the relinquishing mother: A review. *Journal of Obstetrics, Gynecology, Neonatal Nursing,* 28(4), 395-400.

Atwood, Margaret. *The handmaid's tale.* (p. 84). Boston: Houghton Mifflin, 1986.

Australian Parliament Inquiry of Forced Adoption Practices. (2014, September 1). Retrieved December 31, 2015, from http://www.parliament.nsw.gov.au/prod/parlment/hansart.nsf/86ca1d5c167e46c8ca2571ca000080c8/3658

65e805c8670cca257d630021cbb3

Babb, L. (1998). Adoptive parents: Fables, facts, fears, three destructive mindsets of adoptive parents. *Bastard Quarterly*, Spring/Summer.

Babb, L. (1999). *Ethics in American adoption.* (43-44). Westport, CT: Bergin & Garvey.

Baby Scoop Era. Wikipedia. Wikimedia Foundation. Retrieved 11 Jan. 2016 from https://en.wikipedia.org/wiki/Baby_Scoop_Era

Baker, I. (August 1948). Uphold rights of parent and child. *The Child,* 27-30.

Baran, A., & Pannor, R. (1990). It's time for sweeping change. *Concerned United Birthparents Degree, 4,* 511.

Baran, A., & Pannor, R. (1992). It's Time for Sweeping Change. In *The New our bodies, ourselves: A book by and for women* (p. 350). New York: NY: Simon & Schuster.

Barth, R. (1987). Adolescent mothers' beliefs about open adoption. *Social Casework,* 68(6), 323-331.

Bartholet, E. (Spring 1995). Beyond biology: The politics of adoption & reproduction. *Duke Journal of Gender Law & Policy,* (2)1.

Baumler, E. (2003, August 2). Florence Crittenton Home: Girl's best friend for over 100 years. Retrieved from http://helenair.com/news/local/florence-crittenton-home-girl-s-best-friend-for-over-years/article_537cc880-18d1-5c6c-b71f-20e2adc7d22c.html

Bedger, J. (1969). *The Crittenton study: An assessment of client functioning before and after services* (p. 44). Chicago, IL: Florence Crittenton Association of America.

Benedict, L. (1964). *Out of the box: A child is waiting* [Radio Broadcast]. Richmond, VA: Children's Home Society of Virginia. Retrieved from http://www.virginiamemory.com/blogs/out_of_the_box/tag/a-child-is-waiting/

Benforado, Adam. (2015). *Unfair: The new science of criminal injustice.* (p. 84). Crown Publications NY.

Benet, M. (1976). *The politics of adoption.* (pp. 12, 172, 178). New York, NY: Free Press.

Bennett, F. (1964, October 5). *Expansion of maternity home services.* Lecture presented at Florence Crittenton Association of America, Midwest Area Conference, Akron, OH.

Bennett, W. (2001). *The broken hearth: Reversing the moral collapse of the American family.* (pp. 93, 98, 100). New York, NY: Doubleday.

Berkman, Karen & Chapman, Mark & Film Australia. (2006). Gone to a good home [Television series episode]. In *Storyline Australia.* Lindfield, N.S.W.: Film Australia.

Bernard, V.W. (1964). *Adoption*. (pp. 70-73). Washington, DC: Child Welfare League of America.

Bernstein, R. (1962). Gaps in services to unmarried mothers. *Children, 10*(2), 50-54.

Bernstein, R. (1971). *Helping unmarried mothers* (pp. 4, 13-14, 16, 30, 57, 92, 95). New York, NY: Association Press.

Berry, B. (2005). *Why social justice matters*. Cambridge, England: Polity Press. Retrieved from http://gjs.appstate.edu/social-justice-and-human-rights/what-social-justice

Berry, M. (1991) The effects of open adoption on biological and adoptive parents and the children: The arguments and the evidence. *Child Welfare, 70*(6), 637-651.

Biestek, F. (1957). *The casework relationship* (pp. 110-111). Chicago, IL: Loyola University Press.

Blanton, T., & Deschner, J. (1990). Biological mothers' grief: The post adoptive experience in open versus confidential adoption. *Child Welfare, 69*(6), 525-535.

Blatt, M. (1964). Intensive casework with the unmarried mother with her first pregnancy: Emphasis on rehabilitation and prevention of recidivism. In R. Levy (Ed.), *Selected materials on family law: Custody, the unwed mother, adoption, parental neglect (p. 90)*. Chicago, IL: National Council on Legal Clinics.

Block, Babette. (1945). Selected papers. Proceedings of the Family Service Bureau National Conference of Social Work Seventy-Second Annual Meeting. Chicago, IL: United Charities of Chicago.

Boole, L. (1956). The Hospital and Unmarried Mothers. *Children, 6*(6), 211.

Boston Women's Health Book Collective. (1992). New our bodies, ourselves: A book by and for women. New York, NY: Touchstone.

Bowlby, J. (1952). Illegitimacy and deprivation. In *Maternal care and mental health: Monograph Series No. 2.* (2nd Ed. (115, 149). Geneva, Switzerland: World Health Organization.

Bowlby, J. (1961). The Adolf Meyer Lecture: Childhood mourning and its implications for psychiatry. *American Journal of Psychiatry AJP,* 481-498.

Bowlby, J., & Fry, M. (1965). *Child care and the growth of love.* (p. 121). Harmondsworth, UK: Penguin Books.

Braiker, Harriet B. (2004). *Who's pulling your strings? How to break the cycle of manipulation.* Columbus, OH: McGraw-Hill Education.

Brennan, C. (2007). The other mother. Retrieved November 28, 2015, from http://www.oprah.com/relationships/Meeting-the-Biological-Mother-The-Adoption-Files

Bridges, J. (1964). America's problem of sex morality. In C.

Scudder (Ed.), *Crises in morality* (p. 9). Nashville, TN: Broadman Press.

Brenner, R. (1942, May 10). *What facilities are essential to the adequate care of the unmarried mother?* Lecture presented at Sixty Ninth Annual Conference, New Orleans, LA

Brosnan, T. (1996, May 25). Strengthening families. Retrieved from http://openadoption.org/brosnan.htm

Brower, B. (1947). What shall I do with my baby? *The Child, 12*(10), 166.

Brown, M. (1962, May 31). *The Step beyond prevention.* Lecture presented at Florence Crittenton Association of America, National Conference on Social Welfare, New York.

Browning, N.L. (1959, November 1). Problem of the unwed mother. *Chicago Tribune*, pp. 14-16.

Buck, P. S. (1956, June 1). We can free the children. *Woman's Home Companion*, 62-64.

Buck, P. S. (November 1955). Must we have orphanages? *Readers Digest*, 67(403), 57-60.

Buck, P. S. (1972, January). I am the better woman for having my two black children. *Today's Health*, 20-23, 64.

Bye, L. (1959, January 1). *Profile of unwed pregnancy today: Private agency point of view.* Presentation to the

National Conference on Social Welfare, San Francisco, CA.

Canada, R. (1964, November 6). *Changes in adoption services* (3-4) Lecture presented at Western Area Conference, Florence Crittenton Association of America, Scottsdale, AZ.

Caragata, L. (1999). The construction of teen parenting and decline of adoption. In James Wong and David Checkland (Eds.).*Teen Pregnancy and Parenting: Social and Ethical Issues.* (pp. 99-120). Toronto: University of Toronto Press.

Carangelo, L. (1999). *Statistics of adoption.* (pp, 6, 9, 13, 15). Palm Desert, CA: Access Press.

Carp, E.W. (1998). *Family matters: Secrecy and disclosure in the history of adoption* (26, 111, 115--117). Cambridge, MA: Harvard University Press.

Carr, M. J. (2000). Birthmothers and subsequent children: The role of personality traits and attachment history. *Journal of Social Distress and the Homeless.* 9(4) 339-348. doi: 10.1023/A:1009445911090.

Casework papers 1961: From the National Conference on Social Welfare, presented at the 88th Annual Forum, Minneapolis, Minnesota, May 14-19, 1961. (p. 6). (1961). New York: Family Service Association of America.

Chamberlain, D. B. (1995). What babies are teaching us about violence. *The Journal of Prenatal and Perinatal Psychology and Health*, 10(2), 57-74.

Chambers, L. (2006). Adoption, unwed mothers and the powers of the Children's Aid Society in Ontario, 1921-1969. *Ontario History,* (90). 2.

Charnley, J. (1955). *The art of child placement* (pp. vii. viii, 4, 6, 8, 12, 14, 107-108, 116, 279). Minneapolis, MN: University of Minnesota Press.

Chaskell, R. (1967). The unmarried mother: Is she different? *Child Welfare.* (February, 1967), 68.

Cheetham, J. (1977). *Unwanted pregnancy and counselling* (pp. 78-79, 107, 140, 182-183, 192-193, 205, 207, 212-213, 224). London: Routledge & Kegan Paul.

Chesler, P. (1986). *Mothers on trial: The battle for children and custody* (pp. 48, 321, 356-357, 361). New York, NY: McGraw Hill.

Child welfare: Adoption and foster care. (1977). In Turner, J.B., et al. (Eds.) *Encyclopedia of Social Work.* (Vol. 1, p.120). Washington, DC: National Association of Social Workers.

Child Welfare League of America. (1971). *A National Program for Comprehensive Child Welfare Services.* Washington, DC: Child Welfare League of America, Inc.

Child Welfare League of America. (1978). *Standards for Adoption Service, Revised.* Washington, DC: Child Welfare League of America, Inc.

Chippendale-Bakker, V., & Foster, L. (1996). Adoption in the 1990s: Sociodemographic determinants of biological parents choosing adoption. *Child Welfare*, 75(4), 337-355.

Clothier, F. (1941). Problems of illegitimacy as they concern the worker in the field of adoption. *Mental Hygiene, XXV*(4), 584.

Clothier, F. (1943). The Psychology of the Adopted Child. *Mental Hygiene, 27*, 222-226.

Collings, I. (2006). Defensive reasoning and adoption practices. Proceedings paper, Australian Inquiry of Forced Adoptions, 2014.

Comly, H. (n.d.). *A New Look in Providing Services to Unmarried Mothers (3)*. Lecture presented at Florence Crittenton Association of America, National Conference on Social Welfare, Minneapolis, MN.

Condon, J. T. (1986). Psychological disability in women who relinquish a baby for adoption. *The Medical Journal of Australia.* 144, 117-119.

Corea, G. (1985). *The hidden malpractice: How American medicine mistreats women.* (pp. 130, 132-133, 144-145, 174-175, 179). New York,, NY: Harper & Row.

Costigan, B. (1964). *The unmarried mother: Her decision regarding adoption* (pp. 3-4, 32-33, 35, 43, 45-46, 56, 97, 99, 109). Los Angeles, CA: University of Southern California Press.

Costin, L. (1972). *Child welfare: Policies and practice* (pp. 220, 233). New York, NY: McGraw-Hill.

Craigen, J. (1972, May 28-June 2). The Case for Activism in Social Work. In *The Social Welfare Forum, Official Proceedings,* Paper presented at the 99th Annual Forum National Conference on Social Welfare. Chicago, IL. Madison, WI: University of Wisconsin.

Crockett, M. (1960). Examination of services to the unmarried mother in relation to age of adoption placement of the baby. *Casework papers 1960, National Conference on Social Welfare, 87th annual forum* (p. 81). Atlantic City, NJ: Family Service America.

Crowling, E.C. (1968, April). *Adoption services of social agencies during the home study and beyond the completion of the adoption.* (Published dissertation). Virginia Commonwealth University School of Social Work. Richmond, VA.

Cugoano, Ottobah. Narrative of the enslavement of Ottobah Cugoano, a native of Africa, published by himself in the Year 1787. In *The Negro's Memorial, or, Abolitionist's Catechism by an Abolitionist.* Retrieved from http://docsouth.unc.edu/neh/cugoano/cugoano.html.

Cunningham, S. (2010). Smashed by adoption (Baby Scoop Era). Retrieved from http://www.originsnsw.com/id43.html

Cupp, R. (2013). *Miracles on St. Margaret Street, Florence Crittenton programs of SC* (pp. 10, 36). Charleston, SC:

Arcadia Publishing:

Cushman, L., Kalmuss, D., & Namerow, P. (1993). Placing an infant for adoption: The experiences of young birthmothers. *Social Work, 38*(3), 264-272.

Dailard, C. (2003, August 1). Out of compliance? Implementing the Infant Adoption Awareness Act. Retrieved from http://www.guttmacher.org/pubs/tgr/07/3/gr070 310.html

Davies, M. (1997). *The Blackwell companion to social work* (p. 334). Oxford, England: Blackwell.

Dean, C. (1958, June 1). Opinions toward legally required adoption studies done by children placing agencies in Salt Lake County, 1958. MSW Thesis. University of Utah, 1958. Retrieved from http://www.researchgate.net/publication/3463743 2_Opinions_toward_legally_required_adoption_stu dies_done_by_children_placing_agencies_in_Salt_L ake_County_1958

DeSimone, M. (1994). *Unresolved grief in women who have relinquished an infant for adoption.* Unpublished doctoral dissertation. New York University School of Social Work, New York, NY

De Simone, M. (1996). Birth mother loss: Contributing factors to unresolved grief, *Clinical Social Work Journal,* 24(1) 65-76. doi: 10.1007/BF02189942.

Deutsch, H. (1945). *The psychology of women; a psychoanalytic interpretation, motherhood* (p. 380). New York, NY: Grune & Stratton.

Dinniman, L. (1964). *Meeting the needs for services to unmarried mothers.* Paper presented at the Midwest Area Conference of the Florence Crittenton Association of America.

Directory of residences for unwed mothers. (1969). (pp. 5, 54). Washington, D.C.: National Conference of Catholic Charities.

Doctors' trial: The medical case of the subsequent Nuremberg proceedings. Holocaust Encyclopedia. Retrieved from http://www.ushmm.org/wlc/en/article.php?Modul eId=10007035

Dorner, P. (1997). *Catholic Charities searching handbook, adoption search: An ethical guide for practitioners.* Alexandria VA: Catholic Charities USA.

Dubner, Steven. (2016, January 10). The maddest men of all: A new Freakonomics Radio Podcast [Podcast]. *Freakonomics RSS.* Retrieved from http://freakonomics.com/podcast/the-maddest-men-of-all-a-new-freakonomics-radio-podcast/

Due Process. (n.d.). In Wikipedia. Retrieved from https://en.wikipedia.org/wiki/Due_process

Duffield, G. & Graboski, P. (2001, March 1). The psychology of fraud. Australian Institute of Criminology. Retrieved from http://www.aic.gov.au/publications/current

series/tandi/181-200/tandi199.html

Dunlavey, A. (1968). *If you've made a mistake.* Chicago, IL: Claretian Publications.

Edlin, S. (1954). *The unmarried mother in our society: A frank and constructive approach to an age-old problem.* (pp. 9-10, 144, 182-184). New York, NY: Farrar, Straus, and Young.

Eighth Amendment to the United States Constitution. (n.d.). In Wikipedia. Retrieved from https://en.wikipedia.org/wiki/Eighth_Amendment _to_the_United_States_Constitution

Eliot, T., Lundberg, E., & Lenroot, K. (1920). Illegitimacy as a child welfare problem: Part I. *Journal of the American Institute of Criminal Law and Criminology,* 626.

Erichsen, R. (1955). Who are America's 150,000 unwed mothers? *Pageant,* 11(5), 86-92.

Estès, C.P. (1992) *Women who run with the wolves: Myths and stories of the wild woman archetype.* New York, NY: Ballantine Books.

Ferard, M., & Hunnybun, N. (1962). *The caseworker's use of relationships.* (p. 57). London: Tavistock Publications.

Fertility clinics and adoption services: An industry analysis. (2000). Retrieved December 9, 2015, from http://www.mkt-data-ent.com/fertilitytoc2.html

Fessler, A. (2006). *The girls who went away: The hidden history of women who surrendered children for adoption in the decades before Roe v. Wade* (p. 143). NY: Penguin Press.

Fessler, A. (Producer/Director). (2012). *A girl like her* [Motion Picture]. United States: LEF Foundation, Moving Image Fund.

Fingarette, H. (1985). Coercion, coercive persuasion, and the law. In Robbins, Shepherd & McBride (Eds.) *Cults, culture, and law: Perspectives on new religious movements.* (pp. 81-91). Palo Alto, CA: Scholars Press.

Ford, S.P. (1971). *Guidelines for adoption service.* (pp. 2, 9). New York, NY: Child Welfare League of America Committee on Standards for Adoption Service.

Foster Care and Adoption. (1999, September 30). Retrieved from http://www.socialworkers.org/pressroom/features /policy statements/146-153 Foster.pdf

Frears, S. (Director), & Coogan, S. (Writer), & Pope, J. (Writer). (2013). *Philomena* [Motion picture]. United States: The Weinstein Company.

French, M. (1993). *The war against women* (p. 19). New York: Ballantine Books.

Frum, V. (1949). What the medical social worker learns from the patient. *Journal of Social Hygiene,* 329.

Gallagher, N. (1999). *Breeding better Vermonters: The eugenics project in the Green Mountain State* (pp. 4, 52, 54-55,

106, 117-128, 167, 170). Hanover, NH: University Press of New England.

Gallagher, U.M. (1963, June). What of the unmarried parent? *Journal of Home Economics,* 55(6), 401-405.

Gallagher, U.M. (1964, November 6). *Reassessment of Services to Unmarried Mothers (4-5).* Lecture presented at Florence Crittenton Association of America, Western Area Conference, Scottsdale, AZ.

Gaylin, W. (1976). On the borders of persuasion: A psychoanalytic look at coercion. In T.A. Shannon. (Ed.). (pp. 447-461). *Bioethics: Basic Writings on the Key Ethical Questions that Surround the Major, Modern Biological Possibilities and Problem.* New York, NY: Paulist Press.

Germany (Territory under Allied occupation, 1945-1955: U.S. Zone). *Trials of war criminals before the Nuremberg Military Tribunals under Control Council Law No. 10, Nuremberg, October 1946-April, 1949.* Washington, D.C: U.S. G.P.O., 1949-1953.Retrieved December 18, 2015, from http://en.wikipedia.org/wiki/Nuremberg_Code

Gerow, D. (2002). Infant adoption is big business in America. Retrieved from http://www.originscanada.org/documents/infant.pdf.

Gershenson, C. P. In L. Klerman & J. Jekel. (1973). *School-age mothers: Problems, programs & policy,* (pp. x, 2-3, 6-7, 38). Hamden, CT: Linnet Books.

Gianakon, H. (1960 June 5-10). Ego factors in the separation of unwed mother and child. In *Casework papers 1960*. Paper presented at the 87th Annual Forum, National Conference on Social Welfare, Atlantic City, New Jersey. (pp. 61-62, 64, 58). Atlantic City, NJ: Family Service America.

Giedd, J. (2015). The amazing teen brain. *Scientific American,* 312, 32-37.

Gill, D. (1977). *Illegitimacy, sexuality and the status of women* (pp. 99, 103, 106, 260). Oxford: Basil Blackwell.

Gilman, L. (1984). *The adoption resource book* (p. 85, 130). New York: Harper & Row.

Glickman, E. (1957). *Child placement through clinically oriented casework* (pp. vii-viii; 6, 279). NY: Columbia University Press.

Goodacre, I. (1966). *Adoption policy and practice: A study.* London: George Allen & Unwin.

Gouldner, A. (1963, May 19). *The secrets of organizations.* Lecture presented at 90th Annual Forum, National Conference on Social Welfare, Cleveland, OH.

Greenleigh, A. (1961). Does the ADC program strengthen or weaken family life? In *Casework papers presented at the 88th annual forum* (pp. 94-95). Family Service Association of America: New York, NY.

Greil, A. (1991). *Not yet pregnant: Infertile couples in contemporary*

America (pp. 187-188). New Brunswick, NJ: Rutgers University Press.

Hart, H. H. (1924). *Child welfare in the District of Columbia: A study of agencies and institutions for the care of dependent and delinquent children.* New York, NY: Russell Sage Foundation.

Headsten, S. (1969). Maternity care: To hide or to help, that is the question. *Field Reporter,* September-October, 1969, 4-5.

Heiman, M. (1960). Out of wedlock pregnancy in adolescence. In *Casework papers 1960: From the National Conference on Social Welfare.* (pp. 70-71). New York, NY: Family Service Association of America.

Heiman, M. (1964). Motivating the resistant client. In R. Levy (Ed.), *Selected materials on family law: Custody, the unwed mother, adoption, parental neglect* (pp. 14-15, 94). Chicago, IL: National Council on Legal Clinics.

Henderson, D. (2002). Challenging the silence of the mental health community on adoption issues. *Journal of Social Distress and the Homeless, 11*(2), 131-137.

Herman, E. (2002). The adoption history project. Retrieved from http://pages.uoregon.edu/adoption/

Heiman, M. (1960, June). Out of wedlock pregnancy in adolescence. Paper presented at the annual conference of the Florence Crittenton Homes Association National Conference on Social Welfare, Atlantic City, NJ

Henderson, D. B. (2002). Challenging the silence of the mental health community on adoption issues. *Journal of Social Distress and the Homeless,* 11(2), pp. 131-141. doi:10.1023/A:1014311817729.

Hickey, M. (1958, August). More than a place to hide: The Crittenton program. *Ladies Home Journal,* LXXV(8).

Higgins, D. (2014, August 1). Past adoption practices: Implications for current interventions. Retrieved December 9, 2015, from http://www.psychology.org.au/inpsych/2014/augu st/higgins

Himmler, Heinrich. (1943, October 4). Speech to SS group leaders in Posen, Occupied Poland. Retrieved from http://www.historyplace.com/worldwar2/holocaus t/h-posen.htm.

Hoey, J. (1952). Aid to dependent children keeps homes together. *The Child, 16*(6), 87-88.

Hoey, J. (1952). Our common goals. *Journal of Home Economics, 44*(9), 689-690.

Hong, K. E. (2003). Parens Patri[archy]: Adoption, eugenics, and same-sex couples. *CWSL Scholarly Commons,* 40(1), Article 2. Retrieved from http://scholarlycommons.law.cwsl.edu/cwlr/vol40 /iss1/2/

Hood, G. (2012). Dan Rather Reports. "Adoption or Abduction?" AXS TV. Retrieved from http://www.axs.tv/wp-content/blogs.dir/1/files/Salvation-Army.pdf

Howarth, D. (1956, November 22). Mothers not all unhappy. *Toronto Telegraph.*

Howe, D., Sawbridge, P., & Hinings, D. (1992). *Half a million women: Mothers who lose their children by adoption* (pp. 2, 19, 22-23, 30, 44, 48, 50, 64-67, 69-70, 104, 108-109, 111). London: Penguin Books.

Infausto, F. (1969). Perspective on adoption. *Annals of the American Academy of Political and Social Science, Progress in Family Law,* 8.

Inglis, K. (1984). *Living mistakes: Mothers who consented to adoption* (pp. 8, 14-15). Sydney NSW: G. Allen & Unwin.

Isaac, R. (1965). *Adopting a child today,* (pp. 51, 54, 56). New York: Harper & Row.

Jacobs, P., & Schain, L. (2011). The never-ending attraction of the Ponsi scheme. Retrieved from http://digitalcommons.sacredheart.edu/cgi/viewcontent.cgi?article=1003&context=cj_fac

Johnston, P. I. (2004). *Speaking Positively: Using Respectful Adoption Language.* Retrieved from http://www.perspectivespress.com/pjpal.html.]

Jones, M. (1993). *Birthmothers: Women who have relinquished babies for adoption tell their stories.* (pp. 11-12). Chicago, IL: Chicago Review Press.

Josselyn, I. (1955). A psychiatrist looks at adoption. In M. Schapiro (Ed.). *A Study of Adoption Practice* (2). New

York, NY: Child Welfare League of America.

Juliah. (2013, November 8). *At a Loss for Words: How Language Marginalizes the Disenfranchised*. Retrieved from http://serendip.brynmawr.edu/exchange/critical-feminist-studies-2013/juliah/loss-words-how-language-marginalizes-disenfranchised.

Kahn, A. (1964, October 19). *Unmarried mothers: A social welfare planning perspective (5)*. Lecture presented at Florence Crittenton Association of America, Northeastern Area Conference.

Kammerer, P. G. (1969). The unmarried mother: A study of five hundred cases. *Criminal science monograph No. 3. Supplement to the Journal of the American Institute of Criminal Law and Criminology*. (pp. 12, 18, 08, 310, 333-334). Boston, MA: Little, Brown and Company.

Kantor, M. (2006). The psychopathology of everyday life: How to deal with manipulative people. Retrieved from https://en.wikipedia.org/wiki/Psychological_manipulation

Katz, S. (1962). Legal protections for the unmarried mother and her child. *The Child*, 58-59.

Katz, S. (1963). Legal protections for the unmarried mother and her child. *Children, 10*, 57-58.

Kelly, J. (1962). The school and unmarried mothers. *Children, 10*, 60-64.

Kelly, J. (1999) *The trauma of relinquishment: The long-term impact of relinquishment on birthmothers who lost their infants to adoption during the years 1965-1972.* Master's thesis. Goddard College, Plainfield, Vermont.

Keup, C. (2012). *Girls "in trouble": A history of female adolescent sexuality in the Midwest, 1946-1964* (Doctoral dissertation). Retrieved from http://epublications.marquette.edu/dissertations_

Kirk, H. (1984). *Shared fate: A theory and method of adoptive relationships.* (2nd Ed.) (40, 62, 71, 100). Port Angeles, WA: Ben-Simon Publications.

Klerman, L., & Jekel, J. (1973). *School-age mothers: Problems, programs & policy,* (pp. x, 2-3, 6-7, 38). Hamden, CT: Linnet Books.

Krimmel, H. (1991). No: The case against surrogate parenting. In C. Levine (Ed.), *Taking sides: Clashing views on controversial bioethical issues* (4th ed., pp. 53-54). Guilford, CT: Dushkin Publishing Group.

Kunzel, R. (1995). Pulp fictions and problem girls: Reading and rewriting single pregnancy in the postwar United States. *The American Historical Review, 100,* 1467-1468, 1482.

Kunzel, R. (1993). *Fallen women, problem girls: Unmarried mothers and the professionalization of social work, 1890-1945* (pp. 37, 44, 52, 54-57, 89, 127, 129, 151, 155). New Haven, CT: Yale University Press.

Lake, B. (2009). Posttraumatic stress disorder in natural mothers. Master's Thesis. City University of Seattle,

Belleville, WA. Retrieved from http://epe.lac-bac.gc.ca/100/200/300/bryony_lake/posttraumatic/Thesis.pdf [9 Jan 2012]

Landers, A. (1961, April 25). Column. *Democrat and Chronicle*, p. 8A. Retrieved from retrieved from https://www.newspapers.com/newspage/136911580/ May 5, 2016

Lapp, H. (1998). Efforts to Prevent Abuse Too Often Harm Children. In C. Wekesser, B. Leone, B. Stalcup, & S. Barbour (Eds.), *Child welfare: Opposing viewpoints* (p. 115). San Diego: Greenhaven Press.

Lawrence, M. (1979, May 4). *The Demonized Mother*. Lecture presented at First National American Adoption Congress, Washington, D.C.

Lawson, D. (1960). Anxieties of pregnancy. *The Medical Journal of Australia*, 166.

Leone, B., Stalcup, B., & Barbour, S. (1998). Efforts to prevent abuse too often harm children. In C. Wekesser (Ed.), *Child welfare: Opposing viewpoints* (115, 180). San Diego, CA.

Levy, A. (2014, September 14). It was an amazing moment. *Daily Mail Online*. Retrieved from http://www.dailymail.co.uk/news/article-2755853/It-amazing-moment-Social-worker-gloats-Facebook-breaking-family-revelling-massive-rollicking-judge-gave-parents.html#ixzz425PMRHgK.

Levy, R. J. (1964). The Unwed mother, adoption, parental

neglect. In *Selected materials on family law: Custody, the unwed mother, adoption, parental neglect.* Chicago, IL: National Council on Legal Clinics.

Lifton, B. (1979). *Lost and found: The adoption experience* (pp. 45, 273). New York: Dial Press.

Lifton, B. J. (1995). *Journey of the Adopted Self: A Quest for Wholeness.* Hew York, NY: Basic Books.

Lifton, R.J. (1989). *Thought reform and the psychology of totalism.* Chapel Hill, NC: University of North Carolina Press.

Lipke, J., & Bateman, P. (1971). *Sex outside of marriage* (pp. 18, 22, 26-27). Minneapolis, MN: Lerner Publications.

Little, M., & Hillyard, J. (1998). *No car, no radio, no liquor permit: The moral regulation of single mothers in Ontario, 1920-1997* (p. 135). Toronto, Canada: Oxford University Press.

Littner, N. (1955). The Natural Parents. In M. Shapiro (Ed.) Study of Adoption Practices: Selected Scientific Papers. (pp. 22, 31), Washington DC: Child Welfare League of America.

Littner. (n.d.). *Study of Adoption Practices.* Lecture.

Logan, J. (1996). Birth mothers and their mental health: Uncharted territory. *British Journal of Social Work.* 26(5), 609-625.

Lourie, N. (1956, May 29). *The Responsibility of the Maternity Home in Dealing with Personality Problems (5)*. Lecture presented at Florence Crittenton Association of America, National Conference on Social Welfare, St. Louis, MO.

Luker, K. (1996). *Dubious conceptions: The politics of teenage pregnancy* (pp. 20, 22, 24, 36-38, 96, 162-163, 181). Cambridge, MA: Harvard University Press.

Lundberg, E. (1974). Illegitimacy as a child-welfare problem. (pp. 56, 63, 139, 228). New York, NY: Arno Press.

Love, S. (Interviewer) & Pannor, R. (Interviewee). (1998). *PACER Newsletter*. Retrieved from http://pacer-adoption.org/education_editorials/pn_r_pannor_int erview.htm.

Malinowski, B. (1966). Parenthood - The Basis of Social Structure. In R. Roberts (Ed.), *The unwed mother* (p. 35). New York: Harper & Row.

Mandell, B.R. (2007) Adoption. *New Politics*, 11(2), Whole Number 42, Winter.

Mander, R. (1995). *The care of the mother grieving a baby relinquished for adoption* (p. 1). Aldershot, Hants, England: Avebury.

Marshall, A., & McDonald, M. (2001). *The many-sided triangle: Adoption in Australia* (pp. 1- 3, 5, 7-8, 10, 26, 49-59, 103, 208). Carlton, VIC: Melbourne University Press.

Mayo, L. (1962). Social services for children and youth. *Children, 9*(2), 69.

McBroom, E. (1969). Socialization and social casework. In R. Roberts & R. Nee (Eds.), (p. 342) *Theories of social casework.* Chicago, IL: University of Chicago Press.

McCalley, H., & Greenleigh, A. (1961, May 18). *The community looks at illegitimacy.* Lecture presented at Florence Crittenton Association of America, Minneapolis, MN.

McClelland, S. (2002, May). Who's my birth father? Canadians conceived with donated sperm are demanding to know their genetic roots. *Maclean's,* 115(20), p. 20.

McColm, M. (1993). *Adoption reunions: A book for adoptees, birth parents and adoptive families* (pp. 47, 144). Toronto, Canada: Second Story Press.

McConnell, N., & Dore, M. (1983). *Crittenton services, the first century, 1883-1983* (pp. 13-16, 33). Washington, D.C. (1346 Connecticut Ave. N.W., Suite 318, Washington, D.C. 20036): National Florence Crittenton Mission.

Mech, E., & Leonard, E. (1985). *Orientations of pregnancy counselors toward adoption.* Alexandria, VA: National Council for Adoption.

Mercedes, M. (1969). *Catholic maternity residences, Characteristics and trends in facilities and service.* (pp. 10-

11). Washington, D.C.: National Conference of Catholic Charities.

Methodist Mission Home of Texas v. N.___ A.___ B___, 451 S.W.2d (1970). Retrieved from https://www.quimbee.com/cases/methodist-mission-home-of-texas-v-n__-a__-b__

Milotte, M. (2011). *Banished babies: The secret history of Ireland's baby export business.* Dublin: New Island Books.

Missing Piece: Adoption counseling in pregnancy resource centers (n.d.). from http://www.adoptionbirthmothers.com/the-missing-piece-adoption-counseling-in-pregnancy-resource-centers/

Moor, M. (2005). *Silent violence: Australia's white stolen children.* Doctoral dissertation. Griffith University, Nathan, Queensland, Australia, Retrieved from http://www4.gu.edu.au:8080/adt-root/uploads/approved/adt-QGU20070111.172012/public/02Whole.pdf.

Morgenstern, J. (1971, September 13). The new face of adoption, special report. *Newsweek,* 66-72.

Morlock, M. (1938). Socially Handicapped Children, Foster-Home Care for Unmarried Mothers. *The Child, 3*(3), 51-52.

Morlock, M. (1946). Wanted: A Square Deal for the Baby Born Out of Wedlock, 'Our Concern Every Child' should apply to child of illegitimate birth. *The Child,* *10*(11), 167.

Morlock, M. (1946). *Maternity homes for unmarried mothers: A community service* (p. 27). Washington, D.C.: United States Department of Labor.

Morton, M. (1993). *And sin no more: Social policy and unwed mothers in Cleveland, 1855-1990* (pp. 64-66, 70, 83, 87). Columbus, OH: Ohio State University Press.

National program for comprehensive child welfare services; a statement. (1971). (pp. 9, 14-15, 17). New York, NY: Child Welfare League of America.

Nebraska Children's Home Society. (2012) *Adoption questions and answers.* Retrieved from http://www.nchs.org/adoption/adoption-process/adoption-questions-answers.

Nelson, B. (1960). *Elimination of roadblocks in educating school-age unmarried mothers.* Paper presented at annual conference of the Florence Crittenton Homes at National Conference on Social Welfare, Atlantic City, NJ.

Newborn fever: Flocking to an adoption Mecca. (1984, March 12). *Time,* (123 (11), pp. 37, 174.

Ni, Preston. "How to Spot and Stop Manipulators." *Psychology Today.* 1 June 2014.

Nicholds, E. (1966). *In-service casework training* (pp. 99, 206). NY: Columbia University Press.

Nicholson, J. (1968). *Mother and baby homes: A survey of homes for unmarried mothers,* (pp. 41, 69, 86-139, 145). London: George Allen & Unwin.

Oettinger, K. (1965). This Most Profound Challenge. *Children,* 214.

O'Shaughnessy, T. (1994). *Adoption, social work and social theory: Making the connections.* Aldershot, England: Avebury.

Osofsky, H. (1968). *The pregnant teenager: A medical, educational, and social analysis.* (pp. 6, 8, 23, 25, 53-55, 58, 89-90, 248). Springfield, IL: Thomas.

Packard, V. (1977). *The people shapers* **(pp. 17, 355).** Boston: Little, Brown.

Pai-Espinosa, J. (2012, April 29). Adoption or abduction? *Dan Rather Reports, AXS TV.* The National Crittenton Foundation. Retrieved 2016, from http://www.axs.tv/wp-content/blogs.dir/1/files/The-National-Crittenton-Foundation1.pdf

Pannor, R., Sorosky, A., & Baran, A. (1974, December). Opening the sealed records in adoption: The human need for continuity. (pp. 188-195). *Jewish Community Service,* 51.

Pannor, R. (1987, August 1). Comments, 1982 L.A. Adoption Conference. *Concerned United Birthparents Communicator.*

Peck, F. S. (1983). *People of the lie: The hope for healing human evil* (p. 43, 62). New York: Simon and Schuster.

Pelton, L. (1988). The Institution of Adoption: Its Sources and Perpetuation. In D. Valentine (Ed.), *Infertility and adoption: A guide for social work practice* (pp. 1-2, 90, 105). New York: Haworth Press.

Perlman, H. (1964). Unmarried mothers. In N. Cohen (Ed.), *Social work and social problems.* (pp. 154-155, 274-280) New York, NY: National Association of Social Workers.

Perlman, H. (1971). *Perspectives on social casework* (pp. xii, 100). Philadelphia: Temple University Press.

Phyryda, I. (1964, October 26). *Emotional Problems of the unmarried Pregnant Girl and the Patterns of Denial Before and During Pregnancy.* Lecture presented at Southern Area Conference, Florence Crittenton Association of America, Chattanooga, TN.

Pinson, B. (1964). Mothers out of wedlock. In C. Scudder (Ed.), *Crises in morality* (pp. 19, 16-17, 22-23). Nashville, TN: Broadman Press.

Pochin, J. (1969). *Without a wedding ring: Casework with unmarried parents.* (pp. 4, 107, 118, 121-122, 125-127, 129). New York, NY: Schocken Books.

Poinsett, A. (1966, August). A despised minority. *Ebony,* 21(10), pp. 48-49, 52-54.

Polier, J.W. (August 1957). Adoption and law. *Pediatrics.*

(20)2, pp. 372-377.

Politics of adoption. (1994, March 20). *Newsweek* Retrieved from http://www.newsweek.com/politics-adoption-185878

Politics of adoption. (1976). New York, NY: The Free Press.

Pringle, M. (1967). *Adoption facts and fallacies; a review of research in the United States, Canada and Great Britain between 1948 and 1965,* (pp. 29, 129-130). London: Longmans in association with the National Bureau for Co-operation in Child Care.

Projects and Progress. (1955, May-June). *Children,* 2(3), p. 115.

Rains, P. M. (1970). Moral reinstatement: The characteristics of maternity homes. *American Behavioral Scientist, 14,* 219-35.

Rains, P. M. (1971). *Becoming an unwed mother.* New Brunswick and London: Aldine Transaction Publishing.

Rapid adoptions: Stillborn or stolen? (2011). Retrieved from http://www.originscanada.org/rapid-adoptions.

Rawls, J. (2003). What is social justice? Retrieved 2016, from http://gjs.appstate.edu/social-justice-and-human-rights/what-social-justice

Reamer, F. (2012, May 17). Eye on ethics, the dark side of social work: Ethical misconduct. Retrieved 2016,

from
http://www.socialworktoday.com/eoe_051712.sht
ml.

Redmond, W., & Sleightholm, S. (1982). *Once removed: Voices from inside the adoption triangle.* Toronto: McGraw-Hill Ryerson.

Reese, T. (1964, October 19). *Child Care Agencies (pp. 5, 17).* Lecture presented at Unmarried Mothers: A Social Welfare Planning Perspective, Boston, MA.

Reeves, J. (1993). The deviant mother and child: The development of adoption as an instrument of social control. *Journal of Law and Society, 20* (Winter), 420-421.

Reid, J. (1956, May 20). *Principles, Values, and Assumptions Underlying Adoption Practice* (136, 139-140*).* Lecture presented at The Social Welfare Forum, St. Louis, MO.

Reid, J. (1956, June). Why you can't adopt the child you want. *Women's Home Companion,* 37.

Rembis, Michael A. Defining Deviance: Sex, Science, and Delinquent Girls, 1890-1960. Urbana: University of Illinois Press, 2011.

Report of the Rapporteur, Distr. General 6, United Nations, Commission on Human Rights, 59th Session, Item 13, p. 25, A, Adoption 110. (2003). Retrieved December 9, 2015, from http://www.unhchr.ch/Huridocda/Huridoca.nsf/e

6802d4a3d1ddbefc1256610002ee274/217511d4440
fc9d6c1256cda003c3a00/$FILE/G0310090.doc

Reynolds, B. (1963). *An uncharted journey: Fifty years of growth in social work.* New York, NY: Citadel Press.

Rickarby, G.A. (1995). Submission to the New South Wales Parliament Standing Committee on Social Issues Inquiry into Past Adoption Practices. Retrieved from http://www.originsnsw.com/nswinquiry2/id12.html.

Rickarby, G. A. (1998) Testimony to the Social Issues Committee. First Interim Report of the New South Wales Parliamentary Inquiry into Adoption Practices. Retrieved from http://www.parliament.nsw.gov.au/prod/parlment/C ommittee.nsf/0/a4730ea536ad3b20ca256cfd002a63c2/ $FILE/02Sep98.pdf.

Rinehart, J. (1963, March 23). Mothers without Joy. *Saturday Evening Post*, 32-33.

Roberts, B. (1964). *Adoptive Programs and Procedures.* Paper presented at the south regional adoption conference of the Florence Crittenton Association, TN (October 1964) (p. 3).

Roberts, R. (1966). Introduction. In *The unwed mother,* (p. 5). New York, NY: Harper & Row.

Roberts, R., Jones, W., Meyer, H., & Borgatta, E. (1966). Social and Psychological Factors in Status Decision of Unmarried Mothers. In *The Unwed Mother* (pp. 3, 206). New York: Harper & Row.

Robinson, M. (1950, April 23). *Section and Associate Group Meetings (216).* Lecture presented at 77th Annual Meeting, National Conference on Social Work, Atlantic City, NJ.

Rockefeller, J. (1972, March 27). Population and the American Future, the Status of Children and Women, Chapter 10. Retrieved December 19, 2015, from http://www.mnforsustain.org/rockefeller_ 1972_chapter 10_children_women_status.htm# Adolescent Pregnancy and Children Born Out of Wedlock

Roe v. Wade, 410 U.S. 113 (1973) Retrieved from https://en.wikipedia.org/wiki/Roe_v._Wade

Roland, N. (2000). Disenfranchised grief and the birth mother. *American Adoption Congress Newsletter, Spring/Summer*, 9-10.

Roles, P. (1988). *Saying goodbye to a baby: A book about loss and grief in adoption* (Vol. 1, pp. x, 1). Washington, DC: Child Welfare League of America.

Roles, P. (1989). In *Saying goodbye to a baby. Vol. 2: A counselor's guide to birthparent loss and grief in adoption.* Washington, DC: Child Welfare League of America.

Rose, C. (1978). *Some emerging issues in legal liability of children's agencies* (pp. 4-6, 39-40, 59). New York: Child Welfare League of America.

Rowe, J. (1966). *Parents, children and adoption: A handbook for adoption workers.* (pp. 2, 10, 31-32, 48, 51-53, 61-62, 74, 126, 154, 185, 231, 273,). London, England: Routledge & Kegan Paul.

Russell, B. (1929). *Marriages and morals.* London: George Allen & Unwin.

Ryan, W. (1971). *Blaming the victim* (pp. 111, 115). New York: Pantheon Books.

Ryburn, M. (1996). Has Adoption a Future? Presented at Forum Conference on Adoption, Sydney, NSW, Australia. *Concerned United Birthparents Communicator.*

Salvation Army. (1962). "Salvation Army services to unmarried parents and their children." In *Handbook of Information.* New York, NY: Salvation Army National Headquarters.

Samuels, E. (2001). *The Idea of Adoption: An Inquiry into the History of Adult Adoptee Access to Birth Records.* Retrieved January 2, 2016, from http://papers.ssrn.com/sol3/papers.cfm?abstract_id=275730.

Samuels, E. (2006). Adoption consents: Legal incentives for best practices. *Adoption Quarterly,* 10(1), pp. 85-98.

Sandusky, A. (1961). Rehabilitative potentials of families on ADC. *Children,* (3), 93-93.

Schaffer, J., & Lindstrom, C. (1989). *How to raise an adopted child: A guide to help your child flourish from infancy through adolescence* (pp. 5, 7). New York: Crown.

Scherz, F.H. (1947). "Taking sides" in the unmarried mother's conflict. *Journal of Social Casework, 28,* 57-58.

Schur, E. (1983). *Labeling women deviant: Gender, stigma, and social control* (pp. 7-8, 31-32, 38, 187-188, 200). Philadelphia, PA: Temple University Press.

Shapiro, M. (1955). *Study of adoption practices: Selected scientific papers, Vol. 2.* Lecture presented at Child Welfare League of America, Conference on Adoption.

Shaughnessy, T. (1994). *Adoption, social work and social theory: Making the connections* (pp. 21- 22, 95). Aldershot, England: Avebury.

Shawyer, J. (1979). *Death by adoption.* (pp. 29, 35, 49, 60, 62). Auckland, NZ: Cicada Press.

Shiller, A. (1969). The unmarried mother. *The Public Affairs Committee Pamphlet,* (440), 1-6.

Simon, George K. (2016). In sheep's clothing: Understanding and dealing with manipulative people. *Wikipedia.* Wikimedia Foundation. Retrieved from http://fallout.wikia.com/wiki/In_Sheep%27s _Clothing

Singer, M.T., & Ofshe, R. (1990 April). Thought reform programs and the production of psychiatric casualties. *Psychiatric Annals,* (20) 4. Retrieved from https://culteducation.com/group/1153-margaret-thaler-singer-ph-d/995-thought-reform-programs-and-the-production-of-psychiatric-casualtiess.html

Slavson, S. (1956). *The fields of group psychotherapy* (pp. 175, 180, 184). New York, NY: International Universities Press.

Smith, T. (2015, August 16). Children's Traumatic Experiences Can Have Long-Term Effects on the Adults They Become. *Richmond Times Dispatch*, p. G13.

Smolin, D. (2005). *Child laundering: How the intercountry adoption system legitimizes and incentivizes the practices of buying, trafficking, kidnapping, and stealing children.* Berkeley Electronic Press. Retrieved from http://law.bepress.com/expresso/eps/749/.

Snyder, L. (2012, April 12). Dan Rather Reports regarding "Adoption or Abduction?" Catholic Charities USA. Retrieved 2016, from http://www.axs.tv/wp-content/blogs.dir/1/files/Catholic-Charities-USA.pdf

Social Security History: Social Security Related Topics: The Children's Bureau. (n.d.). Retrieved 2016, from http://www.ssa.gov/history/childb1.html

Social workers look at adoption, agencies helping unmarried mothers meet to criticize their own methods of work. (1946). *The Child*, 110-111.

Solinger, R. (1990). The girl nobody loved: Psychological explanations for white single pregnancy in the pre-

Roe v. Wade Era, 1945-1965. *Frontiers: A Journal of Women Studies*, 11(2/3), 45-54.

Solinger, R. (1992). *Wake up little Susie: Single pregnancy and race before Roe v. Wade* (pp. 47-48, 90, 95, 100, 146-147, 158, 254 (fn, Chapter One, note 27, Boston Globe, March 31, 1959)). New York, NY: Routledge.

Sontag, L. (1960). Differences in modifiability of fetal behavior and physiology. In *Casework papers 1960: From the National Conference on Social Welfare* (2nd ed., Vol. VI, p. 151-154). NY: Family Service Association of America.

Sorosky, A., Baran, A., & Pannor, R. (1974). The reunion of adoptees and birth relatives. *Journal of Youth and Adolescence*, 3(3), 195-206.

Sorosky, A., Baran, A. & Pannor, R. (1975). Identity conflicts in adoptees. *American Journal of Orthopsychiatry*, 45, 18-27.

Sorosky, A., Baran, A., Pannor, R. (1978). *The adoption triangle: The effects of the sealed record on adoptees, birth parents, and adoptive parents*. Garden City, NY: Anchor Press.

Spencer, M. (1979). The terminology of adoption. *Child Welfare*, 58(7), 451 459.

Spencer, M. (1980). Understanding adoption as a family building option. *Adoption Builds Families*. Boulder, CO.

Spencer, M. (1988). Post-legal adoption services: A lifetime commitment. In D. Valentine (Ed.), *Infertility and adoption: A guide for social work practice*, New York, NY: Haworth Press.

Stiffler, L. (1991). Adoption's impact on birthmothers: Can a mother forget her child? *Journal of Psychology and Christianity*, 10(3), 249-259.

Stroup, H. (1960). *Social work, an introduction to the field* (2nd ed., pp. 79-80). NY: American Book.

Study of Discrimination against Persons Born out of Wedlock Sales No.: E.68.XIV.3; p. 3. (1971). *Status of the Unmarried Mother: Law & Practice, Report of the Secretary-General, Comm., United Nations, NY*, 1, 3, 57, 88-90, 101-104.

Talukder, G. (2013, March 20). *Decision-making is still a work in progress for teenagers.* Retrieved December 11, 2015, from http://brainconnection.brainhq.com/2013/03/20/decision-making-is-still-a-work-in-progress-for-teenagers/

Taylor, R., & Crandall, R. (1986). *Generations and change: Genealogical perspectives in social history* (pp. 114-115). Macon, GA: Mercer University Press.

Terkelsen, H. (1964). *Counseling the unwed mother* (pp. 82, 84-85, 95). Englewood Cliffs, NJ: Prentice-Hall.

Thirteenth Amendment to the United States Constitution.

(n.d.). Retrieved January 09, 2016, from
https://en.wikipedia.org/wiki/Thirteenth_Amend
ment_to_the_United_States_Constitution

Thornhill, M. (1955). *Protecting children in adoption: Report of a conference held in Washington, June 27 and 28, 1955* (27, 179-180, 183-185). Washington, D.C.: U.S. Department of Health, Education, and Welfare, Social Security Administration, Children's Bureau.

Thornhill, M. (1955). Unprotected adoptions. *Children* 2(5), 179-184.

To better children's chances, the Children's Bureau works with public and private agencies, professional workers, civic groups, and parents. (1953). *The Child, 17*(6), 95.

Tod, R. (Ed.). (1971). *Social work in adoption: Collected papers.* (p. 8). London: Longman.

Tomatis, A.A. (1981). *La nuit uterine.* Paris: Editions Stock.

Trackers International. (2000). *Survey 1000.* Retrieved from http://www.uktrackers.co.uk/ti_survey.htm.

Treadwell, P. (1988). *A parents' guide to the problems of adolescence.* Harmondsworth: Penguin.

Trials of War Criminals before the Nuremberg Military Tribunals under Control Council Law (1949). 10(2), 181–182. Retrieved from http://en.wikipedia.org/wiki/Nuremberg_Code

Triseliotis, J.P. (December, 1988). *Some Moral and Practical Issues in Adoption Work*. Paper presented at the International Conference on Adoption, Melbourne, AU.

Trombley, W. (1963, February 16). Babies without homes. *Saturday Evening Post*, 15.

Troward, T. (1915). *The Edinburgh lectures on mental science: The Edinburgh lecture series*. New York, NY: McBride, Nast and Co.

Troxler, G. (2000). Purely American: Laws, Lies and Love. Retrieved from http://web.archive.org/web/20010620021856/http://www.capitol-college.edu/troxler/essay11.html

Turner, J.B., et al. (Eds.). (1977). *Encyclopedia of Social Work*. (p.120). Washington, DC: National Association of Social Workers.

Tyree, J. (2013, August 21). *A child is waiting*. Retrieved December 9, 2015, from http://www.virginiamemory.com/blogs/out_of_the_box/2013/08/21/a-child-is-waiting/

United Nations Secretary-General. (1971). *Status of the unmarried mother*. New York, NY: United Nations Commission on the Status of Women

United States Children's Bureau. (1953). Quest for knowledge. *The Child,* 17(6), 103.

Unwed parents. In Turner, J.B., et al. (Eds.) (1977).

Encyclopedia of Social Work. (Vol. 2, p.1, 564). Washington, DC: National Association of Social Workers.

Valentine, D. (Ed,) (1988). *Infertility and adoption: A guide for social work practice.* NY: Routledge.

Vincent, C. (1962, May). The unmarried mother in today's culture. In *Papers presented at the Annual Conference of the Florence Crittenton Association of America in conjunction with the National Conference on Social Welfare, New York, NY.* University of Minnesota: Florence Crittenton Archives 10.

Wegar, K. (1997). *Adoption, identity, and kinship the debate over sealed birth records* (pp. 7, 40-41, 52, 54, 69). New Haven, CT: Yale University Press.

Weinstein, K. (1985). Mothers in exile: The aftermath of surrendering a baby for adoption. *Feeling Great,* New York, NY: Haymarket Group, 13, 66.

Wellfare, D. (2009). A sanctioned evil. Retrieved from http://nsworigins.tripod.com/dianwellfare/id13.html.

Wells, S. (1993). Post-traumatic stress disorder in birthmothers. *Adoption and Fostering,* 17(2) 30-32.

Wessel, M. D. (1962, May 31). *A physician looks at professional service for unmarried mothers (7-9).* Lecture presented at Florence Crittenton Association of America, National Conference on Social Welfare, New York,

Wiemo, J. (1966, September 1). Inside a home for unwed mothers. *FACT*, 56-57.

Whitling, N. (2005, April 29). Open doors. *The Columbia Star*. Retrieved from http://www.thecolumbiastar.com/news/2005-04-29/Front_Page/001.html.

Wilson, M., Lordan, N., & Mullender, A. (2004). Family, community, church and state: Natural parents talking about adoption in Ireland. *British Journal of Social Work, 34*(5), 621, 624, 648.

Wilson, O., & Barrett, R. (1933). *Fifty years' work with girls, 1883-1933: A story of the Florence Crittenton homes,* (p. 172). Alexandria, VA: The National Florence Crittenton Mission.

Wilson-Buterbaugh, K. (2001, July-August). Not By Choice. Retrieved March 02, 2016, from http://www.eclectica.org/v6n1/buterbaugh.html.

Wiltse, K. (1966). Illegitimacy and the AFDC program. In R. Roberts (Ed.), *The unwed mother.* (p. 218). New York, NY: Harper & Row.

Wimperis, V., & Witting, C. (1960). *The unmarried mother and her child* (pp. 29, 233, 238, 243, 263-266, 269). London: Allen & Unwin.

Winston, E. (1963, May 23). *Unmarried parents and their children: Services in the decades ahead.* Lecture presented at Florence Crittenton Association of America, National Conference on Social Welfare, Cleveland,

OH.

Woods, G. (2012). Adoption or abduction? *Dan Rather Reports*. AXS TV. Retrieved 2016 from http://www.axs.tv/wp-content/blogs.dir/1/files/National-Association-of-Social-Workers1.pdf

Woolridge, A. (1997, September 7). Eugenics: The secret lurking in many nations' past. *Los Angeles Times*. Retrieved from http://articles.latimes.com/1997/sep/07/opinion/op-29713/2.

Wrieden, J. (1951). To strengthen maternity homes service to unmarried mothers: Part I. *The Child*. 16 (August-September), 5.

Wright, H.R. (1965). *80 unmarried mothers who kept their babies.* (p. 77), Sacramento, CA: State of California Department of Social Welfare.

Why is it called a "baby boom?" (2015, October/November). *Boomer*, 26.

Yeatman, H. Y. (1964, October 16). *Legislation*. Lecture presented at Southern Area Conference, Florence Crittenton Association of America, Chattanooga, TN.

Young, C. J, (2000). *The missing piece: Adoption counseling in pregnancy resource centers.* Washington D.C: Family Research Council.

Young, L. (1953). *Is money our trouble?* Paper presented at the

National Conference on Social Work, Cleveland, OH.

Young, L. (1954). *Out of wedlock: A study of the problems of the unmarried mother and her child.* (pp. 196 211- 213). New York, NY: McGraw-Hill.

Young, L. (1964). Out of wedlock. In R. Levy (Ed.), *Selected materials on family law: Custody, the unwed mother, adoption, parental neglect* (pp. 91, 216-217). Chicago, IL: National Council on Legal Clinics.

Younger, J. (1947, June 1). The Unwed Mother. *Ladies Home Journal*, 102, 105.

Younghusband, E. (1964). *Social work and social change* (p. 60). London: Allen & Unwin.

Zackler, J., & Brandstadt, W. (1974). *The teenage pregnant girl*, (pp. 36-38, 164, 241, 243-244). Springfield, IL: Charles C. Thomas.

ABOUT THE AUTHOR

Karen Wilson-Buterbaugh is one of several exiled mothers whose personal experience of surrendering a child to adoption during the Baby Scoop Era of the 1960s was audiotaped for "Everlasting" a multimedia sound and video installation by Ann Fessler. The stories collected for this exhibition, which showcased the voices of mothers of adoption loss from the 1960s to mid-1970s, are part of the women's oral history collection at the Schlesinger Library. Karen's experience is also a chapter in Fessler's 2006 book, "The Girls Who Went Away, the Hidden History of Girls Who Surrendered Babies for Adoption in the Decades Before Roe v. Wade," and her voice and some of her research appear in Fessler's film "A Girl Like Her."

Karen is co-author of *Adoption Healing: A Path to Recovery for Mothers Who Lost Children to Adoption* (2003); the author of several articles: "Setting the Record Straight," *Moxie* (2001), "Not By Choice," *Eclectica* (2002), "Adoption Induced Post Traumatic Stress Disorder in Mothers of the Baby Scoop Era" (2010) *Associated Content*, "White Washing Adoption, a Critique of Respectful Adoption Language" (2013), *Social Science Research Network (SSRN)*, and co-author of "In the Best Interests of Whom?" (2005) *Associated Content.*

Karen is Executive Director of the Baby Scoop Era Research Initiative, Executive Director of Origins International, co-founder of Origins America, founder and former president of OriginsUSA (OUSA), co-founder of Mothers for Open Records Everywhere (MORE), and a founding member of Mothers Exploited By Adoption (MEBA).

Karen's experience has been featured in the Fairfax, Virginia, *Journal,* the Washington, D.C. *City Paper, Chicago Tribune, Richmond Times Dispatch,* as well as other newspapers around the country. She has been interviewed on National Public Radio (NPR), the Adoption Show on the Internet, and Progressive Radio Network (CA).

In 2012, Karen was interviewed by the *Dan Rather Reports* news program feature "Adopted or Abducted," which discussed Catholic agencies and the coercive aspects of adoption. Some of Karen's research was used in the program, which was nominated for an Emmy.

In 1966, a seventeen year old high school senior, Karen was deposited as an indentured servant in a Washington, D.C. "wage" home before being admitted as a full-time resident ("inmate") of the Florence Crittenton maternity home in Washington, D.C. She gave birth to her daughter, Michelle Renee, at the Washington, D.C. George Washington Hospital on July 22 of that year. Both she and her newborn returned to the maternity home for ten days. Her baby girl was taken from her on August 1, 1966, and offered by a religious adoption agency as available for adoption.

Karen has two raised daughters, Brandi Wilson Brown and Trinity Wilson, is married to her husband, Grant, and resides in Richmond, Virginia. In 1996, thirty years after they were separated, Karen found her taken daughter, Maria/Michelle Renee, also living in Virginia. In August 2007, Karen's daughter, then married with a seven year old son, was taken from her forever as Maria/Michelle Renee lost her battle with ALS (Lou Gehrig's disease).

Contact Karen at karenwb2@verizon.net. Visit her website at www.babyscoopera.com.

Made in the USA
Monee, IL
15 July 2022